PRINCIPLES OF FIRMWARE ENGINEERING IN MICROPROGRAM CONTROL

DIGITAL SYSTEM DESIGN SERIES

ARTHUR D. FRIEDMAN, Editor
George Washington University

S. I. AHMAD AND K. T. FUNG
Introduction to Computer Design and Implementation

MICHAEL ANDREWS
Principles of Firmware Engineering in Microprogram Control

J. E. ARSENAULT AND J. A. ROBERTS
Reliability and Maintainability of Electronic Systems

JEAN-LOUP BAER
Computer Systems Architecture

MELVIN A. BREUER
Digital System Design Automation:
Languages, Simulation and Data Base

MELVIN A. BREUER AND ARTHUR D. FRIEDMAN
Diagnosis and Reliable Design of Digital Systems

ARTHUR D. FRIEDMAN
Logical Design of Digital Systems

ARTHUR D. FRIEDMAN AND PREMACHANDRAN R. MENON
Theory and Design of Switching Circuits

PRINCIPLES OF FIRMWARE ENGINEERING IN MICROPROGRAM CONTROL

Michael Andrews
Computer Science Department
Colorado State University

COMPUTER SCIENCE PRESS

Computer Science Press, Inc.
9125 Fall River Lane
Potomac, Maryland 20854

2   3   4   5   6   87   86   85   84   83

Library of Congress Cataloging in Publication Data

Andrews, Michael, 1940–
    Principles of firmware engineering in microprogram control.

    (Digital system design series)
    Includes bibliographies and index.
    1. System design.   2.   Microprogramming.
I.   Title.   II.   Series.
QA76.9.S88A53   0001.64   80-19386
ISBN 0-914894-63-3

Cover design by Ruth Ramminger

To my Father

PREFACE

Firmware engineering is the practical application of scientific knowledge to the design of computer programs, and the construction and later associated documentation required to develop, operate, and maintain them. This book recognizes the broad implications of firmware engineering which no single text can fully cover. Rather, it is our intent to develop the significant phase of firmware engineering, namely the design and specification of microprogrammable control units. Our hope is to provide the firmware engineer with useful tools.

A new era has emerged for the microprogrammer. Besides being able to generate microprograms at the user level in digital computers, a myriad of LSI circuits now provide an excellent opportunity for ROM-centered designs. Hence, microprogramming of digital machines, of which computers are a small subset, is now possible. This book is written for the engineer who must frequently encounter system designs which incorporate intelligent decision and control mechanisms in digital machines. Such applications extend beyond those typical of general-purpose digital computers. Data acquisition systems, signal processors, transducers, interface and test equipment, and self-diagnostic machines are currently being designed with microprogrammable structures. This book provides the system designer with tools for developing a digital system through the procedures of algorithmic state machine techniques in ROM-centered structures. As noted by Flynn and Rosin[1], the underlying feature of microprogram design is that hardware and software are developed as an algorithmic design. It is only the physical realization which differs.

In the realm of microprogram development, much diversified talent and experience are expended towards the ultimate goal. This great diversity is reflected in the different educational backgrounds, development tools and design languages. Such differences tend to increase the gap between software and hardware. At the microprogramming level the problem is highly sensitive to such differences. The objective of this book is to bring us to a common ground upon which to efficiently design microprogrammable

---

[1]"Microprogramming: An Introduction and a Viewpoint," IEEE Trans. on Computers, July, 1971, pp. 727-731.

vii

machines. This book organizes the many design considerations from hardware and software viewpoints. A new procedural design tool, the algorithmic state machine approach, is employed in the design of microprogrammable machines. Its common language form, the flowchart, should appeal to both the hardware and software engineer, tending to bridge the gap.

Much of the material in this text purposely draws no boundaries between the hardware designer and the user microprogrammer. Both groups must be aware of each other since firmware engineering is a careful blend of these two disciplines. Our horizon encircles both the hardware and software engineer. This is no small task. Formal education (electrical engineering versus computer science), languages (ECAP versus STRUM), and opposing development tools are only a few of the traditional barriers which the firmware engineer must overcome.

The first chapter portrays two classic extremes in the control structure of computers. The first example describes hardware or conventional control. Remaining examples identify microprogram control. By this we contrast the distributed nature of the former with the efficient centralized nature of the latter. More importantly, we suggest that distributed control is inherently difficult. It does not permit an orderly design methodology nor can it lead to clarity in the latter phases of development such as documentation and maintenance.

Regardless of which form of control you use, the control unit must essentially perform two tasks. First, it must declare the current state of the machine. Second, it must determine and identify the next state. These two tasks must be distinctly unambiguous. Recognize that modern digital machines have enormous numbers of "states"; hence, any practical application of state machine concepts must discern only essential states, those which bear on the application at hand.

Control units not only transmit signals but must also receive them. This "feedback" process is essential to intelligent control. These signals represent the implicit/explicit linkage between the control unit and the digital machine.

An engineering discipline distills the practical from the theoretical within realizable costs. The economics of microprogram control, all too often overlooked, are no exception. In the beginning chapter we focus upon such notions as equivalent instructions between conventional and microprogram control. This topic should spark further interest in an essential area of firmware engineering.

Chapter Two is an historical account of control mechanisms found in machines now considered "ancient" as well as machines still found everywhere. Amidst the diversified spectrum of sequencing concepts we can find three basic and distinct structures. The simplest is the two-field configuration, one field for the next address and the other field for the control signals. This earliest configuration was born out of crude technology, diode matrices. In time economical core memory emerged, and today solid state memory has paved the way for improved organizations, single microinstruction, and variable microinstruction. The early two-field concept was very "confining." Hence the later structures are now frequently found in physical designs. In fact, real digital machines frequently employ combinations of these three. Remaining sections in Chapter Two describe such implementations. The internal sequencing hardware has direct impact on the level of flexibility in the eventual development of microprograms. If the microprogramming task is once-only, as in dedicated machines (smart terminals and oscilloscopes, data acquisition instruments, etc.), little flexibility may be sought. Therefore elaborate multiway branches with test and enable branch circuits become superfluous. But, where widespread microprogrammability is expected, the most versatile sequencing scheme implemented in hardware becomes attractive.

Designing control units is multi-faceted. Chapter Three focuses on the second design dimension of the task, that of organizing the microinstruction to facilitate the eventual task of microprogramming. This human engineering problem demands the imaginative use of the designer's talent to portray the inherent power of the digital machine without obfuscating issues. A well structured format does just that. Formats, like sequencing hardware, depend on the intended application. As in the previous chapter, preferences for one design alternative over another are described and supported by examples of real machines, the IBM 360/50, CASH-8, HP 3000, the National Semiconductor GPC/P, and others.

You are encouraged to focus upon the inherent flexibility, speed, and functional clarity of implementations and formats found in Chapters Two and Three, respectively. There exists close coupling between the hardware organization and the microinstruction organization (format) in a control unit. A firm grasp of the topics in firmware engineering can only be acquired by a clear understanding of topics found in both chapters.

For many applications, a significant cost in control unit design is the number of memory devices. It then pays to attempt to reduce the number of bits in each microinstruction to fit the microprograms into a specific ROM or RAM. In general, dedicated applications develop such needs. The bit reduction techniques of Chapter Four provide solutions to these problems. The first methods are simple using obvious techniques such as function extraction. Later, formal techniques employ the notions of "covering." Here classical switching theory is applied to row column reductions in the microprogram. In all procedures, bit reduction methods assume the microprogram has *already* been generated and will most likely remain *fixed* during the lifetime of the product.

On a broader scale, microprogram optimization can be implemented as a top down design tool assuming only the availability of a crude specification of the microprogram sequences. This vague interpretation of the intended task can be used to our advantage by eventually selecting not only narrower ROM's but also shorter ROM's. Chapter Five explores the facets of firmware engineering within the rubric of formal tools available through data dependent graphs, connectivity matrices, and environment dependent factors such as resource conflicts and resource concurrency. A true engineering approach recognizes that microprogram memory is, dimensionally, bits versus words. Minimizing real estate can then be accomplished in either or both dimensions. This chapter focuses on the identification of beneficial attributes of parallel execution which potentially maximizes machine throughput without loss of economy in time and space.

The pioneers of microprogramming hoped that microprogramming as a design tool would close the gap between hardware and software in eliminating the communications problem between the machine designer and the programmer. Unfortunately, this gap developed into a chasm. Each camp spoke different machine languages and used different development tools. In Chapter Six the author proposes a new firmware engineering development tool to narrow the gap hopefully inhibiting further divergence. The notion of employing algorithmic machines as a procedural design technique which couples hardware sequencing information directly into the firmware design is developed. This engineering tool employs the familiar language of flowcharts with descriptive tags or labels in the flowchart elements embedded within simple design rules clearly understandable to the firmware engineer. Three dominant structures are described with implementations on the same problem by example. The chapter demonstrates that careful flowcharting can cleanly couple hardware implementation constraints to the software microprogramming tasks.

The principles of sequencing and architectural organizations of microprogram control units can be found in several physical devices now currently available. These microcontrollers are described in Chapter Seven. The collection of devices, although not complete, is representative of the diversity of available microsequencers and controllers. This chapter serves nicely to couple together the physical implementations of many topics discussed earlier.

The text material can be covered in order, starting with the first chapter, as each succeeding chapter builds on the previous. However, for courses which have an attendant laboratory in which a native microprogrammable machine is used, Chapter Seven may be covered after Chapter Two. Early presentation will greatly assist in the many possible laboratory exercises on a real machine.

The material in this text can be covered in one semester at the senior level, in either the electrical engineering or computer science curricula. The material assumes that the reader is familiar with the basics of computer architecture. A good background in machine or assembly language programming is important to appreciate the powerful capabilities of a well organized microinstruction and microprogrammable machine. Each chapter contains exercises which help to amplify important chapter topics. The complexity of problem sets increases in numerical order.

The author is indebted to the many semiconductor and computer manufacturers who have contributed to this work. The following individuals are especially noted: Nick Tredennick, IBM; Krishna Rallapalli, AMD; Lloyd Maul, Motorola; Subrata Dasgupta, Ohio State University; Stan Habib, CCNY; Mario Gonzales, University of Texas, San Antonio; C. Ramamoorthy, University of California, Berkeley.

The author wishes to acknowledge the many contributions of his graduate students who participated, sometimes laboriously, through the early stages of the manuscript, exercises, and computer programs. In particular, the minimization programs in the appendix were written by Lynn Shimanuki, Kaleen Norris, and William White. Lastly, I acknowledge the sweet support of my wife, Sandra, through the many years with typing, editing, and retyping to bring this text into reality.

Colleagues who have made contributions to this book directly and indirectly include:

S. Bhatnagar   S. Malyscko
T. Brubaker   R. Mueller
D. Dixs   D. Nunnally
D. Eggerding   P. Porter
T. Gale   E. Ruess
S. Henry   D. Ryan
G. Johnson   J. Vermeullen
C. Kelly

CONTENTS

Chapter One

CONTROL IN DIGITAL MACHINES

1.1 INTRODUCTION

The power of digital machines to automatically respond to stimuli in an intelligent fashion, not simply by referring to a tabloid of instructions, but also by executing complicated decisions, has definitely enhanced the role of digital machines in this rapidly changing technological society. Surprisingly, this phenomenon has not been limited to computers. Digital machines such as surveying instruments, intelligent terminals, modems, smart oscilloscopes, and logic state analyzers, while not computers, have all been affected by increasingly sophisticated *large scale integrated* circuits (LSI), some of which even employ microprocessors simply for control purposes with little regard for their inherent computational flexibility. For such machines to perform so remarkably, two prerequisites to designing digital machines stand out clearly. First, efficient programming is necessary. Second, for any machine designer, an intimate awareness of hardware and the structure of that machine is important. This latter task is not trivial; therefore, if we are to "learn" intimate aspects of a digital machine, should we not also be permitted to manipulate the internal structure to best suit our needs? More importantly, does such a mechanism for altering the structure even exist? Indeed it does. This touchstone is the control structure which we will later identify as microprogram control, wherein it is possible to "reprogram" the structure. For the moment, let us examine programming itself.

Although it is obvious that *programming, or the vehicle by which we implement the execution sequences,* is evident in computers, programming for non-computer structures which, until recently, has seldom been possible, now surfaces regularly. This frequency is made evident by increasingly complex operations now possible in digital machines, in general, and demanded in more and more applications, in particular. In the past, these non-computer operations would not even come close to the power of a machine instruction in a computer. Hence, we found no need for a "machine

1

language" or software for such digital machines. With the advent of micro-processors and their innumerable applications to non-computer-like struc-tures, machine instructions became more powerful, partially because the complexity of LSI devices increased. Even in the most trivial of applications for microprocessors, programming is mandatory. While historically this programming has been elementary, being executed at a low level (the machine level), it is not uncommon to find microprocessors employed in many products. Invariably, however, the designer of digital machines which employ microprocessors must not merely be conversant with hardware but also with software.

A more fundamental level of programming activity can be attributed to many digital machines, both computer and non-computer alike. This is the level of microprogramming. *Microprogramming is a form of programming whereupon the apparent architecture of the digital machine is altered.* After microprogramming a digital machine, it is entirely possible that the next user would not recognize its architecture! Thus, the structure or archi-tecture no longer remains fixed. Moreover, in contrast to programming which is generally done at a more sophisticated scale of user software, for instance, ALGOL, FORTRAN, etc., *microprogramming, or programming at the microlevel, manipulates very elementary operations in a digital machine* and is readily accomplished with an intimate knowledge of the hardware and architecture. Microprogramming is similar to allocating rudimentary sequences of operations internal to a machine wherein each step, when considered separately, performs a very simple task. For example, a simple task is a data transfer from one register to another, hence the term *microlevel.* When combined, these internal operations perform such ele-mentary sequences with enough power to execute higher-level program instructions such as a multiply or divide.

Although a thorough understanding of the architecture of a particular digital machine eases the task of microprogramming, such knowledge is not always mandatory. For some computer structures, microprogramming is a relatively simple task because the inherent machine design comple-ments microprogrammability. For instance, user-microprogrammable ma-chines lend themselves to widespread microprogramming applications. These machines possess a readily understandable structure, a logical and orderly arrangement or format in the instruction repertoire, and an ex-tensive software documentation.

The ability to microprogram a digital machine assumes that the machine itself possesses a particular breed of architecture, namely one in which auxiliary storage, which we will call control storage, is accessible by a small set of users. It may be that these select few are only those who initially specify the architecture of the machine. The essential nature of a micro-programmable machine is that some storage medium exists solely for controlling and possibly restructuring the digital machine. Hence, a micro-programmable machine implies an inherent hierarchy of storage mediums much like that shown in Figure 1.1 where smaller areas imply activity encountered by a smaller set of users. Surprisingly, it is common to find microprogrammable machines which are seldom microprogrammed by the user. In fact, often the user is unaware of the microprogrammable nature of such machines, and in some cases manufacturers are hesitant to support such a capability even though it exists.

Embedded in this hierarchy is the notion of controllability. For instance, a high-level language user would program a set of instructions as in FOR-TRAN in a digital machine to exert some influence on the intended task. Subsequently, this set of high-level instructions would be compiled or assembled into a different set of instructions, possibly even at the machine language level, which would then be utilized to execute the sequence of activities that perform the task the user originally intended. This form of control represents one end of the spectrum, whereupon the task, when initially specified, remotely resembles the actual sequence of instructions executed. This contrasts with the user who is microprogramming his tasks and essentially exerts control at the other end of the spectrum, much closer

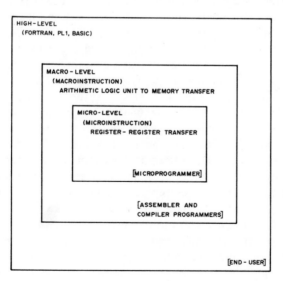

Figure 1.1 Hierarchy of control. (See also Salisbury, "Microprogrammable Computer Architectures")

to actual hardware, specifying elementary steps. His language is very primitive, more basic than machine language. *Therefore, a microprogram exerts a form of control closely related to the "microscopic" activities of a digital machine. We classify this control as microprogram control, utilizing such operations as micro-operations, and programming such code at this level as microcode, all of which imply that microprogramming is executed with instructions closely related to the primitive operations of the digital machine itself, each instruction aptly called a microinstruction.*

Besides the implicit hierarchy of control levels mentioned previously, the degree of centralization also distinguishes control structures. Later we will examine conventional control, wherein we suggest that control is employed by random logic, and we find such control physically distributed throughout a computer. This contrasts with the highly centralized nature of microprogram control, in which a memory unit is specifically dedicated for storage of control information, and all control information can be found in that storage.

Essential to the microprogram control is the relationship of the storage medium of the microprograms to other storage elements in a digital machine. For a computer, microprograms are resident in a fast memory which, generally, is not directly accessible to most users. This memory is commonly called the control memory or control storage and differs from the main memory or user storage in which a higher-level language program resides.[1] The primary distinction between the control memory and main memory rests solely upon functional considerations. Indeed, for some machines, control memory and main memory may *physically* reside in the same unit.

The implicit nature of the dual storage concept in microprogrammable computers rests upon the hierarchy of storage itself. Both the main memory and microprogram storage are "close" to the central processing unit. Both contain instruction control sequences for program execution. However, the microprogram storage contains elementary instructions which can sequence the sub-cycles of the machine instruction repertoire, while the main memory program can only control machine cycles of the instruction set. For instance, in a typical main memory access, such as the READ operation, a hypothetical microprogram sequence of events would be to sequentially open and close data and address paths via the *memory data register* (MDR) and *memory address register* (MAR). It could be possible to dictate destructive as well as non-destructive readout. Each sequential step might be a machine sub-cycle and be separately controllable by bits

---

[1] The level of language stored in main memory is variable. In many instances, the compiled version of machine level can be found in main memory!

in a microprogram instruction word. However, the main memory program when executing a READ instruction from the machine language instruction set could only execute the entire machine cycle to complete a main memory fetch with no provision for separate control of the respective sub-cycles. In essence, microprogram control allows access to the elementary gate and register transfer mechanisms while the control from instructions in main memory allows access to the microprogram instructions.

When employed in non-computer designs, microprogram control does not depend on the availability of two functional types of memory, but rather on the existence of memory for essentially storing microinstructions and on the primary utilization of that memory as a control element in the machine. In some cases, the digital machine may employ a (read-only memory) ROM-centered design, wherein it is assumed that a control memory is the central element for control purposes and that memory locations contain certain microinstructions. A ROM-centered design further assumes that the architecture will employ the ROM to permanently preserve the menu of tasks, which may be trivial or complex, but which, nevertheless, embodies the control sequences available to the user of the machine.

Non-sequential or random access is important to ROM-centered designs. If only sequential access were required, then a simple counter mechanism would suffice for the address generation. A ROM may not even be needed. In some cases, it is also possible to employ random access memory (RAM), which assumes that control storage can be "written into," and which implies that architecture can be redefined dynamically without the need to physically replace the ROM devices. In either case, if control is primarily resident in a seldomly altered storage medium, a ROM-centered design is suggested.

For digital machines, in general, it may be useful to consider the memory locations in the control storage as states of the machine under consideration. These states may depart considerably from the conventional notion of computer states such as RUN, FETCH, EXECUTE, HALT, INTERRUPT, and WAIT. For instance, a state may be described by the specific microinstruction currently in execution. With a ROM-centered control structure, activity may then be specified in a flow chart with state assignments. It is then possible to employ techniques described by the notions of *A*lgorithmic *S*tate *M*achine (ASM) design, a significant topic of this book. An ASM design assumes that we can generate solutions to a problem by devising an algorithm much like solving a series of numerical computations, such as a matrix inversion algorithm, and that the concept of states can then be employed in this algorithm in some flow charting procedure.

In this chapter, we wish to introduce the concepts of control for digital machines which might be classified as either conventional or microprogram control. Our objective is two-fold. First, we intend to draw upon some of the fundamental aspects of microprogramming to contrast conventional and microprogram control. The implication is that conventional control employs very little centralization in the architecture. For instance, hardware for controlling data transfer from the arithmetic logic unit (ALU) may physically reside some distance from the control required for accessing the memory locations in mass storage. Conventional control also implies that the nature of controllability does not reside in a centralized control storage medium. Rather, control is distributed in some fashion, for example, as in tapped delay lines or counters.

Second, our objective is to introduce the notion of control in general terms, the underpinnings of which are recognizable to a large set of readers. For some, the method of design of a microprogrammable control unit is important. For others, the efficient generation of microprograms for an existing machine is paramount. Yet, each reader should be aware of the design considerations inherent to such machines. Hence, in this book the separation of the design considerations from the user considerations is seldom made.

The computer structures we address in this and later chapters are used merely as vehicles for comprehending conventional and microprogram control. It is not sufficient to just understand the difference between microprogram control and conventional control in computers. We need to recognize the difference between these control notions in any digital machine. In later chapters, ROM-centered designs for many non-computer structures will be examined. The notion of computer control mechanisms introduced will carry across to non-computer machines. Because microprogramming implies a hierarchy of control structures, most easily seen in computers, it is simpler to understand the concepts of control for computers. If, then, we understand the control structures in various computer settings, hopefully an extension to non-computers will be straightforward. As we shall soon see, regardless of the nature of the digital machine, the ability to efficiently microprogram requires us to also understand the distinction between architecture and organization of a system.

1.2 ORGANIZATION AND ARCHITECTURE

Until now we have been loosely discussing organization and architecture. However, each concept is distinct and bears discussion. Although both concepts relate to the structure of a system, *organization is a notion of structure largely dependent upon the utilization of individual elements of a system,* while *architecture typifies the actual physical entities and their interrelationships in a system.* This is much like the architecture of an office building even though the building itself is composed of floors or levels, with each floor or level possibly corresponding to occupant usage. For computers we can easily identify the difference between organization and architecture. A computer may be "organized" as a data processing system for the business community. Notice here that elements (disks, printers, tape readers, etc.) are described by their functionality. For instance, if multiple mass storage were available, users would probably not recognize the role of each memory unit in accomplishing a specific task. Thus, as Salisbury points out, such units as elements of organization are of little interest to the microprogrammer even though their functionality is visible to him. The architecture of a computer, in contrast with its organization, relates to physical entities that are directly and knowingly accessible to a microprogrammer. For example, the microprogrammer may exercise a double word length operation on a CPU operation fully aware of the double width feature available to him. Or he may desire to invoke indexed addressing with an index register. Under these circumstances he consciously energizes specific elements in the system. In fact, he desires to capitalize on the power of these architectural features (double width registers for a double operand instruction and an index register for paging memory) rather than resort to awkward programming alternatives (such as repeating a single operand instruction, or generating an offset or base address, which only simulates the desired task).

The distinction between organization and architecture is important to the microprogrammer. As we mentioned earlier, microprogram control exerts some influence on one level of architecture which, in the end, makes the user level of architecture transparent (such as changing from single word length to double word length structures).[2] Therefore, the organization of a system is of little interest to a microprogrammer because he does not intend to merely change the function of the elements (for example, calling up a disk instead of a drum for some bulk storage task which might be accomplished in some higher language). Rather, he expects to actually alter the internal interconnections of a machine.

1.3 STRUCTURE IN DIGITAL MACHINES

The structure of a digital machine relates to its architecture as well as its organization. In terms of organization, we begin by examining the functional role of the machine. For instance, is it a dedicated machine or is it for general applications? Is it strictly a word processing machine or is it a scientific com-

---

[2] To be sure, these levels are distinct and generally separated.

puter? These questions directly relate to the application or environment of some machines (in reality, the higher level usage), but in this book we are more concerned with the architecture of digital machines. Therefore, we would not be overly concerned about the use of an accumulator instead of a memory location for some task, but rather about the functional interrelationship between these elements which would impact upon our programming and, in fact, our microprogramming. We are thus more likely to focus on the available data and address paths of a machine. For convenience we will emphasize computers. Later we will examine non-computers, both groups considered as digital machines.

Basically, a computer architecture is structured as a control unit, central processing unit, interface, and memory unit, as seen in Figure 1.2. Usually the logical power or capacity of each unit is related to its functionality and interconnections between the units. It is even possible to identify an architecture by its interconnect structure. For example, architectures which are bus-oriented tend to emphasize a flow of data and instructions through specific routing or nets. The UNI-BUS® concept of PDP machines[3] is one example of this taxonomy. Alternately, on a functional basis we can describe the architecture by the nature of parallelism of the data path, or even whether binary arithmetic instead of hexadecimal arithmetic is employed internally. In the former we could expect to find variable word length instructions, and in the latter we could expect to find architectures which are basically bit-oriented (binary arithmetic) or byte-oriented (hexadecimal arithmetic), respectively. These aspects of functional and interconnect characteristics are sensitive to a microprogrammer. He must recognize these architectural features if he is to maximize the power of his microprogram. Therefore, we will focus upon the architectural features of

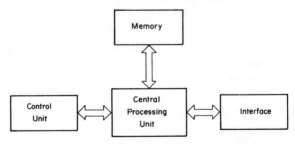

Figure 1.2   Functional activity of a computer

---

[3] See *Processor Handbook, PDP 11/20,* Digital Equipment Corporation, Maynard, Mass., 1971, p. 9.

digital machines rather than on the organization. The interconnect basis and functional basis are only two methods for characterizing architecture. Of course a multitude of architectures and taxonomies now exist and many of these can be found in the annotated references at the end of this chapter.

Digital machines, much like computers which can be as simple as a microprocessor or as complex as a super computer, also have identifiable structures. The major characteristics of digital machines are that they are driven by a clock and they possess distinct states. These states are described by specifications or tasks which are design-driven by the application of the machine. A logical approach to describing the digital machine structure is to directly specify its algorithmic or task-oriented architecture. For example, the simplest application translates output signals directly from input signals, has no memory, and specifies a *combinatorial (or combinational) machine*. Sophisticated applications, and therefore complex digital machines, incorporate memory and feedback output signals, internally, as additional input signals. These digital machines with memory (*sequential machines*) are of primary interest to us.

1.4 CONTROL STRUCTURES

For the moment, we are primarily concerned with the structure of the control unit itself, because we later intend to contrast control structures of digital machines. (Computers are only a small subset of digital machines.) It is beneficial to consider any digital machine as partitioned into two basic units, a functional unit and a control unit, and we will now examine the interplay between these two units. There are essentially two types of tasks performed by a control unit: a) the identification or declaration of the control state during a machine cycle, and b) the establishment of the next control state. *A machine cycle is an elemental period of time in which a primitive activity is being performed.* In some cases, the machine cycle may be the basic clock period of that machine. A *control state is the description of the current primitive activities.* The two essential tasks, current state declaration and next state identification, establish the minimal facility to control a machine. First, there must be storage for information to *declare* the current state; secondly, there must be a translator or decoder to *generate* respective control signals for each state, and there must be decision logic to *choose* the next state identifier.

Such a minimal facility is depicted in Figure 1.3. Here, the control unit contains a state declaration storage element which identifies the current state of the computer and provides signals to the decode logic. The decode logic translates the current state identifier into appropriate control signals

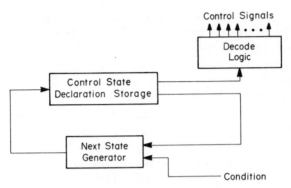

Figure 1.3   Simplified control section

to accomplish a current task. Finally, the control section contains a next state generator whose inputs originate from either the current declaration storage or from conditions imposed on the next state generator by some external element such as an arithmetic logic unit. The next state may even be generated by a combination of conditions and the current state. The next state generator, likewise, takes on varying forms from a simple latch to combinations of latches, counters, and multiplexers.

At present, we are not specifically identifying the architecture of the declaration storage since this depends on our classification of control. Later we will show that conventional control units are typically distributed while microprogram control units are centralized. With a general control structure in mind, then, an implicit internal linkage exists between the functional unit and the control unit of a computer as shown in Figure 1.4. *The implicit link between the functional unit and the control unit is the communications path for describing activity status or conditions which might affect the next state.* For instance, if the control unit had requested the functional unit to execute an arithmetic operation, the functional unit should respond by activating implicit linkage to inform the control unit of the status of a possible arithmetic overflow. This implicit linkage contrasts with the *explicit linkage between the control unit and the functional unit wherein sets of instructions resident to the control unit would activate specific signals in the functional unit.* One generally finds more control signals emanating from the control unit than status signals returning from the functional unit to the control unit. Control signals may activate a sequential data transfer, hold, or data transformation instruction. These signals are explicit. Status signals indicate not only arithmetic conditions (carry, overflow, underflow, etc.) but also physical conditions such as mar-

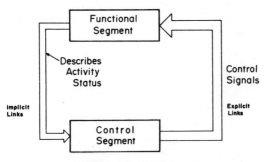

Figure 1.4   Linkage

ginal power, thermal overloads, or interrupt enables and disables. With the simplified control unit and linkage between the control unit and the functional unit now described, let us return to the notion of control for a computer.

The control of a computer can be described in several ways; however, computers intrinsically sequence through several tasks with control signals which emanate from a control unit as shown in Figure 1.5. This control unit receives input instructions from an instruction decoder and multiplexes the resulting control signals to the functional elements of the computer with a clock signal. If all activity is synchronized with the clock within the computer, then synchronous behavior is observed. Where no relationship exists between the clock and the respective functional elements or if the clock itself is nonexistent, then asynchronous behavior is observed. In either case, the control unit transmits specific control signals. In Figure 1.5, for example, five such control signals are identified. One signal, ALU, specifies a particular operation in the ALU. Another control signal, ACC, specifies that data is to be transmitted to or received from the accumulator. A third signal, MQ, activates a data path to some MQ register. Likewise, I_0 and GPR_0 activate data paths to other specific hardware. Now control signals may be either levels or pulses, and in our case we show pulses. In this simple control unit we also show an instruction decoder which represents the mechanism whereby instructions, possibly generated by a user, are decoded or translated for the control unit.

The control of digital machines which are not computers does not differ significantly from that of computers. At the very most, the digital machine may not have an *arithmetic logic unit* (ALU) and, hence, the control unit would not generate ALU-type control signals. Nevertheless, the control unit must perform similar tasks. One such example is depicted in Figure

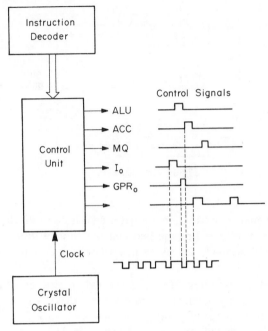

Figure 1.5   Computer control unit

1.6 where a control unit in some general digital machine is assigned the task of monitoring the front panel switches and indicators of the machine, where perhaps, switch actuation is to be controlled by a logical sequence of events. In this example, four control signals are generated by the control unit when various switch actuating sequences occur. A controlled sequencing program (which might be our microprogram) identifies which control signal, ELD_i, is to be generated. These control signals could then activate *l*ight *e*mitting *d*iodes, LED's. And since LED's consume considerable power, a sequencing scheme could be employed which momentarily flashes each LED; hence, the sequential train of pulses is shown in the figure. Should a different switch actuation sequence occur, the control unit would utilize the program controlled sequence in the ROM to establish a new pattern of LED outputs. As we can see, even though this digital machine may not employ an arithmetic logic unit, the application can potentially require a control unit which is ROM-centered. Furthermore, as with computers, the digital machine utilizes both an explicit linkage (from the

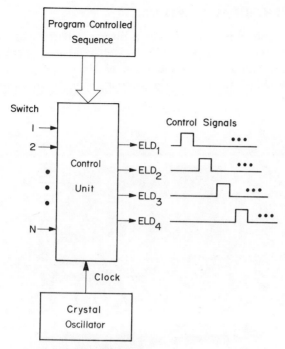

Figure 1.6 Digital machine control unit

control unit to LED's) and an implicit linkage (from the front panel switches to the control unit).

An example of a digital machine which is microprogrammable is depicted in Figure 1.7. This intelligent terminal has many diverse requirements suitable to a flexible control structure. Stand-alone operation includes tape entry, remote print-out, and graphics display edit. As a remote batch data terminal, the microprogrammable control unit must manage remote poll features such as automatic transmission and reception, format control for data entry and correction of user generated errors. The "heart" of the system configuration, Figure 1.8, includes a 4K × 30 bit control ROM for the microprograms.

Regardless of the synchronous behavior or implicit linkage of a control unit, it should be obvious that two main tasks, declaration of the current state and determination of the next states, are necessary for any control unit. Employment of one mechanism over another depends on several factors to be described later.

1.5   CONVENTIONAL CONTROL

Since the computer is comprised of a diverse collection of functional elements and the notion of control is intimately related to operations on these elements, we shall now examine some of these operations. We classify activity in terms of functions or instructions. For instance, *an information*

Figure 1.7   A remote data entry terminal

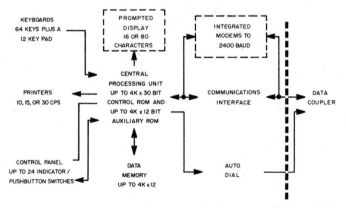

Figure 1.8   System configuration for the data entry terminal

transfer from main memory is called a memory read cycle and the instruction is a memory reference instruction. The design of a control unit then consists of specifications for instructions, timing constraints, and sequencing operation, all of which, of course, are common to both conventional and microprogram control. However, timing constraints and sequencing operations take on different hardware forms in each control mechanism.

Example 1.1: To illustrate the conventional control concepts, examine the simple digital machine shown in Figure 1.9. This computer contains many of the commonly encountered functional elements including a main memory unit, arithmetic logic unit, central processor unit, input-output unit, and control unit. For our purposes in this section, we will be most concerned with the details of the control unit.

Recall that the functions of the control unit are basically to maintain current machine status, identify next machine state, and sequence or branch to the next state. In conventional control, four resources are common: a) a *m*ajor *s*tate *g*enerator (MSG), b) an *i*nstruction *r*egister (IR), and

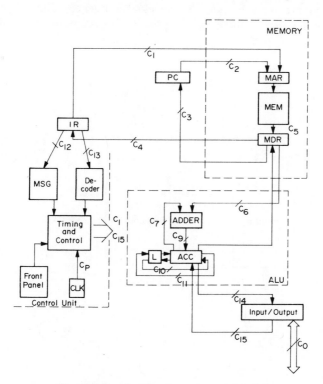

Figure 1.9   Simple computer example 1.1

decoder, c) a control sequencer, and d) a master clock as shown in Figure 1.10. *The major state generator identifies the general status of the computer for each specific instruction.* For example, if a memory reference instruction is currently executed, the "*M*" line would be energized to indicate a memory operation. Or, if the computer is interrupted, the "*I*" line would be energized. The instruction register and decoder store instructions retrieved from memory and, when combined with the major state generator, constitute the control state declaration storage of Figure 1.3, while the control sequencer and instruction decoder are identified with the decode logic of Figure 1.3. Note that this simple computer does not provide for condition inputs to the next state generator nor is the next state generator easily identified by this configuration. The implicit linkage is missing.

The explicit linkage of the control unit is a set of control lines to C_0, C_1, C_2, ..., C_{15}, which enables data or instruction transfer paths throughout the computer.[4] Since control signals must appear at distinct intervals in any machine cycle, internal signals to the control unit must be logically combined at precise sub-cycles in the clock sequence. This requires the specification for timing much like a typical timing diagram shown in Figure

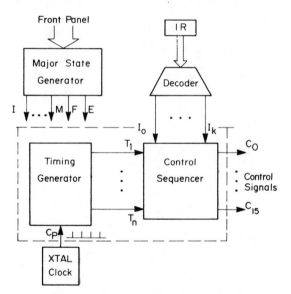

Figure 1.10   Conventional control unit

---

[4] The gates themselves are also called control points.

1.11. Here, T_1, T_2, ... are generated by the timing generator which relates to both major state inputs and the crystal clock, C_p. All T_i are related to C_p by major states of the computer. For example, T_1 denotes the start or initiation of a major machine cycle and may be equated with the initiation of the FETCH state of a computer, since our simple computer must frequently return to memory for the next instruction in a program. T_2 may relate to the EXECUTE state, likewise for T_3, etc. Selection of pulse position and interval duration is determined by ad hoc procedures and most likely only after the functional resources have been specified.

In conventional control we are apt to find that the control sequencer uses an assortment of delay line units or counters which receive inputs from the IR decoder and major state generator, driven by the master clock. For example, if we examine a simple control sequence for an addition cycle of one operand in the accumulator (ACC) to another operand in memory (MEM), the sequential operations for this memory reference addition would require execution of three functions in the computer as shown in Table 1.1. To design conventional control units, we would then specify the hardware necessary to generate C_2, C_6, C_7, and C_9, which requires considering not only path delays (for instance, from ACC to MEM), but also synchronization, among other physical parameters. Assuming that the

Table 1.1   Sequence for memory reference addition

MAR $\xleftarrow{\;C_2\;}$ Memory Address (PC)

ADDER $\xleftarrow{\;C_6\,,\,C_7\;}$ Memory Data (MDR) + Accumulator (ACC)

ACC $\xleftarrow{\;C_9\;}$ Adder

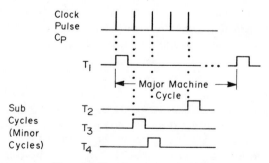

Figure 1.11   Control clock pulses

instruction register (IR) already contains an operand address for the memory reference (instruction fetch is completed) and the ACC contains the other operand, the addition sequence initiates with a call to memory for the second operand. C_2 is now activated in Figure 1.9. After some delay, d_1 (which the designer has hardwired into the sequencer), memory data and ACC data are transferred to the adder via C_6 and C_7. Again, after delay, d_2, which is determined by physical reasoning much like d_1, the result of the addition is latched into the ACC with C_9 activated. The control sequencer hardware then appears as shown in Figure 1.12 wherein T_i, or a minor cycle from the timing generator, drives the tapped delay line. After each delay the pulse appears on the correct control line to enable information transfer among the functional elements. The utilization of this control pulse in a set of AND gates between each element is shown in Figure 1.13 for the MDR to adder transfer. Here, when C_6 is pulsed, data from the MDR is available to the adder via the set of two input AND gates. One input is control signal, C_6. The other input into each gate is the information or data bits for the parallel addition. We call this second input the data signal. Thus, the slash symbols in Figure 1.9 represent sets of two input (dual) AND gates with sixteen sets shown.

As our example suggests, the MDR data transfer must occur within a precise interval governed by delays and sub-cycle clock pulses. However, even if we determine the necessary timing, the C_6 specification is still incomplete. Our design for this data transfer must also include the major machine state control because we need to insure that the MDR transfer occurs during the correct major state of the computer and only after the specific request or command appears from the programmed instruction residing in the IR (which is an ADD instruction in this example). To completely specify the generation of our control signal, C_6, we need to combine several logical control variables (clock pulse, IR decoder, major state, and delay). In this example, our machine should be in the EXECUTE state, and the major state generator must provide a signal to specify this state. The resultant logical Boolean expression for C_6 must therefore combine all necessary control variables. It might appear as

$$C_6 = \text{ADD} \cdot E \cdot T_i \tag{1.1}$$

This Boolean expression for C_6, however, still remains only partially complete. Suppose that a subtract from memory and a data transfer to memory are desired commands. C_6 must again be energized in these cases. Now we must consider additional control events for C_6, and the complete specification for C_6 must include further control variables. If subtract and output

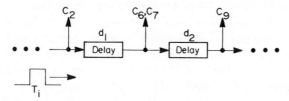

Figure 1.12 Memory add control sequence for conventional control unit

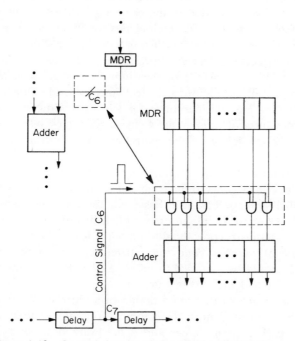

Figure 1.13 Control signal path for addition (MDR Operand only)

functions are to be incorporated in the simple digital machine, our control expression for C_6 could appear as

$$C_6 = (\text{ADD} + \text{SUB} + \text{STA}) \cdot E \cdot T_i \tag{1.2}$$

where SUB and STA are mnemonics for subtract and store instructions, respectively.

This exercise must now be performed for all control lines, $C_0, \ldots, C_{15}$. Upon completion, the control unit may resemble the configuration of a set of delay lines, decoders, and counters partially depicted in Figure 1.14. Note how the control unit closely resembles an asynchronous sequencer. The depicted segment includes the fetch phase for all instructions as well as manual start control. Note further that we have only examined pure sequential control. If we are to include conditional jump control, considerably more structure is required as well as complexity. Not shown are the remaining delay line structures for these other instructions.[5]

Now let us review this design procedure for conventional control. Once the architectural features of our computer were identified, we proceeded to specify sets of control logic and timing chains for functions or instructions executable by the computer. During this process, as additional instructions were identified, necessary Boolean expressions were revised to account for these changes. Although details of the timing considerations (e.g., path delays) were ignored, as additional instructions were identified, the tight coupling of the timing considerations for various instructions would become more pronounced. Until now all of our exercises have merely proceeded to specify the explicit linkage of the control unit, i.e., instructions from the control unit to the functional units.

The equally important task of specifying the implicit linkage (i.e., status signals from functional units to the control unit) remains. And, conceivably after the explicit linkage has been designed, the implicit linkage specifications may force us to reconfigure the explicit linkage. For example, execution of the ADD instruction should also allow for an implicit link to the control unit for an overflow condition. Therefore, the timing chain shown in Figure 1.12 should be modified to reflect a branching operation instead of a sequential fetch of the next instruction.

The main drawback of the above design procedure is the absence of a convenient and readily identifiable mapping from instructions to control signals which both a programmer and a hardware designer may utilize. Use of random logic (AND, OR gates as shown in Figure 1.14) does not lend itself to familiar structures. Consequently, the design process itself has little structure. At best, a first iteration which generates crude specifications precedes exceedingly detailed iterations through tightly coupled levels of specifications, this coupling taking the form of constraints imposed by physical parameters. To impose some structure in the design process, it is entirely possible to tabulate instructions and control signals in some intelli-

---

[5] This example is illustrated further in Salisbury's book, p. 4. See the references at the end of the chapter.

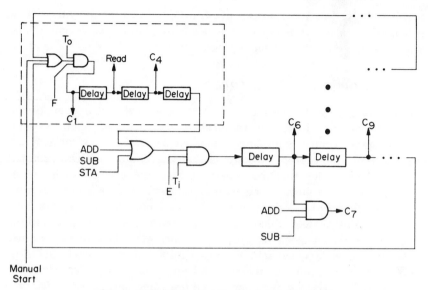

Figure 1.14 Control unit with delay elements

gent fashion with the objective of generating reliable documentation. This tabulation, although incapable of providing a "mapping" technique without further effort, at least would establish a documentary record for subsequent use.

Another disadvantage of conventional control resides in the use of random logic. Employing random logic inhibits the capacity of the design to be "regularized" or, rather, to be composed of common devices throughout which can be easily removed and replaced by similar devices (to reflect intentional architectural modifications for later generations of machines). *Regularity in design is a property of the physical structure that permits the usage of identical circuits which facilitates and even enhances changes in the design itself.* The regularity of design with random logic, unlike a memory device such as a RAM or ROM which is highly regular, is less obvious because random logic is a composition of discrete devices such as gates, latches, or counters. Memory devices are physically structured with an identifiable pattern which makes for regularity. Replacing a gate structure with another gate structure in the control unit is not a trivial task. At the very least, the different path delays in each gate structure will affect the timing specifications, thus requiring changes in the timing. It is also possible that other physical constraints such as size, power, noise, and thermal capacity may limit such changes. These dilemmas in our design procedure for conventional control units were recognized long ago. In fact, these very problems begged for more orderly procedures in which, not only the digital machine, but also the design process itself, should possess structure. The solution led to the notion of microprogram control.

1.6 MICROPROGRAM CONTROL

As we have seen in the previous section, conventional control consists of a decentralized and distributed approach to design of the digital system. Microprogram control represents a marked departure from conventional control. Here, the concept of design assumes a *centralized ROM-centered control* which implies that the essence of microprogram control is the incorporation of a central storage element, commonly called the *control store*. Residing in this control store is firmware or microprograms of individual microinstructions which sequentially control the gating signals in the computer or digital machine. Historically, firmware, in contrast to other software, was code which seldom changed and was most likely found in ROM's, since such code was intended to be permanent and fixed. However, this distinction becomes more vague and less important as user-microprogrammable machines become readily available since every user has the opportunity to alter firmware to best suit his needs. In any event, *firmware describes the microcode of a microprogrammable machine.*

Typically in the microprogram control unit we find hardware similar to that shown in Figure 1.15 in which three basic resources exist: a *microprogram ROM*, a *next address ROM*, which may or may not be incorporated in the control unit, and a *decoder* with the appropriate latches or registers to select the next microinstruction. Two necessary registers include the next address register (or *control store address register*, CSAR) and the current microinstruction register (or *control store instruction register*, CSIR). The control store is sequenced by a master clock via the CSAR.

In the simplest control unit, each microinstruction has at least two fields. As shown in Figure 1.15, we specify the left field as an address field which indicates the next microinstruction address. The right field is the control field which specifies control signals to be energized at the current microinstruction. The next address in this example is 001010 and the current control signal is 001011011 with a binary one indicating that the respective control line is energized. Since the address field is six binary bits wide, 2^6 or 64 locations are directly addressable with each location capable of generating nine control signals. If then, in the control field individual bits are functionally specified (i.e., bit four is assigned to control signal two which enables a specific set of control gates), both the address and control field comprise a "formatted" microinstruction. Our simple format, unfor-

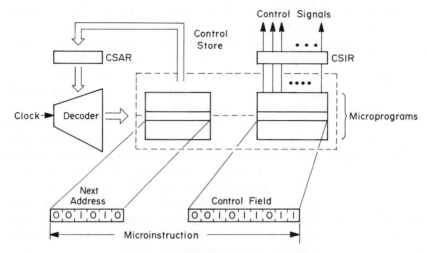

Figure 1.15   Microprogram control

tunately, permits only sequential access or unconditional jump to any microinstruction from the control store. Obviously then, our basic microprogram control unit merely interfaces with the digital machine via the explicit linkage. An implicit linkage simply does not, as yet, exist. Therefore, conditions or status of the digital machine, which require non-sequential access or a conditional branch to an alternate microinstruction, cannot be handled. Even if the implicit linkage similar to that shown in Figure 1.4 were available, we would still need to reformat the microinstruction fields to make use of this facility. For instance, an additional "branch" field would be needed to enable a branch, should such conditions from the implicit linkage warrant access to an alternate microinstruction. Of course, the branch field is not the only extension we may find beneficial. In later chapters, as increasingly sophisticated designs are introduced, the need for additional fields and alternate address-generation mechanisms will become apparent. Assuming that this limited control unit will suffice for the moment, let us examine a typical application of our microprogram control unit with the functional architecture of the previous section.

1.7   MICROPROGRAM CONTROL EXAMPLES

Example 1.2:   Assume that we wish to replace the distributed control unit of the computer in Figure 1.9 with a microprogram controlled unit. Our first task would be to determine the total number of controls we wish to incorporate and how to manipulate them, either singly or in aggregate. The second task would be to microcode our tasks. The microprogram control design begins by assigning specific bits in the microinstruction to particular tasks. Since our simple computer in Figure 1.9 presently employs sixteen sets of control gates or control points, we will arbitrarily specify a bit in the control field for each set. Let us assume that bit zero corresponds to C_0, bit one to C_1, etc. as in Figure 1.16.

This assignment is equivalent to declaring the task or control point which each bit in the microinstruction will individually control. Therefore, if more than one bit is "set" in a given microinstruction, multiple tasks or points can be executed or controlled simultaneously. These tasks are commonly called *micro-orders* (again, because these tasks are commands which relate directly to the "microscopic" or primitive functions of our computer), and a collection of such micro-orders in any given word in our control ROM becomes the microinstruction. We will denote a microinstruction, M_i, as a set of micro-orders, m_{ij}, such that

$$M_i = \{m_{i1}, m_{i2}, \ldots, m_{ij}, \ldots\}$$

where every m_{ij} is an element of the valid set of micro-orders defined for a particular machine. The collection of microinstructions with appropriate address specifications represents a microprogram.

Let us now microprogram the sequence in a ROM for the memory reference addition instruction similar to Table 1.1. The microprogram sequence would appear in a ROM as shown in Figure 1.17.

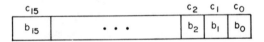

Figure 1.16   Control field specification

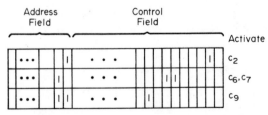

Figure 1.17   A short microprogram for ADD

The sequence of microinstructions for the ADD instruction begins at location zero in our microprogram. For the moment, we will ignore the details by which the CSAR has been loaded with location zero except to indicate that the ADD instruction must point to location zero in our microprogram control unit. Our first microinstruction, now enabled, sends control field signals via the CSIR, and in the first sequence we observe that C_2, alone, is enabled. After this micro-order has been executed, the microprogram control unit automatically places the contents of our address field in the CSAR. This is address 'one.' Now, C_6 and C_7 micro-orders are transmitted via the CSIR. Upon completion of these micro-orders in the computer, address 'two' is sent to the CSAR for the final microinstruction in our microprogram to execute the ADD instruction.

This is a simple microprogram since no branching is required, and, therefore, the address field assignment is merely an increment of each next address while the control field assignment is a one-to-one map of each control bit to a control signal. Furthermore, our three microinstructions are sparsely microcoded (in short, few "1"'s) since few simultaneous tasks are required. Both of these properties are due in part to the simplicity of our machine (one adder, one ACC, PC, MEM, etc.).

Let us review our crude design procedure for control via microprogramming. Our first step was to specify a format for the microinstructions. Here we assigned particular bits in a control field to control signals required by some functional unit. The next step was to generate the microcode for the instructions of our functional unit. In our example, only one instruction, ADD, was implemented in microcode. These two steps partially represent basic operations we will perform when designing a microprogrammable control unit. However, these are by no means the only operations required in such a design procedure.

In the first place, considerably more rationale could have been employed in selecting a format for microinstructions. The format should inherently provide descriptive information about the behavior of a microprogram. In that event, the control field, if formatted properly, is theoretically capable of providing a concise statement of the activity by observing the patterns of "1"'s and "0"'s. This would be possible if we had specified bit assignments, not randomly, but logically, perhaps according to functional behavior! In our example, the designer initially could have partitioned the control field into sub-fields, one of which could be the ACC input field. Here, C_9, C_{10}, and C_{15} would be combined into a contiguous 3-bit field with this control field possibly called "ACCI." This control field partitioning would then be continued for all remaining control signals in relation to the elements of the machine until all groups of bits or fields would easily identify the micro-orders. This simple modification could, potentially, establish a beneficial structure, recognizable by the hardware designer as well as the microprogrammer.

Yet, careful formatting alone is not sufficient to develop a microprogrammable control unit. Returning to our example, we have not provided for any implicit linkage to the control unit, and to do so would require us not only to reformat our microinstruction (to permit branches) but also to more closely observe the timing behavior internal to the functional unit as well as with respect to the control unit. Of course, this latter phenomenon was also evident in our conventional control.

Example 1.3: To say the least, inserting 1's or 0's into a ROM is not microprogramming. In this example, let us look at the simple machine of Figure 1.18. However, we now want to assign codes and meaning to the control points of the machine. The control points in Figure 1.18 are not explicitly shown as in Figure 1.9. It is obvious from Table 1.2 which data paths are accessible by the control storage unit. Note that the code designations directly convey the meaning of each micro-operation. For example, MARM describes the activation of control gates from the MAR to the M bus. Such mnemonics are highly desirable for our understanding of the machine.

A key issue to designing microprogrammable control units is the effective assignment or representation of the micro-operations into a microinstruction; that is, specifying the fields. For our machine, let us choose the seven fields as shown in Table 1.3. The micro-operations from Table 1.2 are tabulated under appropriate fields. A simple microprogram to add the contents of memory to an accumulator is depicted in Figure 1.19.

Example 1.4: Another digital machine is depicted in Figure 1.20 with its micro-orders tabulated in Table 1.4. As with Example 1.3, the labeled control points in the machine have been replaced by enumerated micro-orders. For instance, micro-order 17, or m_{17}, in Table 1.4 when executed places the contents of general register 3, GR3, into the right input of the adder, AIR. Micro-order 7 transfers bits 11 through 0 of the instruction register, IREG[11, 0], into the program counter, PROGCTR. Micro-order 32 executes a single bit right shift in AO, the adder output. Micro-order 33 executes a single bit left shift in AO. Micro-orders 35 and 36 are special types. They enable the microprogram to branch on some condition. Micro-order 35 places some address in the CSAR if AO equals zero. Micro-order 36 increments the CSAR if the AO is positive. Notice that in this example we have not assigned mnemonics to the micro-orders yet.

The following sequential set of micro-orders performs a multiple left shift on ACC1. Assume that the shift count resides in GR3. The micro-

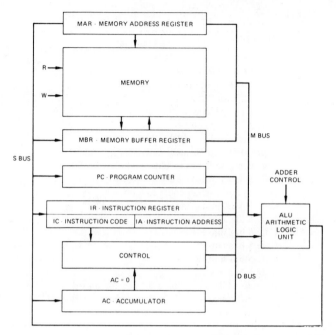

(Reprinted courtesy of Signetics Corp.)

Figure 1.18 Simple microprogrammed machine

CYCLES		MEMORY CONTROL	JUMP INSTRUCTION	ADDER CONTROL	M BUS CONTROL	D BUS CONTROL	S BUS CONTROL	JUMP ADDRESS FIELD
INSTRUCTION FETCH	1	R		DTS		PCD	SMAR	
	2							
	3			MTS	MBRM		SIR	
INSTRUCTION DECODE	4		JOPC					
EXECUTE	5	R		DTS		IAD	SMAR	
	6							
	7			PLUS	MBRM	ACD	SAC	
RETURN	8			ONE		PCD	SPC	
	9		JMP					START

(Reprinted courtesy of Signetics Corp.)

Figure 1.19 Microprogram to add contents of memory to accumulator

Table 1.2   Micro-operations for simple machine

Code	Meaning
MARM	Gate MAR onto M bus
MBRM	Gate MBR onto M bus
PCD	Gate PC onto D bus
IAD	Gate IA (instruction address) onto D bus
ACD	Gate AC onto D bus
R	Read memory into MBR
W	Write MBR into memory
PLUS	Add M bus to D bus in adder and place on S bus
DTS	Gate D bus through adder to S bus
MTS	Gate M bus through adder to S bus
ONE	Gate D bus through adder to S bus and add one
SMAR	Gate S bus into MAR
SMBR	Gate S bus into MBR
SPC	Gate S bus into PC
SIR	Gate S bus into IR
SAC	Gate S bus into AC
JMP	Jump to address in address field of microinstruction
JIFO	Jump to address in address field of microinstruction if AC = 0
JOPC	Jump to address of OP code field

(Reprinted courtesy of Signetics Corp.)

Table 1.3   The fields of the microinstruction

Memory control	Jump instruction	Adder control	M Bus control	D Bus control	S Bus control	Jump address field
R	JMP	PLUS	MARM	PCD	SMAR	
W	JIFO	MTS	MBRM	IAD	SMBR	
	JOPC	ONE		ACD	SPC	
		DTS			SIR	
					SAC	

(Reprinted courtesy of Signetics Corp.)

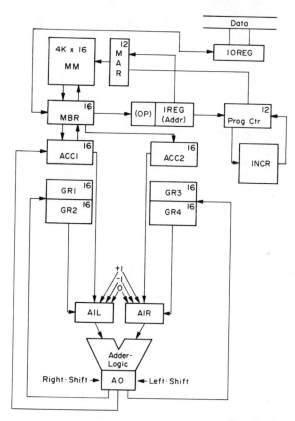

(Reprinted courtesy of ACM)

Figure 1.20 A micromachine

Copyright 1979, Association for Computing Machinery, Inc., reprinted by permission. S. Dasgupta, "The Organization of Microprogram Stores," ACM Computing Surveys, Vol. 11, No. 1, March 1979, pp. 39-65.

program repeatedly executes a single left shift on ACC1 using the AO, decrementing the shift count in GR3 until complete. This microprogram is executed sequentially with a return to the first micro-order at each iteration except the last one. Table 1.5 represents an initial specification for the microprogram. Much remains to be done before an acceptable microprogram appears. For instance, we may attempt to reduce the number of steps by combining micro-orders on the same line. (Each line is equivalent to a microinstruction.)

Table 1.4   Micro-order list for the micromachine

No.	Micro-order	No.	Micro-order
1.	MBR ← MM[MAR]	19.	AIR ← +1
2.	MM[MAR] ← MBR	20.	AIR ← −1
3.	MBR ← IOREG	21.	AIR ← 0
4.	IOREG ← MBR	22.	ACC2 ← MBR
5.	MAR ← PROGCTR	23.	ACC1 ← AO
6.	IREG ← MBR	24.	GR1 ← AO
7.	PROGCTR ← IREG[11, 0]	25.	GR3 ← AO
8.	ACC1 ← MBR	26.	AO ← AIL + AIR
9.	MBR ← ACC1	27.	AO ← AIL + *AIR*
10.	AIL ← ACC1	28.	AO ← *AIL* + *AIR*
11.	AIL ← GR1	29.	AO ← AIL + AIR
12.	AIL ← GR2	30.	AO ← *AIL* + AIR
13.	AIL ← +1	31.	AO ← AIL
14.	AIL ← −1	32.	AO ← shr AO
15.	AIL ← 0	33.	AO ← shl AO
16.	AIR ← ACC2	34.	PROGCTR ← PROGCTR + 1
17.	AIR ← GR3	35.	AO = 0 => CSAR ← address
18.	AIR ← GR4	36.	AO > 0 => CSAR ← +1

(*AIL* is one's complement)

Table 1.5   Multiple left shift microprogram

1. AIL ← ACC1	6. AIR ← GR3
2. AIR ← 0	7. ACC1 ← AO
3. AO ← AIL + AIR	8. AO ← AIL + AIR
4. AO ← shl AO	9. GR3 ← AO
5. AIL ← −1	10. If AO > 0, CSAR ← 1

The point of these examples and the previous discussion on conventional control is two-fold. First, by example, we wanted to describe typical, although somewhat simple control units. Second, we wanted to introduce some of the concepts pertaining to microprogramming, again, by way of example. The designer as well as the microprogrammer should now begin to realize some of the problems related to the subject of control. More importantly, our last example should suggest improvements to be realized by a microprogram control unit.

In practice, microprogram control comes into play for a variety of reasons. The main reason, as noted historically in the conceptual stages of microprogramming, was the need for an orderly approach to the design of a computer. Wilkes first observed the convenience by which microprogram control supports such techniques. Another basis for implementing microprogram control was the capacity to alter the apparent structure of the machine from user to user. In any event, whether motivated by orderliness or flexibility, microprogramming has become popular. In fact, the inherent nature of microprogramming is that we can alter the apparent structure of a computer. This property enhances another application of programming, namely emulation. This is inherently obvious, when we observe that *emulation is basically the process of microprogramming a computer to imitate another computer, the former called a host computer and the latter called a target computer.*

1.8 USER-MICROPROGRAMMABILITY

Unlike the conventional control computers which have only one memory unit, the microprogrammable computer has an additional memory unit, essentially independent of the "main" memory unit. This added memory unit, sometimes called the control storage or microprogrammable storage, serves as the prime sequencer of control within the computer as a whole. The control storage may also have the capability of modifying its contents. *When the end-user of a microprogrammable computer can modify the control storage content, the computer is classified as user-microprogrammable.* At present, user-microprogrammable computers are beginning to appear (e.g., the Microdata series 1600 and 3200, the Intel 3000 microprocessor series, the Hewlett Packard 21mx, LSI 11, and the Varian 73).

Alteration of the contents of the microprogram storage area can be accomplished in two ways, on-line or off-line. Should on-line capability exist, then it is possible for the end-user programmer to modify the microprogram during typical program execution time. Such a storage unit employs a *writable control storage* (WCS), or *random access memory* (RAM), and sufficient software support must then be available to permit the on-line alteration. The Hewlett Packard 21mx and the Varian 73 contain a writable control storage unit. Generally, user-microprogrammable computers incorporate a WCS as the microprogram storage unit. In the case of off-line microprogram modification, a WCS is generally not used. Instead, the microprogram resides in a ROM, which can only be modified by physically replacing the ROM. *On-line microprogramming is commonly called dynamic microprogramming.*

A major concern for the designer of a microprogrammable machine is the degree of microprogrammability available to the user. The designer needs to take into consideration the amount of inherent flexibility he is willing to release to the public. But he must not sacrifice machine diagnosis (when failures occur) and simple maintenance. This requires, besides an orderly design, well-documented drawings. Thus, a trade-off must be made between user-sophistication which is equivalent to the level of user-microprogrammability and the assurance of well-defined diagnostics and machine maintainability.

1.9 COMPARISON OF MICROPROGRAM CONTROL AND CONVENTIONAL LOGIC CONTROL

As we have seen in the previous sections, there are distinct characteristics attributable to each type of control. Redfield mentions some advantages of each. He proposes that microprogram control has the following advantages over conventional control:

1) Inherent flexibility in design alteration by simple replacement of certain ROM pages.
2) Regularity in design by forcing control signal sources to be identified in formatted microinstructions.
3) Physical size reduction via a centrally located control logic element that could be densely packed.

However, microprogram control may tend to penalize a system design since control signal generation may be slow and hardware costs may be non-competitive. Yet, effective utilization of the advantageous properties of microprogram control may provide the following benefits. First, architects can delay binding decisions late in the design process. The inherent flexibility of microprogramming could reduce software development costs by easing "older" software packages into newer generation architectures. Simple firmware changes would be required. The flexibility could assist in emulative exercises where fine-tuning existing software is desirable. And lastly, this flexibility could reduce new software costs by microprogramming frequently used microcode into firmware subroutines. Regularity in design also has benefits that appear attractive. Field maintenance could be reduced to simple parity checks on the firmware while remaining control logic diagnostics could be isolated by identical electronic boards. Any one of these reasons warrants the use of microprogram control. All of these reasons influenced the design of the 68000 microprocessor with a microprogrammed control unit.

While most of this discussion has centered around computers, much the same comparative results apply to digital machines in general. In fact, the capability to trouble-shoot digital machines that are microprogrammable is supported by a host of techniques classified as microdiagnostics. *Microdiagnostics provide the ability to detect and isolate machine malfunction via additional hardware imbedded in the machine to permit diagnosis of the primitive operations.* Since microdiagnostic techniques, like microprogramming, are employed very close to the hardware, we would expect microdiagnostic hardware and microcode to be closely coupled to the microprogram control unit.

In reality, comparing microprogram control with conventional control is similar to comparing it with hardwired control, because a conventional control design is unlikely to change simply because it is difficult to do so. Rewiring circuits is much more tedious than simply replacing memory boards. More importantly, although a ROM-centered design or a microprogrammable machine can potentially contribute to the flexibility of the machine, the notion of flexibility extends beyond simply altering a structure. Of course, microprogrammable machines can be made to do specific tasks with greater efficiency; but, also, future modifications are easier to physically implement. However, hardwired machines which utilize discrete or random logic have traditionally been faster than microprogrammed machines.

Although microprogrammable machines have tended to be slow, at least for generating single instructions like ADD, SUB, etc., the efficient and expedient implementation of higher-level algorithms like Fourier Transforms is possible when such algorithms are implemented in microcode. Furthermore, microprogrammable machines can easily support multiple instruction sets (e.g., emulation) because it is also possible to make corrections in the hardware and extensions to the instruction set by simple ROM replacement.

1.10 ECONOMIC CONSIDERATIONS FOR MICROPROGRAMMABLE MACHINES

If we are to consider the use of a microprogram control unit in place of a conventional control unit, such consideration will depend on several factors. Important among these include the type of application, the level of complexity, and the cost of implementation. Assuming then that we have considered all factors except cost, how do we proceed to recognize the relative cost of implementation of one control unit over another? One method is to identify the equivalence in control between the functional sub-elements in each control unit. For instance, in hardwired control, a conventional small scale integrated (SSI) circuit is most commonly identified as the functional sub-element equivalent to a number of bits in the control storage of a microprogrammable control unit. We would then proceed to accumulate all costs incurred by each implementation taking into account not only the cost of the SSI or ROM, but also the costs of component insertion, connectors, capacitors, wiring, power supply, cabinetry, fans, and the chassis boards. Some manufacturers have proposed that the cost of microprogrammable control, F_M, and conventional (hardwired) control, F_C, are linearly related to complexity, which is a measure of the equivalence in control mentioned earlier. If such an equivalence can be identified, these manufacturers suggest that curves similar to Figure 1.21 are applicable. Note that the conventional control costs rise steeply with complexity while the microprogrammable control costs, although increasing less rapidly with complexity, have an initial cost, C_i, which must be taken into account. C_i reflects the base cost associated with the address sequencing and memory selection circuitry which is incurred regardless of the application. The steeply rising cost of conventional control reflects the high incremental cost of incorporating another small scale integration[6] (SSI) device on a board which generally includes the redesign of the backplane wiring, power source

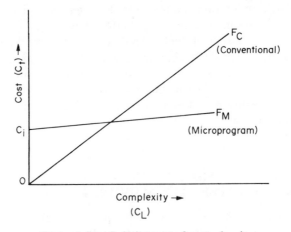

Figure 1.21   Relative cost of control units

---

[6]SSI refers to the number of electronic gates on a particular device or chip. An SSI device has few gates (10-20). MSI devices have 50-150 gates. An LSI or large scale integrated device may have hundreds of gates. Very large scale integrated devices have several thousand gates.

and cooling requirements. Such additional costs are not always evident in microprogram control. Here we may simply need to add another word in the microprogram.

We base our arguments on the ability to identify equivalent mechanisms in either control unit upon which to develop appropriate cost considerations. In Figure 1.21 it has been assumed that the cost of conventional control increases at approximately four times the rate per sequencing cycle of microprogrammed control. Of course, increasing complexity has been assumed to be directly related to the number of sequencing cycles. This notion, although simple, ignores the costly possibility that the equivalence of control for a sequencing cycle in a microprogram control unit cannot be clearly identified with the number of SSI devices in conventional control. Indeed, the diverse collection of SSI devices (gates, flipflops, counters, etc.) partially renders this approach suspect to doubt. Therefore, we need to proceed cautiously. Perhaps a conservative approach would be to identify some "average" *integrated circuit* (IC), i.e., an IC or an IC function which has the greatest commonality in a particular application, and relate its performance to some equivalent number of bits in the ROM. An IC with three gating functions has been proposed with the assumption that anywhere from eight to sixteen bits of a ROM can replace a gating function. The relative cost of one control implementation to another can now be determined by the replacement of an IC with the equivalent ROM bits.

We can analytically express the general relationships for evaluating economic costs. Suppose we define the following

C_m—average manufacturing cost per hardware component
C_d—average design cost per hardware component
C_w—cost of a microprogram word
F_c—total hardwired control unit cost
F_m—total microprogrammed control unit cost

The total cost of the hardwired approach is simply

$$F_c = C_m n_h + C_d n_h \tag{1.3}$$

where n_h is the number of hardware components. The microprogrammed control unit can be partitioned into its control memory and its associated peripheral logic (primarily discrete components). Hence, the logic costs consist of $C_m n_1 + C_d n_1$, where n_1 is the number of components. If we can relate memory costs to the number of microinstructions, n_i, the microprogram memory cost is $C_w n_i$. There also exist coding and design costs, C_c. Therefore, the total cost of a microprogrammable control unit becomes

$$F_m = (C_m + C_d)n_1 + C_w n_i + C_c. \qquad (1.4)$$

The basic fixed cost or initial cost, C_i, (assumes $n_i = 0$ and $C_c = 0$) is simply $(C_m + C_d)n_1$. The proportional cost of increase rate is $C_w n_i + C_c$, which is generally much smaller than the hardwired increase rate.

Another subtle issue arises when we compare program generation to microprogram generation costs. The microprogram development costs are considerably higher initially. Microprogram coding is expensive since effective microprogramming requires us to simultaneously execute several micro-operations. Worse yet, a single main memory instruction could incorporate up to fifty microinstructions! Microprogram coding can also be complex. Statistically coding errors increase.

SUMMARY

In this chapter we have introduced the concept of microprogram control. We have pleaded in favor of this design procedure by briefly contrasting microprogram control with that of conventional control. In this manner we have seen that conventional control is generally decentralized and distributed while microprogram control is highly centralized. We further note that microprogram control represents an orderly design methodology. Further advantages to microprogram control over hardwired or conventional control include multiple instruction set support, regularity in design, and ease of modification. Within each of two examples presented are considerations for both the designer and user of a microprogrammable control unit.

The power of microprogramming relies heavily on the structured nature of the design. Although some minimal random logic is required for any design, it does not increase with new control routines and instructions. The control storage can easily incorporate diagnostics such as found in the IBM 360 and Micro 810. Here the individual elements of the system can be exercised and diagnosed. Pinpointing failures is rapid. Field maintenance is another important reason for selecting a microprogrammable approach. Electronic systems are now functionally packaged. Hence, changes cannot be easily made by simple wiring alterations. Consequently, ROM's appear as attractive alternatives.

Basic to all considerations for a microprogrammable machine is the inherent capacity to be truly general-purpose in nature. For example, many peripheral controllers used on large computing systems must be versatile for any system configuration. Subsequently, nearly all such controllers are microprogrammable.

These points have been noted by Rosin.

"It is also the case that field modification and upgrading will be less expensive, since only the microprogram need be changed in some cases. Consider as a case in point the redefinition of floating-point arithmetic across the entire System/360 line of computers which took place in 1968. Preparation of this change for most of the models involved required only rewriting and debugging the appropriate microprograms and then installing these programs in the vast number of hardware systems in the field. The corresponding change, if made at the hardware level, could have been an economic catastrophe of major impact in IBM. Indeed, in the latter case the change might never have been attempted let alone completed in spite of its generally recognized value."[7]

PROBLEMS

1.1 Describe the "hierarchy of control" concept for digital machines.

1.2 What are the primary functions of the control unit?

1.3 What characteristics do microprogrammable machines possess which are not evident in conventional machines?

1.4 Complete the sequence of steps necessary to calculate

$$\frac{1}{8} \sum_{i=1}^{8} X_i$$

----

[7]Copyright 1969, Association for Computing Machinery, Inc., reprinted by permission. R. F. Rosin, "Contemporary Concepts of Microprogramming and Emulation," *Computing Surveys*, Vol. 1, No. 4, December 1969, p. 197.

where X_i is already in R_0 through R_7 using the computer in Figure 1.22 as follows

Micro-operation	Control Points	ALU Function	REG Select
$ALU_1 \leftarrow R_8 + R_7$	$C_{24}, C_{29}, C_{30}, C_{19}, C_{17}$	Add	R_8, R_7
$R_8 \leftarrow ALU_1$	C_{24}		
$ALU_1 \leftarrow R_8 + R_6$	$C_{30}, C_{29}, C_{19}, C_{17}$	Add	R_8, R_6
$R_8 \leftarrow ALU_1$	C_{24}		

Assume the following

(i) A one-to-one map of control signal to control bit,

(ii) no overflow (i.e., all X_i are previously scaled such that the sum will always be less than the maximum machine number),

(iii) all X_i are positive, two's complement numbers, in fixed-point mode, R_8 is already cleared.

    a) Note that if the MCU of Figure 1.15 is employed, you cannot beneficially execute any "looping" for this problem. Why?

    b) Suppose that extra hardware were available in the MCU. What extra hardware could you use to perform looping?

    c) How does this affect your sequence of elementary steps above?

    d) Now that you have generated the sequence of elementary steps, assign control points to specific bit positions of a micro-instruction word in some logical fashion. Remember that you want a "user-microprogrammer" to readily understand your code.

1.5 Define emulation. What is its relation to microprogramming?

1.6 What is regularity of design?

1.7 Extend the conventional control design (Figure 1.14) in the text to include a branch condition after addition or subtraction to test for all O's in ACC.

1.8 In Example 1.4 of the text, format the microinstruction, not by simply grouping related control signals, but also by encoding the groups. For instance, if a field commands N signals, assume that K bits are to be assigned to these N signals and that $K < N$. What extra hardware is required? (Hint. Use Table 1.3 as organized.)

1.9 What is dynamic microprogramming?

1.10 For the micromachine in Figure 1.20, write a microprogram to perform a two's complement subtraction between GR1 and GR4. Assume the minuend is in GR1 and the subtrahend and the difference are found in GR4. Note that the "+" sign indicates two's complement addition (not a Boolean OR).

1.11 For the micromachine in Figure 1.20, write a microprogram to perform multiple right shifts similar to the procedure of Table 1.5 for multiple left shifts. Use GR3 as a shift counter.

1.12 For the micromachine in Figure 1.20, write a microprogram to perform an indirect memory reference sequence.

1.13 Suppose that X bits of ROM in microprogrammed control can replace a single gating function in hardwired control. Assume that a 4096 bit ROM is used and that each bit costs .025¢ bit. The base cost for all insertion, power, pc card, socket, costs, etc. is $1.75. Furthermore, if an extra control cycle employs only one additional gating function or some additional storage element to distinguish it from all other control states, the direct cost is 35¢ per gate or element. What savings accrue if the 4096 ROM is employed over hardwired solutions?

1.14 Derive a relationship for the single point in Figure 1.21 at which the two curves intersect. What does this mean in terms of the number of gates?

1.15 In the text we suggested that a microprogrammable structure is an orderly design. This orderliness is apparent when certain steps are taken in formatting the micro-orders in the microinstruction. Revise the field specifications of the microprogrammable Example 1.2 to demonstrate some degree of orderliness. For instance, assign all control signals which activate a specific register to a contiguous set of bits in the microinstruction; classify this contiguous set by the name of the register. Do not necessarily assign b_0 to c_0, b_1 to c_1, etc.

1.16 Suppose that we replace the adder and ACC structure in the simple computer of Figure 1.9 with the elements in Figure 1.22. Assign control points to specific bit positions of a microinstruction word in some orderly fashion. Suppose, further, that this section of the computer has designated control functions (e.g., ADD, SUBTRACT, ...) such that each function can be executed by simply activating the respective control line. These control signals to our new ALU section represent the explicit linkage to the ALU (listed below). An implicit linkage from the ALU consists of two signals, BC_0 and BC_1, which indicate an all zero result in the ALU or a positive result, respectively. If BC_1 is not activated, a negative result has occurred. These two signals can be combined with test enable signals from a special control field in the microinstruction to enable a branch. How would you include the ALU functions and test signals in a microinstruction format? Note, R_0, ..., R_{31} are general-purpose registers. Data paths, ALU's and registers have equal word length.

ALU Functions	Branch Conditions
ADD	ALL ZERO $- BC_0$
SUBTRACT	POSITIVE RESULT $- BC_1$
COMPLEMENT	
OR	
AND	
SHIFT LEFT ONE BIT	
SHIFT RIGHT ONE BIT	

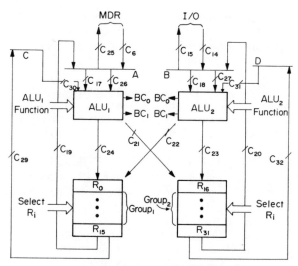

Note: General Purpose Registers from
Groups I and 2 are Selected by
Control Bits Not Shown.

Figure 1.22   Architecture for Problem 1.16

REFERENCES

A basic yet comprehensive study of digital systems is provided in two books: G. R. Peterson and F. J. Hill, *Digital Systems: Hardware Organization and Design*, John Wiley & Sons, New York, 1970; and H. W. Gschwind and E. J. McCluskey, *Design of Digital Computers*, Springer Verlag, New York, 1975.

An early discussion of microprogramming can be found in a paper by Wilkes which is reprinted in *Computer Structures: Readings and Examples*, Bell and Newell editors, McGraw-Hill, New York, 1971, pp. 335–440. This book also contains a substantial collection of computer architectures with informative remarks preceding each section.

The notion of Algorithmic State Machine design is introduced by C. R. Clare, *Designing Logic Systems Using State Machines*, McGraw-Hill, New York, 1972.

For additional coverage of the material on levels of control, see A. B. Salisbury, *Microprogrammable Computer Architectures*, Elsevier, North Holland, New York, 1976. The example in the section on conventional control is further described in Salisbury's book.

Discussions relating to relative performance of microprogrammable machines is provided by S. R. Redfield, "A Study in Microprogrammed Processors: A Medium Sized Microprogrammed Processor," *IEEE Trans. on Computers,* July 1971, pp. 743–750.

Recognition of the emulative power of microprogramming is discussed by S. H. Fuller, V. R. Lesser, C. G. Bell, and C. H. Kaman, "The Effects of Emerging Technology and Emulation Requirements on Microprogramming," *IEEE Trans. on Computers,* October 1976, pp. 1000–1009.

Example 1.3 is an adaptation of the simple microprogrammed machine briefly described in the Signetics Application Note SMS0052AN entitled "Design of Microprogrammable Systems," Signetics Memory Systems, 740 Kifer Road, Sunnyvale, CA 94086, December 1970.

An elaborate discussion of relative cost for microprogram control can be found in A. M. Beisner, "Microprogramming Study Report," Department of Computer Mathematics, Center for Exploratory Studies, IBM—Federal Systems Division, Rockville, Maryland, September 1966. A summary of his analysis can be found in S. S. Husson, *Microprogramming Principles and Practices,* Prentice-Hall, Englewood Cliffs, New Jersey, 1970, pp. 67–72. These discussions relate to computers. An analysis of costs related to digital machines is provided in the *Signetics Memory Systems Application Note* entitled "Economic Advantages of Microprogramming," January 1971.

For more comprehensive coverage of the UNI-BUS [T] concept of PDP machines, see *Processor Handbook*, PDP 11/20, Digital Equipment Corporation, Maynard, Mass., 1971, p. 9.

More on the flexibility of ROM-centered designs is covered in "Field-Programmable Patches Simplify Firmware Maintenance," EDN, April 29, 1981, pp. 139–144.

Chapter Two

SEQUENCING INSIDE THE CONTROL UNIT

2.1 INTRODUCTION

At the lowest architectural level, the sequencing of control signals which actuate primitive activity in a machine is absolutely necessary (e.g., a data transfer between two registers or a clearing of a particular bit in the accumulator). At the highest architectural level, the flexibility in microprogrammability of the end-product is desirable. Regardless of which level we are studying, there are some considerations common to every level. These include: a) flexibility, b) speed, c) functional clarity, and d) suitability for the intended application.

This chapter is directed to the original equipment manufacturer. We shall study the notion of control inside the control unit itself. We will assume that the control architecture basically possesses a control memory and control memory access. In particular, we will analyze the types of hardware configurations that are employed in microinstruction access.

The hardware notions in this chapter are especially of interest to the designers of original equipment. Recognize, of course, that any LSI design is still a moving target. In an engineering sense, the fundamental question is, "Does the final design meet the performance specifications of the intended applications well within the alloted costs?" Here the architect needs to understand the impact on a user-microprogrammer of selecting one sequencing scheme over another. This chapter focuses on such considerations.

The architecture of microprogram control employs a ROM for generation of control signals in a digital machine. Yet, the ROM alone is insufficient to execute the two essential tasks necessary for any control mechanisms: *declaration of the current states and generation of the next state.* Additional hardware is often necessary, and even found desirable, to sequence through the ROM locations. Furthermore, as we previously observed, the need for an implicit linkage suggests that conditional as well as unconditional branches or jumps are desirable even in simple digital machines. In this chapter, we focus on this latter task of next address generation, or in other words, the sequencing hardware for microinstructions. In the next chapter, we will study the mechanisms for declaring the current state. Then we will examine microinstruction formatting in greater detail.

It is important to realize that designing a microprogrammable control unit requires us to examine both tasks simultaneously. In reality, neither design task can be performed without the other. Therefore, careful design of a control unit suggests that current state declarations and next state generations be considered together. This coupling of control tasks reflects our desire to centralize control and to design the control unit in an orderly fashion. To do so, we will find that the format of a microinstruction (the use of each bit) strongly influences the sequential behavior of addressing. Likewise, the hardware or logic peripheral to the ROM which enables the next address generation is highly dependent on the address field specifications in the microinstruction format. This coupled nature between the hardware addressing logic and the field format must eventually be reconciled before we can completely specify a microprogrammable control unit.

This coupling is further made evident by briefly describing the spectrum of formats and next address mechanisms. In one sense we can view a format consisting of two explicit or distinct fixed fields,[1] the control field and the next address field. In this setting, the logic peripheral to the ROM may consist of simple latches or registers to "hold" the next address and prevent anomalous timing behavior in the sequencing. The sequencing logic is simple and distinct from the logic necessary for the control field which may be just another latch and behaves much like any memory data register (MDR). In more complex situations, formats from one microinstruction to another are capable of multiple interpretation. The fields themselves, although explicitly defined, have variable meanings. As a result we can expect to find elaborate peripheral sequencing and control logic. Here, we commonly find additional fields which specify the interpretation of other fields. This interpretation task impacts on hardware because these additional fields must utilize more peripheral logic to physically "switch" the destination of signals initiating from these variable-meaning fields.

In this chapter, we will assume some microinstruction format without discussing considerations for our choice. Format selection is left for the next chapter. Emphasis will be placed on the sequencing logic internal to

---

[1] That is, a field in one microinstruction can never be redefined in another microinstruction.

the control unit with concern for the flexibility of each addressing scheme. Since a major benefit of including more hardware into a microprogrammable control unit is to enhance the microprogrammability, we must be careful not to build structures which are so rigid that flexibility, which is also highly desirable, is lost to an elegant, yet inflexible architecture. Therefore, in this chapter, we focus on the role of hardware surrounding the ROM. Our hope is to provide a control architecture which the microprogrammer finds comfortable to program, free of possible nuances that arise within the confines of rigid control architectures.

The above discussion highlights the dual nature of the tight coupling between sequencing and formatting concepts. On one end, this coupling means designing hardware which can potentially make efficient use of both concepts. On the other end, this coupling is evident in user-microprogramming which must be capable of satisfying the intended applications of the digital machine, always with a view towards ease of programming. For instance, it makes no sense to employ a simple two-field format and sequencing logic in applications where several conditional branches are anticipated. Obviously, the microprogrammer will soon become frustrated by the inability to conveniently program branches (even if he is unaware of the control hardware). Likewise, the microprogrammer, who intends to merely sequence through microinstructions with little concern for conditional branching (because the applications rarely execute branches), will experience similar frustration with a conditional branch format that may be extensive and confusing. In the former case the microprogrammer is hampered by the sparcity of hardware and in the latter case the microprogrammer is bewildered by its profundity.

Returning then to candidate schemes for sequencing hardware, generally speaking, three basic schemes are possible: a) the two-field schemes, b) the single microinstruction scheme and its extension, c) the variable microinstruction scheme. The two-field scheme is the simplest, and, historically, was introduced first. With advancing technology of transistors, memory devices and LSI, the devices themselves altered the picture. This subsequently led to refinements in the sequencing techniques and further inclusion of memory devices for control storage. These technological improvements also stimulated more sophisticated schemes. Single and variable schemes became more popular because they were both cost and speed competitive. In parallel developments, next address selection began to assume complex forms. This transition from simplistic to complex microprogrammable control paralleled not only developments in technology, but also the understanding of the nature of microprogramming. At first microprogramming was considered to be simply a design tool for hardware implementation relegated to the private preserve of the engineer. But later, as the complexity of LSI technology increased, the power of microprogramming as a versatile design tool for programming became evident. In the process, emulation was given new life.

Let us briefly consider an alternate viewpoint to next address selection mechanisms; that is, from the perspective of either explicitly or implicitly identifying the next address. *We say that the next address is explicit if it is fully imbedded in the current microinstruction word as a field of its own with minimal logic external to the ROM; otherwise, the next address is implicit if it is imbedded only partially in a ROM field of the current microinstruction.* Note that the implicit notion may require extensive logic external to the ROM. The explicit notion was common in the earliest microprogram sequencing schemes. In these implementations we directly identify the next address by observing the next address field of the current microinstruction. No modification is made to that address field. One simply chooses the next address from one or more available sources (there may be more than one next address field in a given microinstruction). This scheme is the simplest to implement yet appears somewhat restrictive because branching is cumbersome. Hence, it may be quite adequate for a *"microprogrammed machine"* (*non-user-microprogrammable*) but is ill-suited for a *"microprogrammable machine"* (*user-microprogrammable*). Consequently, the explicit method gives way to less explicit addressing schemes; that is, through indirect or implicit schemes.

The implicit method of sequencing and branching assumes one of several schemes. The simplest of these schemes is a method for next address selection by address generation with a simple counter (e.g., incrementing the microinstruction address register) for sequential access. Counter usage, however, is only a rudimentary example of implicit addressing. Increasing levels of complexity in the implicit method can and do occur especially as we incorporate various alternatives to handling conditional branches coupled with the counter access mechanism. For instance, we could pre- or post-concatenate bits to the current address (high order/low order address bit selection), force a pure address replacement from external registers, and lastly imbed branch bit fields coupled with any or all of the previous schemes. The former techniques (concatenation) are commonly employed in applications where microinstructions tend to be sequentially ordered in the firmware, while the latter techniques are found in applications where branching is emphasized.[2]

As we shall see later, the implicitness of the next address selection is a

---

[2] We will examine these notions in greater detail later.

measure of the amount of peripheral hardware logic. Simply stated, more implicit schemes require more logic. In future sections we examine this relationship, proceeding initially with explicit schemes and concluding with implicit schemes which assume increased peripheral logic. These notions will become clear there.

Our first sequencing architecture is the Wilkes control scheme which uses basically a two-field scheme mentioned earlier. This scheme is followed by refinements to the microinstruction scheme which assume, at the very least, the incorporation of a branch or jump field. Here, as before, a single microinstruction scheme is proposed. That is, all control unit tasks (generation of control signals and identification of next address) are completed within a single microinstruction access. But now additional peripheral logic is necessary to implement some of the addressing selection tasks. The peripheral logic may consist of an address incrementer or counter and a selector driven by a control field in the new format to switch from the counter to the jump field.

If we permit even further logic as well as assume that the format itself may vary from microinstruction to microinstruction, we can derive another sequencing scheme, namely the dual microinstruction control scheme. Here, one format for the entire word may be a control field and another format for the entire word may be an address field, hence the name dual microinstruction, since two microinstructions must be retrieved. Of course, the three sequencing schemes just mentioned do not exhaust all possibilities. In later sections, various other alternatives are introduced. Yet, even these alternatives can be shown to be extensions of the three basic schemes.

2.2 WILKES CONTROL

The microprogrammable computer was first conceived by Wilkes in 1951. At this time he was primarily concerned with the lack of orderly design procedures for complex computer architectures. His approach led to the notion that the control functions could be centralized in some independent storage element. This storage element was called upon to perform basically two tasks. The first task was to identify or declare the current machine state, while the second task was to determine the next machine state. The simplest configuration for a microprogram control unit consisted of a ROM, address latch, and decoder, shown in Figure 2.1. The decoder and address latch assist the ROM in preserving the next address while the ROM stores the microinstructions which perform the two main tasks. These tasks are represented in the format which can be identified by one field as the next address of the microprogram and by another field as the

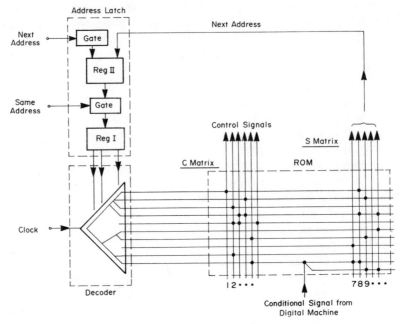

Figure 2.1   Microprogram control unit

control signals to the digital machine itself. Any conditional branches that are required during machine computations are executed by testing conditional branch lines which select the next address by activating the address field in the next microinstruction. The microprogrammer would then recognize that the ROM activates respective control lines for a particular machine instruction, generates the next sequential address of the microprogram in the same microinstruction if branching is not required, and if branching is required, fetches the next address in the next microinstruction.

The address latch, equivalent to the CSAR in the previous chapter, is conceptually depicted with two registers, REG I and REG II, which are enabled by signals, "SAME ADDRESS" and "NEXT ADDRESS." The details of this configuration are not important except to note that the decoder is a combinatorial device (contains no memory) and, therefore, the current address must be provided to the decoder during the full microinstruction period. However, the next address field in the current microinstruction generates the next address (assuming no branches) which must be saved before the current microinstruction is disabled. REG II serves to temporarily store this address. Obviously, "SAME ADDRESS," "NEXT

ADDRESS," and the "CLOCK" signals must be coupled to load and transfer addresses from REG II to REG I. Furthermore, if a branch request appears, the relative timing of these signals must accommodate the additional delay. Regardless of the additional delay, relative timing for each signal should consecutively activate "CLOCK," "NEXT ADDRESS," and "SAME ADDRESS" with no overlap and with the three-step sequence repeated continuously.

Referring now to Figure 2.1, each horizontal line in the grid matrix represents a microinstruction. The dots on the horizontal lines represent the bit patterns or microcode of each microinstruction. For instance, in the first line (first microinstruction) we see that there are eleven bits in the word, and that the first and eighth bits are opposite to that of all remaining bits. Thus when the first microinstruction is executed, control signal C_1 is activated (by the first bit). At the same time, the next address is specified by the second grouping of vertical lines which indicate a bit pattern of 01000 (assume that the first line is at address zero, the second line is at address one, and so on). Each subsequent line characterizes respective microinstructions which are words formatted with two fields. One field generates the control signal and is six binary bits long, while the second field issues the next address for the microprogram and is five bits long. In this control unit there are eleven microinstructions in the ROM. The ROM is, therefore, an 11x11 memory device. Also note that one conditional branch is allowed with the tenth microinstruction. When no conditional branch is required, the next sequential microinstruction executed after the tenth instruction has the address 11000. When a conditional branch is required, the next sequential microinstruction is accessed from location 00101. Typical hardware for accomplishing the conditional branch is shown in Figure 2.2. For this case of a two-way branch condition, two additional AND gates and an inverter are required for each conditional branch.

The advantages of the Wilkes control unit are obvious. The architecture is simple since only three functional elements are required, namely ROM, address latch, and decoder. The format of the microinstruction is also straightforward. It uses two fields and this simplicity is further evidenced by the distinctively disjoint usage of each field. Neither field has dual roles. However, this simplicity also obscures penalties. First, repetitive execution of the current microinstruction can only be accomplished by physically programming the same microinstruction in the ROM as needed.[3] This

---

[3] Of course, if more branch control circuitry were included, a microinstruction could loop to itself until commanded to do otherwise.

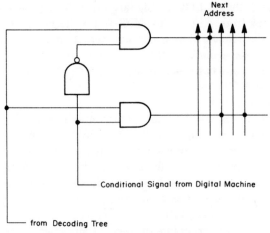

Figure 2.2   Two-way branch control

tends to increase the length of a microprogram. Secondly, branching, although simple, also requires that each branch address physically reside in a different microinstruction. Unfortunately, the control fields of the micro-instruction which contain these branch addresses are empty! These instructions are essentially *no op*eration (NOP) microinstructions. Hence, if the Wilkes control unit is configured with a single ROM and branching is frequently encountered, several locations in the ROM may be only partially utilized, thus wasting ROM words. To overcome these deficiencies, we can either increase the peripheral control logic or "reformat" the micro-instruction.[4]

The organization of the Wilkes control unit, when first proposed, was implemented at a time when memory devices were relatively slow and expensive. Therefore, in order to generate signals at least as fast as a register-to-register transfer, hardware control units incorporated diode arrays instead of core memory planes (solid state memory was not available in the 1950's). As a result, few restrictions were placed on the actual layout of a word in control "memory." Hence, changing the width of the microinstruction that would be necessary for the eleventh word in Figure 2.1 impacted only slightly on the hardware design. In fact, it was simply a matter of including another diode in the arrays. The two arrays were called the S matrix and the C matrix, for sequencing and for control, respectively.

---

[4] Formatting is the subject of the next chapter.

Diodes were placed at junctions indicated by dots in each array of Figure 2.1. When an additional connection was required to enable an alternate or branch address (as in the eleventh microinstruction), the circuit of Figure 2.2 was employed instead of a diode.

When memory devices became both reliable and economical, attempts were made to include them in the control unit storage. Storage dimension became an important design factor.[5] Subsequently, the organization of the control unit became sensitive to fixed word lengths and memory access speeds because memory devices were used instead of diode arrays. It then became necessary to consider the relative speed of the microinstruction access to the macroinstruction access. Furthermore, the microinstruction word length became more restrictive within a particular machine from word to word. Simply stated, it was fixed! Therefore, with advancing technology, questions arose concerning the need for additional fields in the ROM and how best to incorporate refinements while maintaining the inherent flexibility of microprogram control. Additional peripheral hardware became necessary and the simplicity of the two-field format blossomed into more elegant structures.

2.3   SINGLE MICROINSTRUCTION CONTROL

In the single microinstruction control sequencing scheme, we assume that individual microinstructions in a typical microprogram are generally retrieved sequentially or repeated. But we also expect to encounter jumps or branches which alter the desired sequential access. In making effective use of these assumptions, we will employ a simple modification to the microinstruction format as well as some additional peripheral logic. For instance, suppose that the sequential retrieval of microinstructions is no longer provided solely by generating an address from a field internal to the microinstruction but rather, also, by an additional incrementer or counter in the address latch region of the Wilkes scheme. Because this incrementer will always generate the next sequential address, our address field in each microinstruction can now serve principally as the branch address or *target* address field. Now the addressed location is no longer restricted to the next sequential location. Notice that if branches are seldomly encountered, our ROM remains under-utilized. The branch field will appear empty most of the time. So we really have not overcome one objection of the previous scheme, namely a sparsely coded control storage!

---

[5] The storage dimension of a memory is the product of the width of the words by the total number of words.

To employ this new scheme with an incrementer and branch address field, we include some additional peripheral logic (besides the incrementer) to choose between the incrementer and the branch address field. An implicit link is necessary from the functional elements of the digital machine under control to the control unit itself. For example, suppose that the signals via the implicit linkage are generated by "branch conditions." The additional field in our microinstruction is provided by enabling branch condition tests. A typical configuration appears in Figure 2.3 and utilizes the branch control circuitry of Figure 2.4.

The configuration provides two addresses to the decoder, one from a counter (CNTR) and another from a *branch address register* (BAR). Either address is selectable by branch control signals, S_c and S_r, generated by the branch control circuit. For sequential access, the S_c line activates the counter, while for branch access, the S_r line activates BAR. The branch control circuit receives signals from the functional elements of the digital machine through *branch condition lines*, BC_1, BC_2, and BC_3. Moreover, the current microinstruction word enables the branch control through the branch test lines, which are test bits in the microinstruction word. We see from Figure 2.4 that unconditional branches are ORed with all conditional branches. Thus, if it is necessary to execute an unconditional branch or simple jump, then that particular bit in the branch test field is set in the microinstruction word. Also, the S_r line is activated regardless of the status of the branch condition lines. The branch address located in that microinstruction is then passed from the BAR to the decoder. For this control method, an additional AND gate is required for every conditional jump. In our illustration, three AND gates are required for the three conditional branches.

Let us now compare the previous Wilkes scheme with that of the current control scheme. In each scheme, how many branch addresses are available at the end of the current microinstruction? With the Wilkes scheme two branch addresses remain, while with the current scheme any number of branch addresses potentially remain. Of course, this depends on the complexity of the branch test lines, conditions, and branch address field of the microinstruction word. For example, suppose that we concatenated four extra bits to the address field. These bits serve merely to provide a jump to any location between the current location and the sixteenth location from the current location. This concatenation procedure, when properly implemented in hardware, could then generate the N-way branching.[6] This inherent flexibility of sequential control encourages more versatile micro-

---

[6] N equals sixteen in our case.

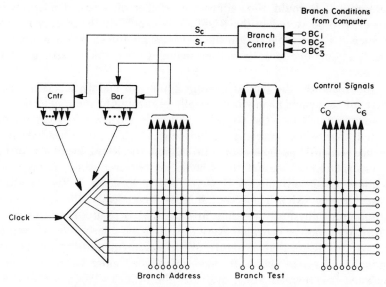

Figure 2.3   Single instruction sequence control

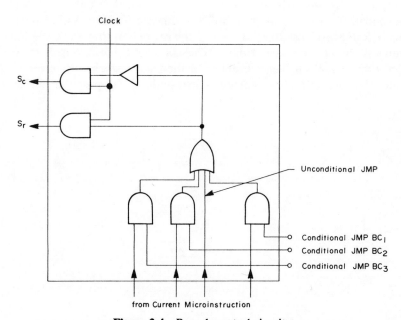

Figure 2.4   Branch control circuit

programming. It could also reduce the number of repeated microinstruction words to be stored in the ROM. This capability becomes most effective when it is desirable to use the repeated microinstruction by inserting the code at only one location and branching to that microinstruction when necessary.

In this instance, the typical microprogram will mainly access the incrementer for sequencing, only occasionally branching to the repeated microinstruction, much like the sequence shown in Figure 2.5. Here we have assumed that some microinstruction (e.g., "ASR") is executed in the sequence shown. The flow chart also depicts the ROM locations for each microinstruction. Note that the scheme we are proposing in this section will allow us to conveniently branch back to location 3 after location 4 (to execute the ASR). Therefore, at least theoretically, the length of our microprogram physically residing in the ROM is reduced, since the code for ASR need not be repeated every time that the micro-order is required. Of course, to insure that we return to the incremented address rather than a branch address in the ASR microinstruction, more peripheral control logic must be provided which overrides the branch. This peripheral logic could be driven by a new bit in the branch test field which will automatically return us to the incrementer.

Even though the current scheme improves upon the Wilkes approach to sequencing, as it now stands, it still has inherent drawbacks illustrated in Figure 2.6. Most important of these is the restriction that any branch must return to the next counter address. The example in Fig. 2.6 depicts both a legal branch and an illegal branch. In the legal branch, just prior to the jump, the counter address was microinstruction 2. Suppose that the condi-

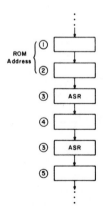

Figure 2.5   Microprogram flow chart with repeated instructions

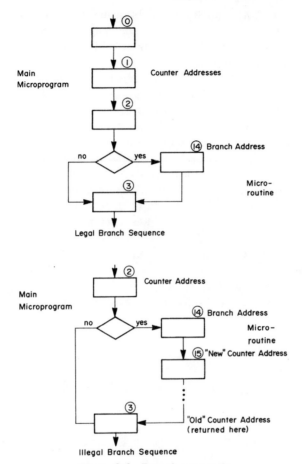

Figure 2.6 Branch sequences

tional branch requires a jump to location 14, and after microinstruction 14 is executed, a return to location 3 is required (the main stream of the microprogram). This is permissible since the counter is incrementing through the "main stream" of the microprogram. But now suppose the branch sequence contains several microinstructions as in a microroutine. *A microroutine is simply a subroutine in the microprogram.* An illegal branch sequence will occur since the counter address cannot be preset to the "new" counter address (location 15). Furthermore, this illegal branch sequence requires the counter address to be reset to the main stream location or microinstruction 3, shown here. Since no hardware exists to support this additional capability, all branches must be one line micro-routines with an immediate return to the main stream (clearly, this is intolerable). To overcome this limitation, additional hardware must be provided to facilitate longer microroutines.

Suppose we add a latch and control gates to preserve the "old" count in the counter. Upon return from the microroutine, a signal from the control branch circuitry or another bit in a ROM field (possibly called the ENABLE RETURN FIELD) would indicate that a return from microroutine is desired. To insure that a microroutine call has occurred and a return from microroutine is desired, the bit in the special ROM field must be enabled by some circuitry in the control branch box. This additional control logic might take the form shown in Figure 2.7. Here, a simple D flipflop generates a gated signal of the special field to the counter to restore the "old" count (incremented by one). The flipflop is set when S_r goes high indicating a branch is in progress. The restore "old" count signal is not generated until the ENABLE RETURN FIELD bit is high (accomplished by micro-programming).

The reader should observe, by now, that all of the above can be partially provided by microprogram software as well as by the hardware scheme

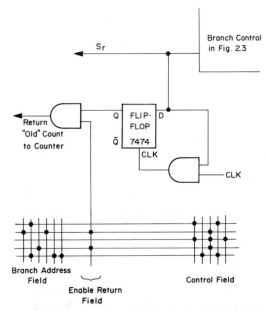

Figure 2.7 Return from subroutine control

shown above. That is, when a return from microroutine is desired, the microprogrammer may simply program a branch to location 3 (by "writing" a 3 into the branch address field). This enables the counter with the next executable microinstruction if the address field is also tied to the counter (this is also new hardware). But now we have placed a constraint upon the microprogrammer. He must specify the return jump address to be the "old" counter address. This constraint may not be desirable in all cases. Finally, we remark that the hardware scheme, with the modifications proposed by Figure 2.7, prevents any microroutine nesting, since we have not provided a stack nor any hardware to support nesting. Again, we could continue to provide more peripheral hardware to the single microinstruction scheme. Or we must rely on microprogramming software with some additional programming constraints. The choice is not always obvious to the designer since many factors must be considered (timing, power, number of devices, etc.).

The above sequencing methods assume that if repeated microinstructions are frequent and if efficient bit assignment requires sequential ROM access, then the single microinstruction method is superior to the Wilkes basic scheme in terms of bit efficiency. Let us examine this assertion. Although it is true that the current scheme, like the Wilkes scheme, requires an address field, this field in the single microinstruction scheme contains either a sequential address or a non-sequential address. Note further that conditional branches in the Wilkes scheme require an "extra" line of microcode for each conditional branch. Consequently, this "extra" line of microcode has an empty control field specification (the dotted extension line of Figure 2.8). Therefore, the Wilkes scheme essentially

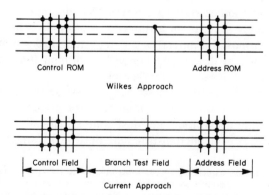

Wilkes Approach

Current Approach

Figure 2.8   ROM Length reduction by single instruction

requires a no operation (NOP) microcode for every branch microcode. In contrast to this, the current control scheme requires no extra code. Thus, a line of microcode is "saved" for every branch line. If, then, several branches are required in a typical microprogram, the Wilkes scheme would be disadvantaged in terms of ROM storage requirements. The Wilkes scheme requires a longer ROM. However, the longer ROM in the Wilkes scheme is offset by the additional peripheral logic in the current scheme. Before, the address latch consisted of two simple registers. Now, the address latch contains a counter with appropriate control selection between the counter and branch address register provided by an additional branch test field.

Additional hardware is not the only solution. We need to organize the branch test field. We should clearly identify the branch tests by coupling or directly mapping the target address to the conditional branch tests. For example, suppose we format this field of our previous example (Figure 2.4) as shown below. Now the infrequent user-microprogrammer need only

Branch Test Field

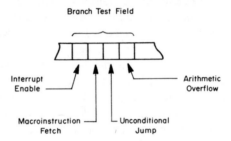

Interrupt Enable — Arithmetic Overflow

Macroinstruction Fetch — Unconditional Jump

observe the bits set in this control field to immediately determine whether an interrupt is permitted, the microprogram sequence is returning to the user program for another starting address of a microprogram sequence, or an ALU anomaly such as an arithmetic overflow is being monitored.[7] Note that the leftmost bit refers to an important task. Remaining bits refer to lesser tasks in descending "order" (assuming that the rightmost bit is of the least significance in some sense).

The current control scheme is described as a single microinstruction sequence control because the two essential tasks of a control unit, namely current control state declaration and next state specification, are provided by a single retrieval of a microinstruction. Both tasks are simultaneously

---

[7] It is difficult to discuss sequencing mechanisms internal to the control unit without considering the format. This example with branch tests is only one case which dramatizes the tight coupling between microinstruction organization and sequencing. More will be said in the next chapter.

accomplished even though a single microinstruction access is made. Suppose, however, that it is desirable to further reduce the width of a ROM, possibly because both the current scheme and the Wilkes scheme require microinstruction widths which are excessive and only available in custom ROM's. The motivation to implement a narrow ROM leads to the following control scheme which we call the dual microinstruction control scheme.

2.4 DUAL MICROINSTRUCTION CONTROL

In the single microinstruction control scheme for sequencing through a microprogram, we assumed that every word in the ROM has an identical format. In that case, the activity or micro-order specified by each field in any word was obvious. The control field was used solely for generating the micro-orders. The address fields were sequential (as in the Wilkes model) or nonsequential (as in the single microinstruction). The branch enable field identified the selection between unconditional and conditional jumps. However, as we desired more flexibility, we also increased the relative width of the microinstruction word. Suppose, now, that we cannot accept a long word length (maybe the physical dimensions of the ROM's themselves cannot support it). Could we find a flexible sequencing architecture which supports a narrower ROM?

One solution is to stagger the fields in a ROM in the vertical dimension. That is, assume that a particular microinstruction can be either a control field or an address field. A complete control word access would consist of two microinstruction accesses: one for control and another for next address, hence the name, dual microinstruction. Successive words in a microprogram would only generate either control signals or next addresses much like that shown in Figure 2.9. Of course, we need not be restricted to a simple repetitive alternation from a "control" to an "address" microinstruction if some mechanism were imbedded in each word to identify the type of format desired. This may consist of a single bit field labeled the format key or *format designator* field. Even if this extra field is too costly to implement, we can still provide for a dual microinstruction scheme if we assume that "control" and "address" always alternate. In that case, the peripheral logic would keep track of the current format instead of relying on a designator field. However, employment of the extra peripheral logic instead of another control field does not necessarily lead to a less expensive design.

A typical architecture for the dual microinstruction scheme with a format designator field is shown in Figure 2.10. The essential features of this control unit include the ROM, decoder, next address and control

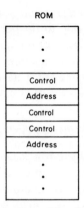

Figure 2.9 Microprogram with a dual microinstruction

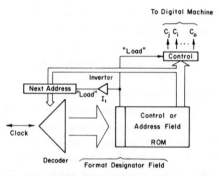

Figure 2.10 Dual microinstruction control architecture

latch, and, finally, a format designator signal which generates a "LOAD" signal to either the address latch or the control latch, but not both simultaneously (hence, the inclusion of the inverter, I_1, which insures that only one latch is activated). Notice how closely this control architecture appears to resemble the Wilkes control scheme. In fact, if we remove the inverter, the outward appearance depicts nearly identical architectures. We should obviously expect a high degree of parallel behavior between each control scheme, including the limitations, one of which is the awkward branching mechanism in the Wilkes scheme. What, then, could be added to this architecture to overcome the deficiencies in the Wilkes scheme?

A more effective control architecture, which still makes use of the dual format notion, could include the refinements of the single microinstruction scheme. At the very least, an additional field in the "address" microinstruction should be included which would enable branches. The control architecture for the refinement is illustrated in Figure 2.11. Here another signal, called the BRANCH ENABLE, is utilized to switch from one address to another. Note also that the "address" microinstruction is partitioned into two address fields, ADDR A and ADDR B, to provide two alternate address sources. However, these additional address fields require peripheral control logic to switch between ADDR A and ADDR B. Gates A_1 and A_2 activated by the branch control circuitry and enabled in the branch enable field of the "address" microinstruction provide such control.

One limitation of this sequencing scheme, as noted before, is the small number (two) of branch paths possible with each microinstruction. Of course, we could "nest" the "address" microinstruction such that the first address microinstruction jumps to another address microinstruction, and so on. However, this nesting sequence requires multiple microinstruction access which slows the execution of a microprogram. To overcome this problem, we may introduce three or more address fields until the word length of the microinstruction approaches the physical limits of our design. Another refinement is to include an address incrementer or counter to replace one of the branch address latches. Then a narrower ROM is possible.

These three sections complete the discussion of the basic sequencing schemes for microprogrammable control units. Naturally hardware extensions can be found in every direction from simple counters and latches to small RAM stacks and multiplexers which can nest microroutines and handle priority interrupts at the micro-order level. The next sections describe derivatives of our three sequencing schemes.

Section 2.5 describes an extension to the single microinstruction scheme. Priority in branch addressing selection is desired. Here the design philoso-

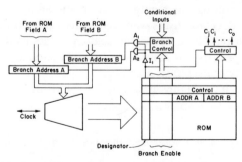

Figure 2.11   Branching refinement to dual microinstruction control

phy is predicated on classifying micro-orders into groups in relation to
their control tasks.[8] Section 2.6 discusses a truly flexible implicit addressing
scheme proposed by Schlaeppi. As we shall soon see, the notions of the
dual microinstruction scheme are only vaguely recognizable. Here the
design philosophy assumes that microprogramming is essentially modular
and "subroutine-like". Hence, the control unit should facilitate the handling
of the entry and exit of subroutines. The last sequencing scheme, microinstruction interleave, is discussed in Section 2.7. Here multiple ROM's are
employed in parallel fashion. Motivation for such an architecture stems from
the potential increase of the sequencing access speed of a microinstruction.[9]
Both the advantages and disadvantages for this approach are identified. These
three remaining sections introduce specific control sequencing schemes.
However, the reader should focus on considerations for choosing such schemes
as much as on understanding the architectural details. Less obvious details
can then be found in the references at the end of this chapter.

2.5   PRIORITY BRANCH CONTROL

Suppose we desire to impose an additional constraint on microprogramming.
For instance, perhaps a branch control scheme may be warranted with
some inherent priority mechanism. One possible application for this sequencing structure can be found in digital machines which must support
several users or tasks simultaneously. Here it may be desirable to selectively
provide rapid access to the microprogram control unit from several sources.
In one case, user access to the microprograms would appear as macroinstructions generated at a higher-level language. These macroinstructions
would serve principally as the starting addresses to microroutines. Upon
exiting from a microroutine, control must return to the next macroinstruction or, perhaps, to another user/task. With several user/tasks dynamically
accessing the microprogram storage unit, a hierarchy of control events
may be encouraged. Those users who frequently access the control may be
given a high priority. Those users who seldom access control may be pre-
assigned a lesser priority. Of course, this priority should not depend solely
upon the frequency of user/task access.

In some cases, it is highly desirable to interrupt the current micro-

---

[8] This is a format notion of considerable importance in the "organization" of a microinstruction.
[9] This is a rudimentary form of pipelining.

instruction. Suppose that a major machine malfunction is pending. For instance, cabinet cooling fans have stopped and sensitive circuits are in danger of overheating. The control unit should interrupt current activity, preserve important register contents, and place the machine in a WAIT state with minimal power consumption in order to prevent physical damage to the machine from overheating. To be effective, the control unit must be capable of generating several branch addresses simultaneously in every microinstruction. Furthermore, the many status signals from the digital machine must inform the control unit of conditions which warrant a branch to an alternate microinstruction.

The following scheme for a control unit, proposed by Gerace, effectively allows for a four-way branch with priority in the branching control. The configuration is illustrated in Figure 2.12 and the four-way branch is indicated in Table 2.1 with the priority structure. Two features of this sequencing scheme are noteworthy. *First,* alternate branch addresses are defined explicitly in every microinstruction, requiring the ROM to be relatively wide. *Second,* additional peripheral control logic provides for priority hardware branching. The impact of the first feature is obvious. Branching is fast since the address is immediately available. Of course, the

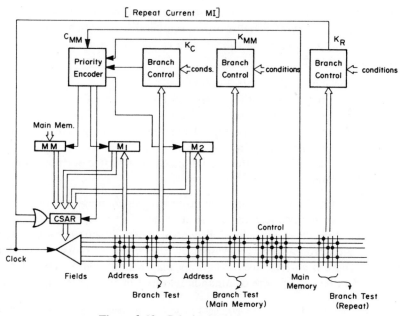

Figure 2.12   Priority branch control unit

Table 2.1

Address	Priority
Current (CSAR)	High
Main Memory (MM)	↑
Conditional Branch (M_2)	
Unconditional (M_1)	Low

gain in speed is offset by a wide ROM. The impact of the second feature is not obvious since, on the surface, it would appear that priority hardware is desirable, but this is not always true. In fact, for some applications, the priority hardware scheme may appear overly restrictive to the user-microprogrammer.[10] And, at best, we may find that a wide ROM (for multiple branch fields) without the priority hardware is more attractive. For the moment, let us assume that both features, a wide ROM and priority hardware, are permissible.

Our design philosophy implied by the priority branch control scheme assumes that the micro-orders can be classified according to their functionality. Hence, if "general" classes can be identified, then the micro-orders in each class should be combined in some fashion. This may either be in the microinstruction fields or in peripheral logic which must support each class. Suppose, in either case, that it is desirable to arrange the classes into four main tasks:

1. Information for the control unit.
2. Control operations in the control unit and intervening at the end of the current microprogram.
3. Control operations in the digital machine and/or intervening during the current microprogram.
4. Control operations in the digital machine which determine physical cycle timing.

The first class identifies those micro-orders which must aid the control unit during such instances as initial start-up of the machine. Or, more commonly, this class provides for control when a starting address for another microprogram is generated by the main memory or working memory where high-level user-programs may reside. The second class of micro-orders belongs to the commands required of the control unit which,

---

[10] Hence, this kind of architecture may not be found in user-microprogrammable machines. At least, the capability may be opaque to all but the original equipment manufacturer.

for example, may facilitate the return from a microroutine in the micro-program. Here the microroutine return address may be activated by appropriate control signals in this second class. The third class of micro-orders serves to execute respective commands which might be required during the execution of a current microprogram. For instance, an interrupt external to the control unit may request a change in the sequence of microinstruction executions. The fourth class of micro-orders comprises those commands which primarily serve to partition the timing cycles of microinstructions. This mechanism frequently appears when either the control unit or the user environment is asynchronous. Such would be the case when, for example, many peripheral devices such as magnetic tapes or disks are used and such devices dominate communication to the computer.[11] In the current control scheme, three of the four classes have been utilized to group conditional and unconditional branch enable fields. Each enable field is then combined with its appropriate branch address field. Finally, the enable fields are controlled by a priority scheme which makes use of control information provided both by the control unit itself (e.g., the "repeat" current micro-order) and by the digital machine (e.g., a main memory address request).[12]

The multi-branch control unit permits conditional input control from the main computer through three control circuits, K_C, K_{MM}, and K_R. Each control circuit is also tied to a respective control field in the microinstruction word. Table 2.2 lists the condition code combination and address selection for this control unit. The priority encoder circuit selects control signals from each K to specify the choice of the next microinstruction address. Four sources for this next address are available: the current microinstruction address (CSAR), main memory (MM), conditional branch (M_2), and unconditional branch (M_1). To repeat the current microinstruction, the contents of the control storage address register, CSAR, are held until a new address is needed. Repetitious words are selected by K_R. This address source has the highest priority. If it is desired to execute an unconditional jump from a microprogram to the main memory of the computer, then register MM is activated by the C_{MM} line through the priority encoder block. This address has the next highest priority. Conditional jumps to main memory are enabled by K_{MM}. Should it be desired to branch internally within the microprogram conditioned by the machine

---

[11] These classes are likely to be found in microprogrammable machines such as Input/Output Controllers (IOC).

[12] Our present discussion relates to the next chapter. We again mention formatting here because it is important to the understanding of the current sequencing scheme.

Table 2.2

	Condition Code			Address Selection
K_C	C_{MM}	K_{MM}	K_R	
X	X	X	1	Repeat (CSAR)
X	X	1	0	Main Memory (MM)
X	1	0	0	Main Memory (MM)
1	0	0	0	Conditional (M_2)
0	0	0	0	Unconditional (M_1)

status, the contents of register M_2 are loaded into the CSAR. This activity is controlled by K_C and a computer condition status. Of lowest priority in the address source selection is the unconditional access via register M_1.

Table 2.2 lists the condition code combinations for each address selection. If it is desired to perform an unconditional branch, then K_R, C_{MM}, K_{MM}, and K_C must be zero. When a conditional branch is required, the condition code combination must be 1000. Others are further indicated in the table. Of course, even though the condition code combination may allow a condition branch, this may not take place unless warranted by the actual status of the machine. This multi-branch control scheme with its inherent priority structure internal to the microprogram controller is most effective when the priority is mapped carefully to the condition status of the machine itself. Extreme care must be taken to insure that these priorities be properly exercised by the microprogrammer. Otherwise, effective controller behavior may be defeated.

We summarize the characteristics of this next address scheme below:

Priority Branch Control

No counter
Fixed number of branch paths
Explicit branch priority
Encoded branch control

Observe the natural capacity of this scheme to support increasing interaction between the digital machine and the control unit. Of course, all of the control schemes in this chapter can provide for some implicit linkage from machine to control unit. Naturally, this linkage may appear in various forms to the microprogram control unit. For instance, the macroinstruction op code field might serve as a starting or map address for a microroutine in the microprogram. Another example is the need for the control unit to respond to high priority machine interrupts (as in a power failure). In this case, graceful degradation would require all active control elements throughout the digital machine to preserve status. And, control should permit a return to a simple restart state when operator reinitiation occurs. This scheme may well support such tasks. We briefly list possible implicit linkage signals which apply to our scheme:

Implicit Linkage Paths to Microprogram Storage from Main Machine

---

Macroinstruction op code as target microinstruction address
Mode control (master machine state in FETCH or EXECUTE)
Interrupt
Initialization (of ROM by some hardwired microprogram bootstrap routine)

The current sequencing scheme is similar to the single microinstruction control scheme. In both, a single access provides all of the necessary functions for control. But, the similarity ends here because the physical structures possess striking differences. For one, the ROM is much wider in the current scheme because several branch addresses are found in every microinstruction. Correspondingly, we need more peripheral logic to take into account, not only the selection of the next address, but also the priority structure of the selection.

Suppose, then, that we desire to return to a narrow ROM yet retain some of the flexibility capable in the current scheme. With that in mind, let us extend the dual microinstruction scheme in Section 2.4 (which does not require a multiple microinstruction access), by assuming that the fields in *every* microinstruction serve dual roles *simultaneously*.

2.6 VARIABLE MODE CONTROL

Of all the microprogrammable control schemes presented so far, the variable mode control scheme is the most implicit of next address techniques. This design is an adaptation of control proposed by Schlaeppi at IBM. In the variable mode scheme, as portrayed in Figure 2.13, we assume that no single segment of each ROM word is designated solely as an address field. The same is true for the control field. All fields of the ROM are dual-purpose fields implementing both control and next addressing.

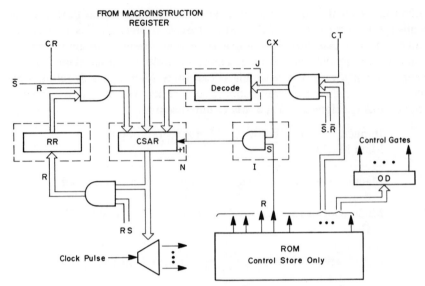

Figure 2.13   Variable mode microprogram control

However, unlike the dual microinstruction scheme which requires two ROM accesses, the variable mode scheme requires only one access. Because this is the case, each microinstruction must serve both as a microword commanding certain micro-orders and as a code for the implicit next address.

In practice, significant peripheral decoding is required to generate several micro-orders as well as the next address. In Figure 2.13, we observe that the control field of the microinstruction is the full width of the ROM and, further, that an output decoding matrix, OD, is required. The control bits of the microinstruction (again, the entire microword) must eventually pass control information to the individual micro-orders in the digital machine, *but* only after significant decoding by the OD. Although we show simply a block for the OD, more than simple combinatorial logic may be required. For instance, the OD may also contain a latch to hold the current microcode after decoding. Certain bits in the microinstruction such as the "S" or "R" bits may be used to latch the code. S and R have other important functions as we shall soon see. We could also expect the OD matrix, at times, to inhibit all control bits. Some mechanism must be able to decode this microword as the null microcode. This is simply a *no* operation (NOP) for the digital machine.

For the present discussion, we need to understand the function of the sequence inputs in Figure 2.13. This logic is depicted in the peripheral hardware as the control storage address register, CSAR, the return register RR, and associated control gates. Our particular variable mode scheme (there are, of course, many varieties) has four modes for the next address with a protocol listed in Table 2.3. They are the Normal mode, Prepare Return mode, Execute Return mode, and Jump Target mode. The design philosophy of this sequencing technique assumes that individual micro-programs are essentially microroutines to be accessed by a variety of tasks. Hence, the control unit should enhance the entrance, exit, and interrupt of microroutines.

Normal Mode

The Normal mode of next address sequencing has two sub-modes, the increment mode and the repeat mode. The increment mode assumes that the next microinstruction to be retrieved from the microprogram is the next sequential location in the ROM itself. Thus, we simply need to increment the current address to determine the next address. However, should it be desired to repeat the current microinstruction, we must enter the Repeat sub-mode in the Normal mode for this provision.

Prepare Return Mode

The Prepare Return mode for our implicit next address sequence assumes that the microprogram is currently in a closed loop much like a subroutine. Therefore, we need to be able to return from the loop micro-routine to the main microprogram sequence. To do so, we require a return microinstruction address. This address should be the address at which we left the main microprogram to enter this microroutine. To return, we need simply to remember the current address before branching. A special

Table 2.3 Next Address Modes

Normal	S	R	CX	CR	CT
a) Increment	1	X	1	0	0
b) Repeat	X	X	0	0	0
Prepare Return	1	1	X	X	0
Execute Return	0	1	0	1	0
Jump Target	0	0	X	X	1

register, RR, is used to latch the current address (before we enter the microroutine). RR is then incremented by one and held constant until a "return to main" microprogram signal is issued. Hence, the name Prepare Return mode.

Execute Return Mode

Upon receipt of the "return to main" microprogram sequence (which may be internal to the variable mode scheme but most likely is not), the next address sequencing mode enters the Execute Return mode. Here the preserved return address in RR is now latched into the CSAR. Both the Prepare Return mode and the Execute Return mode require the RR register.

Jump Target Mode

The last mode of next address sequencing is the Jump Target mode. In this mode we have assumed that a branch is desired from the current address. But, beyond this, we are not required to preserve a return address. Such would be the case in a jump to all unconditional branch sequences. We control the four modes with five sequencing control signals, S, R, CX, CR, and CT. The first two, S and R, are control bits in all microwords. Therefore, they are internal to the variable mode control storage unit. In a user-microprogrammable machine, they would be available for coding by the end-user, while in a microprogrammed machine they probably would not be accessible. The various logical combinations for both S and R are shown in Table 2.3. Note that S must be a logical "one" to enable the increment sub-mode of the normal next address sequencing (see "I" dotted block in Figure 2.13). Besides S and R, three external control sequencing signals are required in our variable mode control store unit, CS, CR, and CT. The increment sub-mode is entered when CX is a logical "one".

At this point we should begin to ask where the source exists for the external signals, CX, CR, and CT. These signals may emanate from several locations in the digital machine depending on the type of machine architecture. In a microprogrammed machine, some of these signals may be accessible to the user. In a microprogrammable machine, access is desirable. In the latter case, for example, CX, CR, and CT may be generated by certain decoded bits in the macroinstruction op code. In this case (see Figure 2.14), if the specified op code for all unconditional jumps in the main program required bits 2, 3 and 7 of all op codes to be set to "one", then a simple three input AND gate tied to these bits in the instruc-

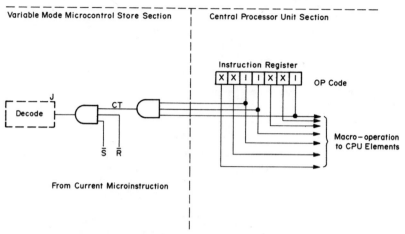

Figure 2.14 External CT signal generation

tion register of the main computer could generate CT. Assuming that these op code unconditional jumps required a Jump Target mode in the microprogram, the appropriate CT signal would be generated. Similar configurations exist for the remaining signals, CX and CR.

2.7 INTERLEAVE CONTROL

During the early development of microprogrammable control, the control storage was rather slow. At that time, a significant improvement in speed was achievable by simple instruction interleave. One implementation was incorporated in the RCA Spectra 70 computer illustrated in Figure 2.15. This microprogrammable controller used two memories and microinstructions alternately accessed from one and then the other. A two-phase clock synchronized both address decoders and latches. With this scheme we can, theoretically, halve the memory access time of a microinstruction. However, we must realize that interleaving complicates conditional branches. Although sequential access is conceptually fast, in practice this speed increase is seldom achieved because non-sequential access is sometimes required in the interleave scheme.

The two-ROM scheme could eliminate the double latch requirements in earlier schemes. Furthermore, the microinstructions could be interleaved to within the fetch phase of each microinstruction as in Figure 2.16. This interleaving is achievable only if microinstructions are alternately fetched from each ROM. In practice, however, we must recognize that branching

Address
Latch I
Control Matrix
Address Matrix
Phase
2
Two - Phase
Clock
Conditional
Branch
Control
Phase
1
Address
Latch 2

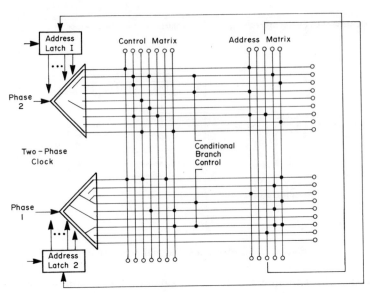

Figure 2.15 RCA Spectra 70 microprogram control

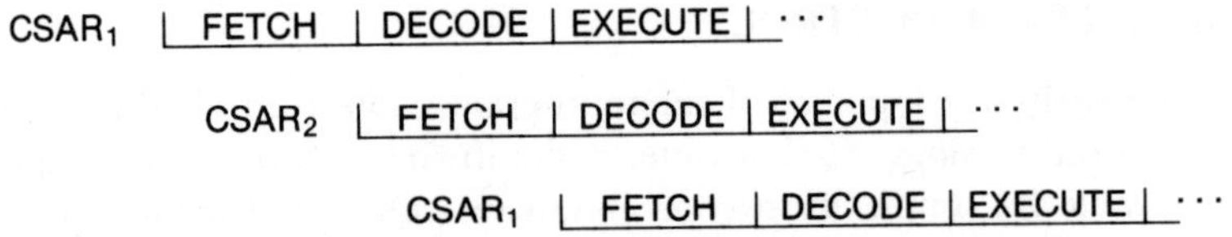

CSAR₁ FETCH DECODE EXECUTE · · ·
CSAR₂ FETCH DECODE EXECUTE · · ·
CSAR₁ FETCH DECODE EXECUTE · · ·

Figure 2.16 RCA Spectra 70 microinstruction interleave

requires additional logic. This logic may consist of two latches on each ROM for the conditional jump address within the currently activated ROM. Automatic control must then be provided to insure that the next microinstruction is inhibited from the ROM not currently addressed. This additional circuitry does not come without additional delay in microinstruction access. Hence, the interleave timing portrayed in Figure 2.16 is an idealized specification seldomly achieved.

In principle, dual microinstruction interleave can be extended to an n-manifold interleave (see Figure 2.17), however, an increasing cost in complexity must be recognized. At the very least, the clocking pulses, CPM_i, must be carefully timed, otherwise the simple "ORing" of the

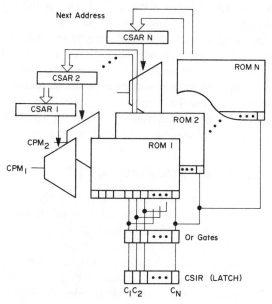

Figure 2.17   N-Manifold microinstruction interleave scheme

ROM outputs does not work. We can expect even more complications when our microprograms are no longer resident in a single ROM but are now interspersed within several ROM's. This interleave, although reducing ROM access time drastically, likewise amplifies the microprogrammer's instruction management problem. Furthermore, peripheral logic grows with each manifold. It is not even clear that the simple branch and counter control schemes (described previously) are applicable here. In fact, for the RCA Spectra 70, the rule of alternate ROM fetch was relaxed in specific instances.

Obviously, branching must be skillfully employed in the n-manifold microprogram control scheme. Otherwise, the simplicity of design may be lost. What is not as obvious here is that we may have to take a closer look at decision making and branching. Gardner points out that the two are not synonymous, and he further suggests that branching delays in a microprogram can be minimized by restricted usage of branch tests in the microprogram control section. This can be achieved by grouping data flow conditions into: a) those generating only minor changes in data path flow (e.g., the difference for ADD, SUBTRACT, and COMPARE), and b) those that require gross changes in path flow (e.g., differences between ADD and EDIT). Then the control unit should not have to consider branching when minor changes occur at the data path flow level. However, major changes occurring anywhere in the digital machine should be addressed by the control unit and branching permitted where necessary. The branch delay problem can subsequently be minimized by allowing gross changes to modify the address of the control word to be fetched. Otherwise, minor changes simply modify contents of control words already fetched. These notions for branching and control relate directly to the significance of the internal functional activity in the digital machine. However, such notions are very sensitive to the current configuration.

2.8 INTEL 8086 MICROPROGRAMMED CONTROL

At some point in the design, one needs to temper enthusiasm for regularity of design in return for raw speed. The microprogrammed control unit of the Intel 8086 (See Figure 2.18) is a case in point. In fact, the classic trade-off between microinstruction width and execution rate forced some, otherwise, microprogrammable functions back into random logic control. Second to speed was the need to reduce required ROM space on the device itself. Fine-tuning of the control unit led to adjusting microcode for mathematical macroinstructions. Specifically, the often used data type specifications for such instructions (eight bit versus sixteen bit) are left to other resources (namely, the group decode ROM). Mathematical source and destination operands are also controlled elsewhere (the M and N resources in the execution unit). Furthermore, the mathematical operator is determined directly via the X operator resource. Such mechanisms are aimed at reducing costly look-up and execution chores of the microprogrammed ROM.

The 90 short microroutines of the 8086 are stored in a 504 × 21 bit ROM. Where possible, repeated microroutines are eliminated. The effective address and data-read (from memory) procedures are combined into a common microroutine. Another unique feature of the control unit is the use of the ROM as a sort of programmed logic array (PLA) to assist in deriving the ROM starting address from the macroinstruction op code. The leading byte of the op code is used. Sequencing through microroutines is facilitated by post-concatenating a 4-bit incrementing register to the address. For SHORT jumps, this is sufficient. For LONG jumps, the full address is modified by the AR and CR registers.

The 8086 microprogrammed control unit represents a collage of the sequencing schemes presented in this chapter. Yet, this is not markedly different for other microprocessors which are microprogrammed. At one end of the spectrum, the fully microprogrammed control unit, lies the

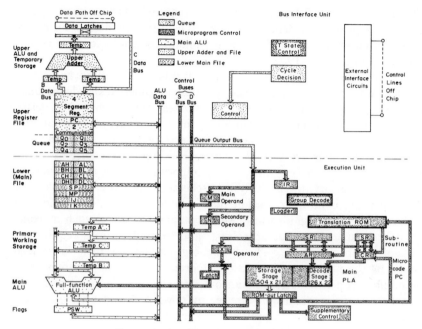

Figure 2.18   8086 Functional Diagram

Copyright © 1979, by the Institute of Electrical and Electronics Engineers, Inc., reprinted, with permission, from IEEE Spectrum, New Option from Big Chips, James McKevitt, John Bayliss, vol. 16, no. 3, 1979.

Motorola 68000 with virtually no random logic. Here a two-tier ROM control structure generates a 10-bit control word from the first ROM, which is later decoded into seventy control signals by a second ROM. At the other end of the spectrum, some microprocessors, like the Z8000, are controlled almost entirely by random logic, in spite of the fact that its predecessor, the Z80, was microprogrammed.

SUMMARY

This chapter has focused on hardware for sequential control schemes for generating the next address. Next address sequencing is a hardware problem involving a trade-off between the width of the ROM and the amount of peripheral control logic. When a narrow ROM is desired (as in implicit addressing), more peripheral control logic is required. Thus, some control implementations suggest a significant investment in the control hardware adjacent to the ROM. Decode logic, both for the next address as well as the control signals themselves, may be required. The implicit address approach represents a departure from ROM-centered design since most of the design effort is placed in the peripheral control logic. This relation is depicted in Figure 2.19.

Each addressing approach has both advantages and disadvantages. In the elementary sequencing schemes, the designer must acknowledge that a simplistic implementation (such as the Wilkes control scheme) is desired by the hardware designer. But, simplicity must not destroy user flexibility.

The choice of which control sequencing architecture to use in any given application depends on several factors. However, the choice is mainly application driven. Access time is also important. When mere sequential access is satisfactory, the basic Wilkes scheme is adequate. In some sense, the sequencing is no more elegant than a table look-up. No decisions are made. Access is straightforward. More complicated access such as conditional branching, interrupt branching, and subroutine links require considerably more hardware. The branching mechanism then is typically chosen by the number and selection of branch condition variables. Also, the number of permissible simultaneous branches plays a major role in the branch selection mechanism because, by now, it should be obvious that the hardware to implement multi-way branches increases rapidly.

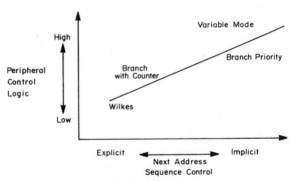

Figure 2.19   Peripheral control logic versus next address sequence control

PROBLEMS

2.1 How is conditional branching performed in the basic Wilkes control scheme?

2.2 Give three examples where conditional branching would be employed.

2.3 What is inefficient in the ROM layout for the Wilkes control scheme?

2.4 In the single microinstruction control scheme, how are unconditional jumps implemented?

2.5 How can repeated microinstruction control be implemented in the single microinstruction scheme.

2.6 Can you prioritize branch control in Problem 2.4 above?

2.7 In a microprogram control scheme, why are repetitious microinstructions given highest priority?

2.8 In a control scheme, why would the unconditional or sequential microinstructions be given lowest priority?

2.9 The microinstruction interleave control scheme requires additional buffering. Identify these latches and explain their function.

2.10 All address schemes in this chapter have ignored the problem of initializing the microprogram address register. In each scheme, design the necessary additional hardware to incorporate some initialization technique such as firmware bootstrap.

2.11 Which addressing scheme is most amenable to microwords which are predominantly stored in sequential ROM locations? What hardware aspects in each case support this feature?

2.12 What additional problems can you foresee with the variable mode control scheme?

2.13 What currently available microsequencer chips are functionally similar to those schemes discussed in this chapter? Describe the significant departures.

2.14 Design an op code set to generate CX, CR, and CT for the variable mode control scheme. Identify the level of user-programmability.

2.15 A scheme for next address sequencing, not discussed in this text, uses the op code of the macroinstructions as starting addresses for microroutines. Design such a scheme. Is it implicit or explicit?

2.16 You are given a counter, latch, decoder, and 256 word by 20-bit ROM and miscellaneous circuitry (gates, flipflops, wires). Assume that a ROM format with eight bits of control, eight bits of address, and four miscellaneous bits is provided.

   a) "Sketch" a microprogram control unit with the elements above. Show briefly but clearly the connections.

   1. What are the four bits used for?
   2. Explain your branching mechanism.
   3. How "far" can you branch? Why?
   4. To what is this branch addressing relative?
   5. How do you go into and return from a microroutine?

   b) Suppose that the ROM must remain at twenty bits; however, you now need sixteen bits for a control field.

   1. Redesign the architecture above to meet this requirement adding only the minimum necessary peripheral logic.
   2. What limitations now exist in microprogramming this configuration?

2.17 Microinstruction access time is sometimes very important. For each of the sequencing architectures below, determine the worst-case access time.

   1. Wilkes scheme
   2. Single microinstruction with modifications (Figure 2.7)
   3. Dual microinstruction with branching refinement (Figure 2.11)
   4. Priority branch control (Figure 2.12)
   5. Variable mode control (Figure 2.13)
   6. Interleave control (Figure 2.15)

REFERENCES

A general discussion of specific microprogrammable machines mentioned in this chapter can be found in four references: C. R. Campbell and D. A. Neilson, "Microprogramming the Spectra 70/35," *Datamation,* September, 1966, pp. 64-67; *Microprogramming Handbook,* 1972, available from Microdata Corporation; *Hewlett Packard 2100 Computer,* 1972, *Microprogramming Guide,* available from Hewlett Packard; and the *Varian 73 System Handbook,* 1972, available from Varian Data Machines.

An interesting comparison of user-tasks is discussed by C. V. Ramamoorthy and M. Tsuchiya, "A Study of User-Microprogrammable Computers," *AFIPS Conference Proceedings,* 1970, pp. 165-181, as well as by P. L. Gardner, "Functional Memory and Its Microprogramming Implications," *IEEE Trans. on Computers,* July, 1971, pp. 764-775.

Lastly, historical developments on the subject of control for microprogrammed machines are available in two articles: G. B. Gerace, "Microprogrammed Control for Computing Systems," *IEEE Trans. on Elect. Computers,* 1953, p. 733; and A. Graselli, "The Design of a Program Modifiable Microprogrammed Control Unit," *IRE Trans.,* 1962, p. 336. The basic notions in the variable mode control scheme can be found in S. S. Husson, *Microprogramming—Principles and Practices,* Prentice-Hall, Englewood Cliffs, 1970, pp. 29-30.

Chapter Three

MICROINSTRUCTION ORGANIZATION

3.1 INTRODUCTION

Recall that a microinstruction consists of "bits" stored in a ROM which executes two general tasks: a) sequencing/branching of microinstructions, and b) specifying control signals for the digital machine. Certainly, both tasks must be efficiently executable in the particular machine application. Such efficiency can be measured by the ease with which a machine can be microprogrammed. Efficiency implies the complete exploitation of the internal resources of the digital machine. In the final analysis, this effectiveness depends upon how well we initially specify control signals to the microinstruction. Effective organization of individual tasks in a microinstruction is the goal of this chapter.

Previously we were more concerned with the impact of hardware on the control unit. Now we are concerned with the subtleties of organization in the individual microinstruction. That is the second design dimension of microprogram control. We call this dimension *formatting*. To do so, we must focus on aspects of the architecture of a machine which relate to its functionality. To be sure, we must identify a logical basis by which we will organize the microinstruction around functional roles of our machine. Then our format, if properly organized, will make the flexibility of microprogramming evident.

In the previous chapter we studied basic sequential schemes internal to microprogrammable control units solely from the hardware viewpoint. In that sense we assumed that our role as the designer was much like that of a structural engineer who initiates a task by identifying available raw materials for his or her specific application. Likewise, the computer architect, and in particular the control unit architect, studies the available resources (latches, counters, ALU's, ROM's, gates) and formulates a construction plan of the control unit, never forgetting the particular application of his or her machine. If the architect is essentially applications-driven, he or she will initially establish the importance of each control resource, identify its relationship to the application, and finally, assess the relative gains of employing or not employing each resource. Once the task of identifying the architecture is completed, it is then possible to build upon this structure (generate high-level software, interface peripherals, etc.).

It is important, then, to always remember why we format microinstructions. *A microinstruction represents the window through which the physical resources of a digital machine are made visible to the user,* much like that depicted in Figure 3.1. Here the digital machine is "representable" to several user-communities. They are high-level language designers, microprogrammers, maintenance personnel, and architect designers. This representation is the microinstruction format which governs the usage of internal resources. Hence, it is important to make these resources highly visible. However, no user-microprogrammer should be burdened by intensive study of the architecture before generating microprograms. Therefore, a major benefit to be derived from organizing a microinstruction format is to relieve us of the burden of "learning" every intimate detail of the hardware. Some formats do just that! Good formatting should allow us:

a) to build a format with a minimal set of programming constraints,
b) to make internal resources readily identifiable to the largest community of users, and
c) to support user flexibility.

The physical resources of the digital machine which a user intends to employ in an application must be readily identifiable in the format. The actual layout of the control signal assignments into relative bit positions of

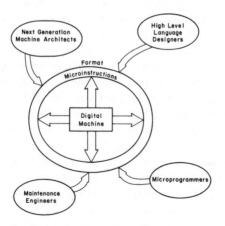

Figure 3.1   The format window

the microinstruction should be such that control functions can be readily understood. For example, a "readable" format for a microinstruction in a digital computer may be the following. Each zone or field in the micro-

Microinstruction

Sequence	ALU Control	Memory Control	I/O Control

instruction identifies control activity for a particular functional resource. Hence, a bit set in the ALU control field would not be expected to activate an I/O resource and vice-versa. This simple grouping helps us to meet the first two goals of formatting mentioned before. Note, however, that the second goal of "illuminating" resources to the largest community of users may not be desired in some cases, by the very nature of the machine application. In fact, some microprogrammable machines are not intended for user-microprogrammability. The IBM 360 is one notable example. Hence, we, as designers, must be careful how to interpret the second goal. The third goal, support of user flexibility, is also measured by the intended set of users. Factory microprogrammers will find a different set of criteria by which to measure user flexibility than field maintenance personnel.

Whereas the previous chapter addresses itself to considerations for the computer control architect from the hardware standpoint, this chapter addresses itself to the organization of microinstructions from the software standpoint. We do not generate any software, per se. Rather, we acknowledge the eventual multitude of software that rests upon our microinstruction set, namely FORTRAN, BASIC, PL/I, etc. But remember, the user-community comprises many personalities, with more varied levels of understanding of the machine. The levels stretch across the intended applications to the actual hardware of the machine. Therefore, we will not be primarily concerned with the hardware impact on the user-microprogrammer (it should have been minimized before user-microprogramming ever begins). It is far more important to portray the powerful features of the digital machine to the user without confusing him or her by requiring an extensive study of the architecture. As we shall see, one particular format speaks to this issue for each group of users.

In a previous chapter we implemented micro-orders imbedded in microinstructions. These micro-orders, m_p, m_q, ..., refer to the control point signals, C_i, C_j, ..., which are issued by microinstructions to hardware resources. In this chapter we will be concerned with microroutines, or equivalently, user-specifications which "call up" the micro-orders for any given task. Notice that micro-orders are physical control signals emanating from the microprogrammable control unit. But microroutines are tasks which the microprogrammer intends to employ in any given situation. Hence, microroutines emanate from microprograms designed specifically by the user-microprogrammer. If the user-microprogrammer is also the designer of the microprogrammable control unit, micro-orders are likely to be equivalent to a microroutine. If, however, that is not the case, no apparent correspondence may exist. In fact, one commonly finds the former to be rare and consequently more than one micro-order may satisfy a given microroutine. To emphasize this point in the chapter, we naturally call *the primitive tasks desired by a microprogrammer as a microroutine.* The intent, of course, is to focus on the needs of the user-microprogrammer.

A number of formatting taxonomies have been established. These concepts are generally referred to as packed or unpacked, vertical and horizontal, direct encoded and indirect encoded, monophase and polyphase, and hard and soft microprogramming. Although, in theory, each concept is distinct, in practice this distinction is not always clear. Such taxonomies will be explored in this chapter with the intention of identifying various structures for a microinstruction format. For now, only the general features of each format type are described. All but the last concept bear directly upon the format of microinstructions and all but the last two concepts are closely allied with the physical dimensions of the ROM (the number of bits, B, and the number of words, W) containing the microprogram.

The degree of "packing" relates to the quantity of control information imbedded in a set of bits in a microinstruction. Highly packed microcode contains much control information. Hence, the physical width of a ROM is more likely to be narrower with packed code than with unpacked code. The same relationship exists between the ROM width and horizontal/vertical formats. Vertical formatted microprograms tend to reduce ROM width requirements. Like the previous formatting concepts, encoded formats rely on the general notion of the relationship of the micro-orders in a machine. When it is desirable, *micro-orders may be grouped into fields each of which possess a logical property which makes each field use immediately recognizable by a microprogrammer.* The concept of phase formatting departs from the previous formatting concepts in that phase formatting considers the timing relationship among the individual micro-orders. Hence, physical resources which are capable of parallel execution may be effectively utilized by employing phase formatting when the relative length of each execution interval for each resource is considered. Then the notion of concurrency, the intrinsic capacity of a machine to simultaneously execute multiple tasks, comes into play. Hard/soft microprogramming relates to the behavior in a particular application.

In all of the above concepts, the format itself represents the structure of a microinstruction and, to some extent, the degree of flexibility in writing microprograms. Each format has advantages and disadvantages which will be partially identified. However, preference for one format over another is not always obvious. In fact, in some machines, the distinctions become blurred, and we find that a combination of formats is applicable.

In simplest terms, the intrinsic format of the microinstruction is equivalent to the degree of identification made between a given control task in the digital machine and a specific bit in the microinstruction. If a specific bit directly controls a given task and all bits in the microinstruction possess this characteristic, then an *unpacked* format is identified. If, however, a specific bit controls more than one task and many bits in the microinstruction possess this characteristic, then a *packed* format is identified. Notice that in order to unambiguously specify control tasks in a packed format, other means must exist in which to identify the control of each task. One such method is to assume that bits are encoded in some fashion and that additional peripheral logic will decode the control bits for each task.

An unpacked microinstruction is commonly referred to as a *horizontal* format simply because unpacked microinstructions tend to generate microprograms in wide ROM's which literally tend to be horizontal when documented.[1] This contrasts with packed microinstructions which literally tend to be vertical in terms of documentation. Consequently, packed microinstructions have been referred to as having a *vertical* format. However, it is not always necessary to have encoded fields in vertical formats because the nature of a vertical format is more fundamental.

Vertical format microinstructions tend to control tasks which are sequential in time. Hence, by specifying a single microinstruction with a vertical format, the user-microprogrammer expects to execute several sequential micro-orders. Furthermore, he or she expects to specify fewer details of each micro-order since the designer of the format has previously incorporated such details into the formatted structure. The motivation for choosing this type of packed format over an unpacked format is sometimes to reduce the width of the ROM. But remember that packing can reduce the inherent flexibility in microprogramming. This inflexible nature of packed formats in some cases may not exist while in other cases it may be

---

[1] Because there is so much to describe when we "write" each microinstruction in a microprogram, the documentation (e.g., flow chart description, lists, tables or whatever "forms" we employ) is literally spread out across the page.

evident that the microprogrammer is severely constrained. In other cases, the loss of flexibility can only be measured by designing a horizontal format and by comparing the horizontal format with the vertical format.

The unpacked format is certainly not free of microprogramming nuances either, even though flexibility tends to be higher than that found in packed formats. For example, since any single control task has a single assigned control bit, many simultaneous tasks can be executed. Thus, the inherent parallelism in the machine architecture can be more fully exploited. However, few mechanisms exist to prevent the microprogrammer from executing conflicting tasks that may use the same data path or physical resource. Even though the unpacked format supports a high degree of flexibility, it also may support the same degree of potential microprogramming hazards.

3.2 MICRO-ORDER SPECIFICATIONS

It is now necessary to examine probable sets or classes of micro-order specifications we could encounter. The first set of specifications assumes that our digital machine consists largely of only two types of resources. The second set of specifications assumes that our digital machine is a computer where more detail is desired at the micro-order level. The last set described belongs to the class of digital machines portrayed as process controllers. As we shall see, the set which we choose is highly dependent upon the intended application and the resources of our particular machine.

Micro-order specifications directly relate to executable operations in the digital machine. However, these operations taken individually are not commonly encountered in high-level language operations such as DIV, MULT, etc. Recall that the operations we are describing belong to the "primitive" set of instructions at the microprogram level. These operations are intimately related to the available hardware, whether the hardware is a storage resource or a functional resource. In fact, the *simplest designation or specification for micro-orders assumes that a digital machine largely consists of either registers or combinatorial execution resources (address, shifters, etc.).* Registers are *temporary* or local storage resources while combinatorial circuits are *functional* resources. The hardware interconnections between the storage and functional resources are called *data paths.* Data paths may be distinguishable by the existence of a functional resource between two storage resources as in Figure 3.2. Hence, micro-orders may simply connect storage resources or else connect and transform data between storage resources. The former is sometimes called a *link* or *transfer* micro-order and the latter, an *operation* or *function* micro-order.

For many digital machines, these two types of specifications suffice.

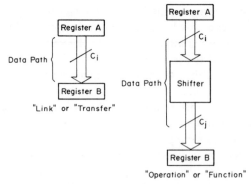

Figure 3.2   Data path types

However, when it is desirable to organize specifications to be more explicit, we need to identify the various species of functional resources and storage resources. In digital computers, a convenient set of field specifications can be developed from the following five types:

    a) Successor Fetch or Transition Rules
    b) Arithmetic Logic Control
    c) Storage and I/O Control
    d) Status Control
    e) Constant

These five sets of field specifications are representative of a general set of specifications we may encounter in a computer. For a computer, a format employing these five sets of microroutines may appear as shown in Figure 3.3. Although the successor fetch microroutine is primarily determined by the architecture of the microprogram control unit, the linkage between the computer and the control unit is also important.

Recall that some communication is required between the high-level user-program in main memory and the microprogram.[2] For instance, the op code in the *macro*instruction conveniently serves as a starting address in the microprogram subroutines. Likewise, the storage and I/O control have been combined into one group of microroutines even though it is certainly possible to isolate a storage microroutine from an I/O control microroutine. The status and control field microroutines may relate to machine status (e.g., RUN state, low power state, diagnostic "mode", etc.) and loop count (e.g.,

---

[2] The explicit and implicit linkage mentioned in Chapter One is an example of such communication.

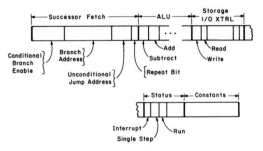

Figure 3.3   Computer microinstruction format

looping in a micro-subroutine, or repeating microinstructions). The five sets, themselves, relate to a general-purpose computer configuration. For machines intended primarily for scientific computation or word processing, the sets may look entirely different. For instance, our representative set above is well-suited to scientific applications; however, for other applications another set may be more effective. For file management applications, a set which makes less conspicuous use of the ALU control and more obvious use of string manipulation (packing, unpacking, etc.) is better.

Similar to the computer subset of digital machines, the process controller subset of digital machines may find sets of field specifications that are application dependent. In general terms, we may identify a useful set of field specifications for process controllers according to the expected control events. Hence, a candidate set of microroutines may be generated from field specifications such as the following:

a) Successor Fetch
b) Timing
c) Next Event
d) Event Enables
e) Event Monitors

For a process controller, a format employing these five sets of microroutines may appear as shown in Figure 3.4. This choice is highly dependent upon the notion of "event-driven" control. In other words, the process controller initiates some activity (Event Enable), maintains current event activity (Event Monitor), and sequences through events (with a combination of Successor Fetch, Timing, and Next Event). Since process controllers tend to find application in asynchronous environments (because events occur at random), a field specification for variable timing may be desirable.

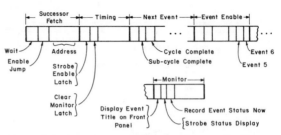

Figure 3.4   Process controller microinstruction format

3.3 HORIZONTAL MICROINSTRUCTIONS

Recall that any microinstruction is a specification of information required to control hardware resources. In a totally horizontal format microinstruction, each bit is identified specifically with a single control point in "direct" fashion. Therefore, a one-to-one mapping exists between a bit in the microinstruction and a control bit in the digital machine. For instance, suppose we have an ALU as shown in Figure 3.5. The ALU has four input registers to the adder. Each input register is tied to a BUS which also has two accumulators connected to it. A horizontal organization for microinstruction control of this ALU could look like that of Figure 3.6. Note that each control gate, c_i, in the ALU is specified by a single bit in the microinstruction. The actual control signal for each gate is transmitted directly from its respective control bit position in the microinstruction. As such, no decoding logic is used to generate the c_i control signal. Since no decoder is necessary for a fully horizontal organization, timing delays from the microinstruction to the control gate are minimized. And in this respect, the purely horizontal or direct control represents the fastest microprogram control.

Furthermore, because each bit is dedicated to a control gate and every control gate has a bit, the purely horizontal format is the most flexible organization to microprogram. Virtually any set of microroutines may be microprogrammed (if the specified control gates exist). Although it is not obvious from our simple ALU example, purely horizontal formats are the most difficult for the user-microprogrammable machines to implement. This difficulty arises when the user begins to microprogram with a totally horizontal format, and soon realizes the enormity of the task even in moderately small digital computers. It is not uncommon to find over fifty bits in horizontal organization. In short, this implies that the user-microprogrammer must be intimately familiar with over fifty micro-orders in the machine. In no way does horizontal microprogramming become a casual exercise, and for

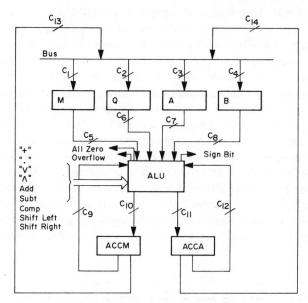

Figure 3.5 Arithmetic logic unit

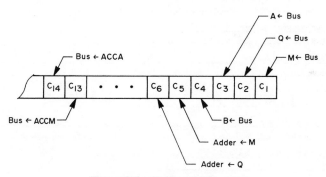

Figure 3.6 Horizontal format

this reason, few digital computers with totally horizontal formats are user-microprogrammable.

Our previous example of a horizontal format represents one field of the typical horizontal machine format; that field concerned principally with the ALU. The next example is representative of an extremely, but not totally, horizontal format. Our digital computer is an IBM 360/50[3] which is a medium to large scale member of the 360 series which employs horizontal encoded fields. Encoding is discussed in a later section. Model 50 is intended as a general-purpose computer; hence, it is capable of handling a variety of data formats (half word, full word, decimal numbers, etc.) as shown in Figure 3.7 with an equally wide variety of macroinstruction formats shown in Figure 3.8. The 360 series represents a unique departure in computer design in that every attempt was made to build a series of upward compatible architectures with microprogrammable control units. A primary goal of the designers was to permit execution of a fixed instruction set spanning similar machines in a wide range of performances. Simultaneously, common user level architectural features were sought for all models and these are represented in Figure 3.9. This hardware commonality coupled with hoped-for software commonality (emulation, diagnostic routines, etc.) led to a high level of machine series compatibility at the microcode level.

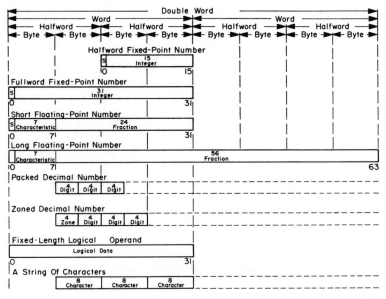

(*Reprinted Courtesy of IBM Corporation*)

Figure 3.7   360 Series data format

---

[3] Reprinted by permission from IBM Systems Journal, 1967 by International Business Machines Corporation, Tucker, S. G., "Microprogram Control for System/360," IBM Systems Journal, 6, 4, (1967).

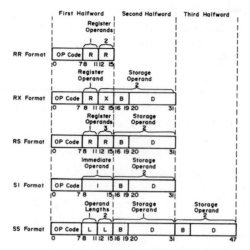

(Reprinted Courtesy of IBM Corporation)

Figure 3.8 360 Series instruction format

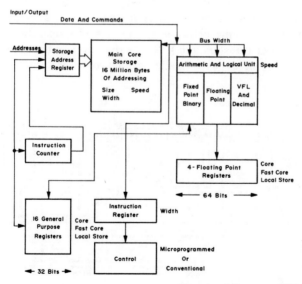

(Reprinted Courtesy of IBM Corporation)

Figure 3.9 Common architectural features of 360 Series

Hence, reprogramming for the next generation machines (IBM 370's) was made possible with less manpower and time than would have resulted otherwise. As a result, a horizontal encoded format was chosen in general, and the model 360/50 format for the CPU is as depicted in Figure 3.10. Note that ninety bits are required.

The model 50 series is a classic example of a computer with a horizontal format and represents a noteworthy effort to insure flexibility in microprogramming. This flexibility is desired for many reasons. Most important of these is the need to support architectural commonality and to implement efficient microdiagnostics. Since the 360 series represents a wide spectrum of low, medium, and high performance machines, common design features were imposed upon the 360 which were facilitated by the horizontal control word format. Also, during the course of machine development, architectures were chosen such that advances in electronic technology could be easily incorporated.

In fact, it was desired to efficiently extend the machine characteristics into the next generation of computers. This upwards compatibility was desired to some extent both in hardware and in software. The second reason for choosing a flexible microinstruction format was to incorporate hardware and software features in the 360 series to facilitate field maintenance. Hence, a form of diagnostics at the microprogram level was developed in order to return malfunctioning machines to operational status without excessive down periods. *Microdiagnostics* is a microprogrammable tool which tests machine behavior at the primitive operation level (gates, register-to-register transfers, etc.). Notice than even in the above situations, the physical resources were made visible to several user-communities,

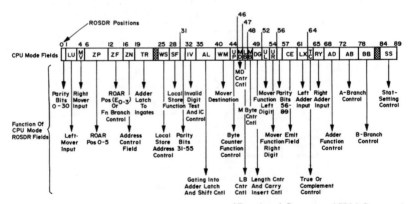

(Reprinted Courtesy of IBM Corporation)

Figure 3.10   Horizontal microinstruction format for 360/50

including field engineers, software support programmers and microprogrammers. And yet, the 360 is not available as a user-microprogrammable machine.

Three major field specifications were made by the manufacturer in the model 50 series: static control, emit, and sequence. Control signals were included in the static control specification if such signals activated input and output gates of physical resources such as the ALU, floating-point registers and general-purpose registers. Any subfields in this specification had to be "mutually exclusive." For instance, since the ALU has left and right inputs as shown in Figure 3.11, the set of left input gates was included in one subfield and the set of right input gates was included in another subfield, both fields being mutually exclusive. The emit field included control signals which enabled branch condition latches (the STATI-CIZER in the 360), set the program status word and, if so microprogrammed, injected four binary bits into the arithmetic data stream. The sequence field specifications included all control signals for microinstruction access.

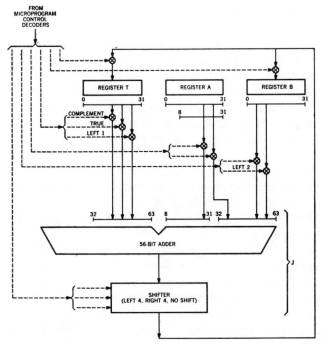

(Reprinted Courtesy of IBM Corporation)

Figure 3.11   IBM 360 ALU

3.4   VERTICAL MICROINSTRUCTIONS

The major advantage to a totally horizontal format machine is the flexibility that it provides in microprogramming. This is true simply because every micro-order is controlled by a single bit. Hence, any microroutine can be programmed in a given microinstruction. Unfortunately, for many digital machines of significant computing power with horizontal formats, it is necessary for the microprogrammer to become very familiar with the many micro-orders. This is especially evident in machines which have resources that can be operated simultaneously or concurrently. In these same machines, even though the microprogrammer theoretically can specify any or all control bits in a given word, such microinstructions may be invalid. They may even result in sequences of operations which cause machine malfunctions. Therefore, not only must the microprogrammer recognize all valid microroutines, but he must also be aware of invalid sequences and combinations in the particular machine.

For some digital machines, it is less important to have a high degree of flexibility than to have a readily understandable microprogram. Furthermore, many machines are intended for dedicated applications, where user-microprogrammability is non-existent. And in these situations, simple microprogramming features that are both rich in microinstruction repertoire and easy to use are favored. One solution is to employ a vertical format in the microinstruction. Here, it is possible to reduce the number of fields in each microinstruction, which can be accomplished in several ways. One method would be to designate resources in the digital machine which are independent of each other. This may reduce some of the timing considerations for a typical microprogram at the user-microprogramming level. Another method would be to identify similar functional resources in the digital machine and specify fields by function type. This would make it easier for the microprogrammer to implement microinstructions by assigning mnemonics to fields which specify similar activity. Such consistency greatly aids the occasional microprogrammer in the generating and debugging of microprograms.

For example, in a typical digital computer, it is possible to employ either a functional encoding format as in Figure 3.12 or a resource encoding as in Figure 3.13. The meaning of bits in the control word is different for each operational mode. In the functional encoding format shown, a designation by ALU activity is described. A separate field exists for the input and output fields. This encoding method is quite easy for data flow machines. In the resource encoding format, similar resource activity is combined in the

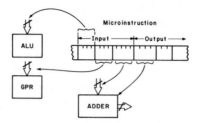

Figure 3.12   Functional Encoding

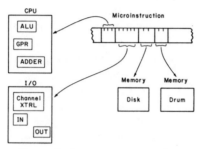

Figure 3.13   Resource encoding

same field. For instance, all I/O device activity specifies one field; all CPU activity defines another field. Then all main memory activity defines a third field.

These organizations are two simple examples of the types of encoding which are possible in a vertical microinstruction organization. In all cases, we need to insure that the task of generating and debugging microprograms remains simple. But simple field encoding does not necessarily imply an efficient vertical format. Recall from the introductory remarks that vertical microprograms tend to be literally vertical in the "documentation." Furthermore, a vertical format relies more on the timing specifications to be imbedded in the field and less on the encoding of the fields themselves. A format tends to be vertical if the sequence of executable micro-orders which constitute any microinstruction are predominantly sequential in execution. Hence, careful consideration of the timing specifications between micro-orders has already taken place and has been designed into the microinstructions. *Micro*instructions tend to take on the appearance of typical *macro*instructions. For instance, MULT and DIV, which are mnemonics commonly found at the *macro*instruction level, could be found at the microinstruction level in a vertical format machine.

Assuming, then, that the notion of encoding is to be employed in a vertical machine, one important question must be addressed. What is the degree of dependence in the grouping of the fields themselves? For instance, in Figure 3.12 we arbitrarily designate one field as the ALU output field and another field as the ALU input field. This represents field specifications which are independent of each other. The ALU output field is not dependent on the ALU input field and vice-versa, since the output field would not be energized simultaneously with the input field because results would not be available at the output field until the input operands have been logically combined by the ALU. As such, these field designations represent sets of mutually exclusive micro-orders within each set. Micro-orders in the ALU output field depend on the destination requirements of the microprogram, while micro-orders in the ALU input field depend solely on the source operand designation in the microprogram. Grouping mutually exclusive micro-orders is the answer.

As an example of encoded fields, let us return to the horizontal ALU format of Figure 3.6. We will encode the adder in the ALU according to source and destination as in Figure 3.12. We are motivated by the fact that no more than two adder inputs may be specified in any given microinstruction. The adder input may then be encoded as shown in the following table:

Adder Source Field

Micro-order	Control Bits	Control Point Signal
ADDER ← M, A	001	c_5, c_7
ADDER ← Q, B	010	c_6, c_8
ADDER ← Q, ACCM	011	c_6, c_9
ADDER ← B, ACCA	100	c_8, c_{12}
NOP	000	—

Here we have combined two input registers as source operand pairs into four micro-order functions. The first micro-order function decodes three control bits as 001 and designates registers M and A as operand inputs to the adder. When the control bits are set at 001 in this adder field, both registers M and A will be input to the adder. The second micro-order uses control bits 010 and sets registers Q and B as adder inputs. Likewise, 011 designates Q and ACCM while 100 designates B and ACCA. We may also include one more micro-order in this field, the NOP, which uses the control bit assignment 000. This NOP designates the no operation for this field. This vertical format encoding now requires extra hardware which is shown in Figure 3.14. Since three bits in this field can select one-of-eight micro-orders, a 3:8 decoder is utilized and, in terms of control gate signals, the first micro-order, 001, simultaneously energizes control gates c_5 and c_7 in Figure 3.5. The second micro-order, 010, energizes gates c_6 and c_8, and so on. Note that no single control bit in this field specifically designates a single control gate, but rather, the three control bits collectively designate one-of-eight possibilities. We specified only five possibilities in Figure 3.14 and, therefore, we have not fully utilized this field. Three possibilities remain. Perhaps these can be used to designate single operand micro-orders.

One field specification for the adder input micro-order was selected assuming that no more than two inputs to the adder are needed. This requirement alone essentially isolates the remaining two adder inputs from the two currently specified in the input field for the current microinstruction. This isolation is equivalent to an independence which takes on the form of non-concurrent activity. There are other ways to insure some independence in the functional resources. For instance, it should be obvious that data cannot simultaneously be passed from the ALU to the ACCM register and from the ACCM register to the ALU since a race condition

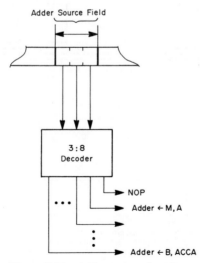

Figure 3.14   Adder source decoder

may result. A vertical format is chosen primarily for this reason, wherein, c_9 and c_{10} (in Figure 3.5) cannot be simultaneously specified in a micro-instruction because the hardware is unable to operate in that fashion.

The Standard Logic CASH-8 machine represents a low priced vertically microprogrammed machine intended as a controller and/or a computer. In controller applications, the microprogrammable features of the machine lead to flexible reconfigurations for each dedicated application. In computer applications, the same microprogrammable features were employed in the CASH-8 to build a general-purpose minicomputer. The essential resources in the organization of the CASH-8 are depicted in Figure 3.15. An 8-bit parallel ALU is supported by selector circuitry via X and Y buses for data-instruction transfer from sixteen general-purpose registers and the control store. The 16-bit wide microprogrammable control unit consists of

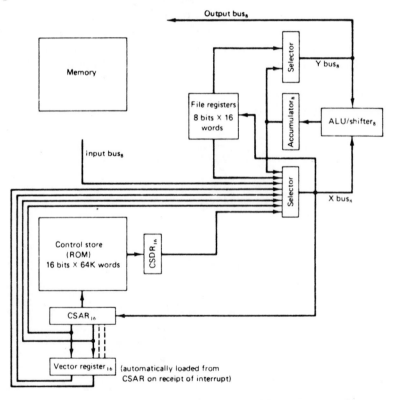

(Reprinted Courtesy of PRIME Computer Corporation)

Figure 3.15   CASH 8 machine

the CSDR, CSAR,[4] and a vector register (which primarily serves to hold the return address from an interrupt). Four formats for the microinstructions were chosen: ALU/Logic, Branch, Register, and Shift as depicted in Figure 3.16.

Again, the CASH-8 architecture is intended to support applications at two ends of the spectrum, as a dedicated controller and as a general-purpose minicomputer. For either situation, the designers chose a vertical format microinstruction to best suit their needs. Hence, relatively few, yet carefully specified, microinstructions were employed.

The 16-bit HP 3000 depicted in Figure 3.17 is another vertically organized microprogrammable machine. Here, the microprogrammed CPUs utilize a procedure-oriented stack architecture to serve in Hewlett Packard's first full-scale multi-purpose computer. Since the HP 3000 is an integrated software-hardware design, careful attention to software power was made jointly with hardware design considerations. As a result, program segmentation, relocation, reentrancy, code sharing, recursion, user isolation and system protection are enhanced by the integrated design approach.

Each CPU has a special microprocessor and control storage unit, with each word from the 32-bit ROM coded into seven fields as shown below.

R-Bus	S-Bus	Function	Shift	Store	Special	Skip

The R and S bus fields control source registers. The function field redefines other fields.

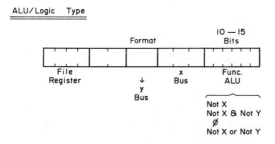

Figure 3.16a   Vertical format for CASH 8 machine

---

[4] The CSDR is a control *s*torage *d*ata *r*egister and the CSAR is a control *s*torage *a*ddress *r*egister. The CSDR is identical to the commonly used CSIR or control *s*torage *i*nstruction *r*egister.

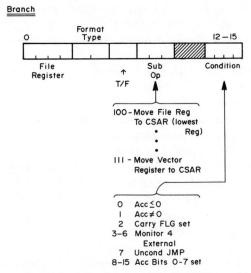

Figure 3.16b Vertical format for CASH 8 machine

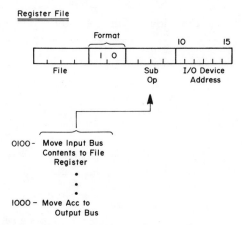

Figure 3.16c Vertical format for CASH 8 machine

For instance, branching is provided when the R-bus, shift, and special fields are interpreted as a branch address. This occurs when a JUMP or

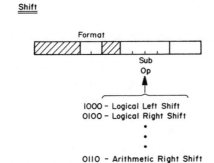

Figure 3.16d   Vertical format for CASH 8 machine

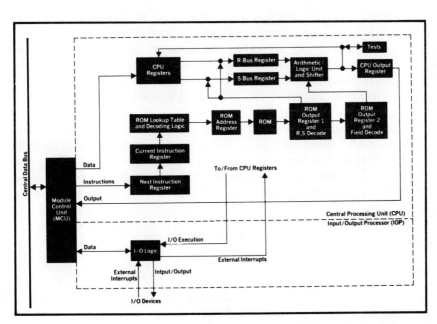

(Reprinted Courtesy of Hewlett Packard Company)
Figure 3.17   HP 3000

JUMP subroutine microcode is found in the function field. Constants formed by other fields are generated in the same fashion by the function field. Although a slight reduction in speed results, the trade-off in ROM cost savings apparently outweighs the loss of speed.

3.5 DEGREE OF ENCODING

The degree of encoding microinstructions in any digital machine is a field composition problem, the desirable goals of which are to a) reduce the width of the ROM itself, b) maintain the regularity and flexibility of micro-program design, and c) establish simple microprograms. We can achieve these goals by designing into the encoded format a rationale which is immediately obvious or intuitive to the user-microprogrammer. Hence, less time will be required of a microprogrammer to learn the code. Also, by encoding we can eliminate the timing considerations which may be otherwise required by the microprogrammer. Unfortunately, this encoding may lead to a less flexible microprogrammable machine. Some loss of concurrency may also result. *Concurrency is the ability of a digital machine to simultaneously execute multiple tasks.* For example, if a machine were to have two ALU's, a concurrent operation would result if both ALU's were activated simultaneously. However, the trade-off between flexibility and ease of microprogramming must be compared with the degree of user-microprogrammability sought and the narrowness of the machine application. Both of these considerations merit a highly encoded structure.

There are two common hardware structures for encoded formats, the direct encoded and the indirect encoded. Depicted in Figure 3.18 is the direct encoded control. Such bits in a microinstruction are decoded through, at most, one level of decoding logic and are subsequently sent directly to the digital machine as control signals. In this manner the time delay between the microinstruction accessed and the control signal point[5] in the

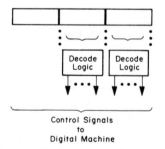

Figure 3.18   Direct encoded control

---

[5] A control signal point is the physical location in the machine where the control signal executes the intended control activity.

digital machine consists of the path delay in the decode logic itself. In the indirect encoded control, another field exists in the microinstruction which further interprets the decode logic of another field before eventually being transmitted as a control signal to the digital machine. As an example in Figure 3.19, field C serves as a field decode logic which further interprets or "steers" the decode logic of field B before finally permitting transfer of control signals to the digital machine. The indirect encoded control is more sophisticated than the direct encoded control. Obviously, more hardware structure is built into the indirect encoded control which can be useful sometimes at the design architectural level of the machine. This type of control, sometimes called "bit steering," is used in the RCA Spectra 70 and the Honeywell H1700 and to some extent in the IBM 360. Unfortunately, this additional structure may further reduce the speed of a micro-programmable control unit because additional gate delays exist between the microinstruction and the eventual control signal destination. However, encoding reduces the width of the ROM. Redfield[6] suggests that micro-instruction width reductions by a factor of two to three are possible with this indirect encoded control format.

In many digital machines it is important to insure that the microprogram controller operates at least as fast as the slowest functional resource in the digital machine. For example, in a digital computer, the microprogram control should permit microinstruction execution to be as fast as main memory access, and in most instances it is desirable to access at a factor three to five times faster than the main memory. Relative speed places a

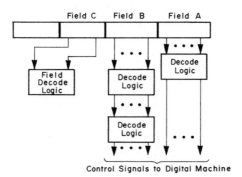

Field C   Field B   Field A

Field Decode Logic

Decode Logic

Decode Logic

Decode Logic

Control Signals to Digital Machine

Figure 3.19 Indirect encoded control

---

[6] See Chapter One's references.

burden on the amount of decoding required of each microinstruction before eventual control signal generation. If a substantial amount of encoding is incorporated in the vertical format, an equally substantial amount of decoding logic must be required. Therefore, in this case we should enforce narrow vertical fields as in Figure 3.20, rather than wide vertical fields as in Figure 3.21. Wide fields require multiple level decoding logic. Wide fields increase gate delays between the microinstruction and the control signal destination. Furthermore, not only do we pay a penalty for the additional gate delays, but as additional format structure is designed into the vertical machines, more sophisticated assemblers and compilers are required to generate or support the microcode itself.

The widest possible field spans the entire microword. In such cases, a *maximally encoded* ROM results. Maximal encoding incurs a subtle penalty in speed. Suppose that W is the number of microinstructions in some microprogram and q is the number of distinct states. Then the microprogram can be maximally encoded into $W \lceil \log_2 q \rceil$ [7] bits. The decoder is then a $\lceil \log_2 q \rceil$ input, q output device. For large q, the decoding delay can be excessively long!

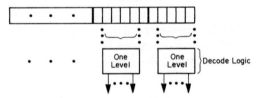

Figure 3.20   Narrow vertical fields

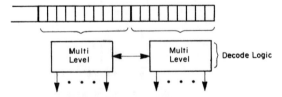

Figure 3.21   Wide vertical fields

---

[7] $\lceil R \rceil$ means the smallest integer larger than R.

If then, encoded control is desirable, what architectural configurations in the digital machine lend themselves to beneficial encoding? The answer is simple for modern computers. The architecture should possess functional resources and data paths which are mutually exclusive and which theoretically can be operated in parallel (concurrently). A data flow structure is a natural choice. For digital machines in general, the answer is not as obvious since architectural features of digital machines cannot always be readily classified into recognizable categories. In either event, it is important to utilize a rational approach to field composition selections, and control signals should be placed in control fields according to their functional independence.

3.6 MONO-POLYPHASE ORGANIZATION

Up to now we have been considering the microinstruction format solely on the basis of the interrelationship between functional resources and the degree of encoding. Microinstruction organization also may be highly dependent upon the timing behavior of the digital machine itself. Timing was only partially discussed in the vertical format section. Now suppose that we are able to describe the functional activity of a digital machine by virtue of the various execution intervals of each micro-order. We would assign a specific time interval to each micro-order, and then we might specify control signals which execute these micro-orders in some orderly fashion that minimizes the time delays required of micro-orders which otherwise might be sequentially activated. In the most conservative fashion, the micro-order with the longest execution interval might dictate the major clock cycle rate. All faster micro-orders would then be assigned minor phases in the major clock cycle. By careful assignment of valid micro-order intervals to requirements, it may be possible to organize microinstruction fields in order to execute microprograms faster. This is the essence of organizing a format in terms of *phase control* methods. A typical microprogram which includes timing specifications would appear as

Microword	Micro-Orders With Timing Specifications
M_1	$\{m_1(t_1),\ m_4(t_2),\ \cdots\}$
M_2	$\{m_3(t_1),\ m_5(t_2),\ m_7(t_4),\ \cdots\}$
$\vdots$	$\vdots$

where $m_1(t_1)$ implies that micro-order 'one' is valid at t_1 time, $m_4(t_2)$ implies that micro-order 'four' is valid at t_2 time, etc.

There are basically two kinds of phase control, monophase and polyphase. The monophase control assumes that a single clock pulse is available for all micro-orders. Any combination of micro-orders would be energized at these clock pulses and only at these clock pulses, much like that shown in Figure 3.22. Here three fields, A, B, and C, or combinations of these three, would be valid only at the clock pulses shown. The designer also organizes the fields so that micro-order executions are valid only at these clock pulses. However, if it is desired to make use of micro-orders which require *different* execution durations, then a polyphase structure generally results, much like that shown in Figure 3.23. Here a major clock cycle is shown at t_1 with four minor clock cycles or clock phases at t_2, t_3, t_4, and t_5. During the major clock cycle t_1, m_1, m_7, and m_6 are valid.[8] Similarly m_8 and m_{10} are valid at instance t_2 and so on.

The user-microprogrammer does not consider the inherent timing constraints of his digital machine since these will be satisfied by assigning micro-orders to various intervals. For instance, if we know that m_8 and m_{10} control extremely slow micro-orders, then assignment of m_8 and m_{10} to the t_2 interval would be made. If, however, a combination of m_1 and m_3 cause the generation of a rapidly executable micro-order, then t_5 may be assigned as the interval of m_1 and m_3. *Our purpose is to initiate slower executable micro-orders as early as possible in the clock cycle.*

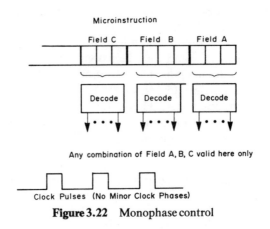

Figure 3.22   Monophase control

---

[8] A control, m_i, is valid if the specific bit in the microinstruction for that control is micro-programmed.

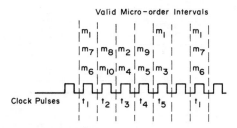

Figure 3.23   Polyphase control

The user-microprogrammer need not consider valid control bit intervals since they are already imbedded in the machine clock cycles by the hardware design. Of course, extra timing hardware is required to insure that control bits become valid as specified.

The polyphase control is more flexible than the monophase control; however, in most digital machines that employ polyphase control, the microinstruction width is relatively longer than the microinstruction width of monophase control.

Monophase and polyphase control are limiting extremes of phase control formatting in microprogramming. In most cases, a combination of the two is employed. A strictly monophase approach would be a worst case or pessimistic approach to microprogrammable control design. At the conceptual stages of a machine design process, we want to employ the faster micro-orders more efficiently, but cannot. Furthermore, for a typical *macro*instruction, many *micro*instructions may be required. Hence, this may result in a large number of ROM accesses which subsequently increases the execution time of the macroinstruction itself. At the other extreme, polyphase control tends to facilitate concurrent micro-orders (if the architecture permits it), but generally requires a wider ROM. Furthermore, since several phases are possible in the polyphase control scheme, every microinstruction may be valid for an inordinately long time, even those which would otherwise require short intervals. And, unless concurrency is physically possible, many bits in each microinstruction would most likely be under-utilized. In other words, the ROM is very sparsely coded (few bits actually microprogrammed). Certainly this would make for very inefficient ROM utilization!

The General Purpose Controller/Processor (GPC/P) depicted in Figure 3.24 manufactured by National Semiconductor is one example of a polyphase microprogrammable controller. The microprogram residing in the ROM contains an instruction fetch routine which fetches the next macro-

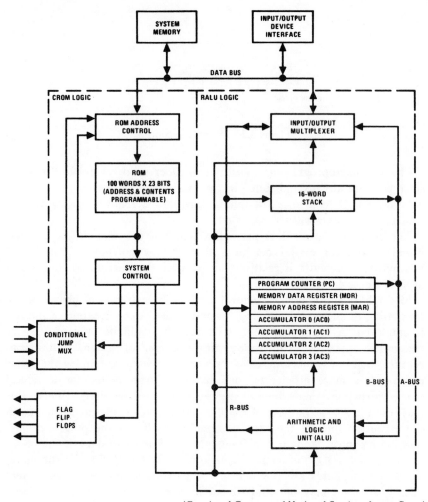

(Reprinted Courtesy of National Semiconductor Corp.)
Figure 3.24   Functional block diagram of a GPC/P

instruction. The nine most significant bits define a starting location in the ROM. The last step of the fetch routine causes a microprogram branch to this starting location in the ROM. Normally, the GPC/P is partitioned as shown in Figure 3.25 and the polyphase timing is illustrated in Figure 3.26.

Since the control bus is time-multiplexed, control bits have been encoded for each of the four time phases. Only during these phases does control information pass from the CROM to the RALU (Figure 3.24).

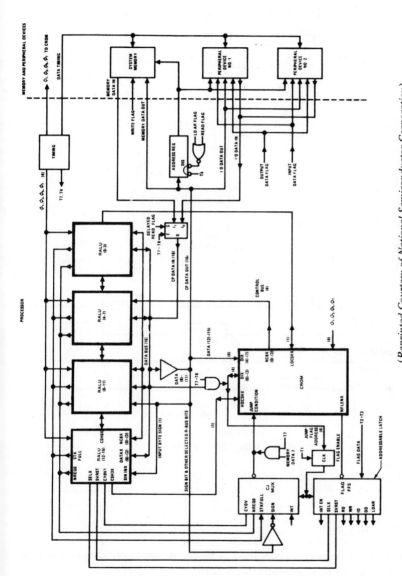

(Reprinted Courtesy of National Semiconductor Corporation)

Figure 3.25 "Example" system logic partitioning, simplified schematic diagram

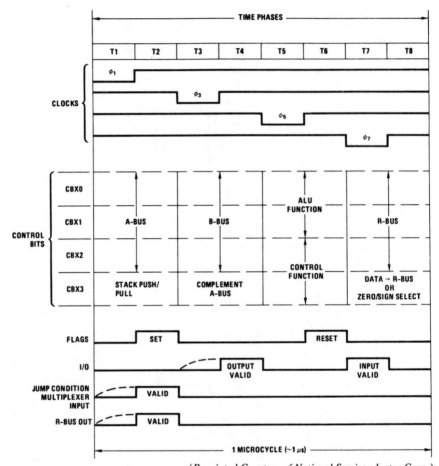

(Reprinted Courtesy of National Semiconductor Corp.)
Figure 3.26   GPC/P Timing

Phase 1 Control Bits.

If the 3-bit A-Bus address field is nonzero, the contents of the designated register is gated onto the A-Bus.

If the A-Bus address field is zero and the push-pull control bit is "1", the LIFO Stack is pulled and the contents of the top of the stack is gated onto the A-Bus.

If the A-Bus address field is zero and the push-pull control bit is "0", then, a value of zero is gated onto the A-Bus.

Phase 3 Control Bits.

If the 3-bit B-Bus address field is nonzero, then, the contents of the register designated is gated onto the B-Bus.

If the B-Bus address field is zero, a value of zero is gated onto the B-Bus.

The Complement A-Bus bit causes the A input to the ALU to be complemented.

Phase 5 Control Bits.

The ALU bits designate a function according to Table 3.1.

Table 3.1 ALU Function Bits

Code	Function
00	AND
01	XOR
10	OR
11	ADD

The Control Function bits designate a function according to Table 3.2. The no-op function applies only to the Control Function field. The expression R ← 0/SIGN means that either zeros or the sign of the less-significant byte of the word being transferred to the R-Bus is propagated throughout the more-significant byte. (If the fourth control bit CBX(3) is "1" during phase 7, the sign is propagated; otherwise, zero is propagated.)

Table 3.2 Control-Function Bits

Code	Function
00	No-Op (no operation for control bits only)
01	R ← 0/SIGN (zero or sign propagation)
10	LSH (Left SHift)
11	RSH (Right SHift)

Phase 7 Control Bits.

If the 3-bit R-Bus field is nonzero, the contents of the R-Bus is gated into the register addressed by this field.

If the Control Function bits transferred during phase 5 do not specify R ← 0/SIGN (see Table 3.2), then, CBX(3) specifies the source of the data gated onto the R-Bus:

(1) If CBX(3) is "0", the source is the output of the ALU.
(2) If CBX(3) is "1", the data comes from an external source via the Input/Output Multiplexer.

If R ← 0/SIGN is specified, then, CBX(3) specifies whether zero or the sign is propagated throughout the more-significant byte.

If the R-Bus address is zero and the Push/Pull Control bit was active (during phase 1), data is pushed onto the LIFO Stack from the R-Bus.

Figure 3.27 is a block diagram of the CROM, which receives control signals from the microprogram in the ROM. Likewise, the ROM generates signals across the control bus to the RALU. Starting microprogram addresses (upper nine bits) appear at DIX(0)–DIX(7) and NJCND1. Note that each bit in the ROM word specifies data flow paths and operations to the registers and RALU.

3.7 HARD/SOFT MICROPROGRAMMING

Previously we have been discussing microinstruction organization in terms of the control bit assignments, timing considerations, and field combinational concepts (i.e., generic properties). On a broader scale, vertical and horizontal microinstructions can be studied in relation to a philosophy of microprogramming itself. In a horizontal format, the microprogrammer is concerned with individual control bits and their relationship to respective micro-orders. Thus, he or she focuses upon the set of primitive operators in the digital machine. In this sense the microprogrammer is very close to the hardware. This type of microprogramming may also be called *"hard"* microprogramming. Here the microprogrammer is openly concerned with the optimal generation of the micro-orders themselves, and is intimately familiar with the actual hardware of the digital machine and is potentially capable of fine tuning microcode to best suit a specific application. Microprograms are then typically stored in permanent memory such as ROM's, thus becoming "hard."

DATA LINES FROM DIGITAL MACHINE(RALU)

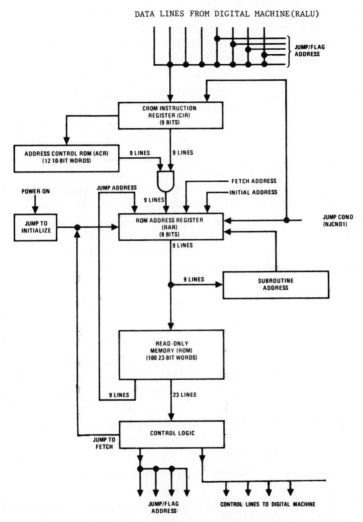

(Reprinted Courtesy of National Semiconductor Corp.)

Figure 3.27   CROM Block Diagram

In contrast to this programming philosophy, the situation naturally arises where the microprogrammer resorts to a vertical format to generate, possibly, a "universal" set of microinstructions. For example, the micro-programs could be used in an algorithmic setting to implement macro-instructions. But this microprogrammer, who now generates *"soft"* micro-programs, is more concerned with problems generally associated with machine language programming, and is not concerned about control gates, signals or levels. Nor is he or she concerned with the timing constraints of the system because, hopefully, these have been imbedded in the vertical format. Since it is likely that soft microprograms may be changed (a clever user might find a better way to do a task), soft microprograms are typically stored in writable control storage.

Whatever the philosophy, whether it is hard or soft microprogramming, the objective of formatting should be to eventually enhance execution of *macro*instructions. But, whereas the former strives towards more efficient operation at the data path logic (primitive operation level), the latter strives towards an optimal algorithmic structure in microprogramming. Hard microprograms tend to rely on the maximum exploitation of concurrency in a digital machine, benefited by wide microinstructions. Soft microprograms are generally characterized by shorter microprograms and narrower microcode. Slower macroinstruction execution may result since less optimization of control signal selection (if concurrency is possible) is made at the primitive hardware level.

SUMMARY

In this chapter we have examined the organization of microinstructions and considered the functional activity and/or timing specifications of the digital machine. When organization by functional activity is desired, mutually exclusive sets of micro-orders may be encoded into separate fields. Encoding, whether maximal or minimal, strives to combine the flexibility and potential parallelism inherent in horizontal or direct control. However, decoding complexity as well as microword length must be considered. Hence, a vertical or encoded format is sometimes employed. If very little organization is desired, a horizontal machine generally results. In the former situation, it is much easier for the user-microprogrammer to generate microcode. In the latter situation, the user-microprogrammer may need to be intimately familiar with both the hardware and the software of the digital machine before even beginning to generate efficient microcode. This is not a simple task in large scale general-purpose digital computers. As can be seen in the IBM 360/370 series, microinstructions beyond fifty bits are commonly encountered. Therefore, we find that user-microprogrammability is seldom found in horizontal machines. In fact, the eminent requirement in the marketplace for user-microprogrammability has led many manufacturers to design machines which portray many characteristics of both horizontal and vertical machines. Such machines, which we have not discussed in this chapter, are sometimes called diagonal machines. The HP21mx, META 4, INTERDATA model 85 and MICRO-DATA 3200 are noteworthy examples. The Honeywell H4200, although not strictly diagonal, combines both minimal encoding and direct control to achieve greater flexibility than pure minimal encoding.

To reduce timing considerations at the user-microprogrammer level, both a degree of encoding as well as phase control are employed. In the monophase control with a high degree of encoding, the respective fields of each microinstruction are designed to incorporate timing constraints and specifications which allow for microroutine execution at specific clock intervals in the absence of minor phases. In the polyphase control structure, the major clock cycle is further divided into minor clock phases to allow certain control bits to become valid at these minor clock phases only. Here the architectural designer has specified valid control bit instances for the micro-orders. Slowly executable micro-orders would then require many clock phases and tend to be made valid early in the clock cycle time. Rapidly executable micro-orders would become valid late in the clock cycle (They need less time!). In each case, the designer specifies valid control intervals in the microinstruction which no longer must be considered during microprogramming. Note that maximal encoding together with polyphase timing is a potentially hazardous design combination, which tends to severely complicate matters. Polyphase alone, however, is useful in pipelined machines and appears favorable when control memory is slow relative to the speed of the remaining machine.

Finally, a general philosophy for microinstruction organization has been described, dependent upon whether microprogramming is hard (in ROM) or soft (in WCS or RAM). If the microprogrammer generates code, he or she fully expects to minimize data path delays through efficient choice of current micro-orders. Alternatively, in a soft mode, the micro-programmer is concerned with the algorithmic structure of microinstructions which implement particular macroinstructions. In general the microprogrammer wants to solve machine language problems such as subroutining, nesting, reentry, overhead, etc. Notice that in each case, be it hard or soft, organization of the microinstructions should be dictated ultimately by the need to support efficient implementation of macro-instructions.

PROBLEMS

3.1   What is the window of microprogramming?

3.2   What is a microroutine? How does it differ from a micro-order?

3.3   In Figure 3.14 an encoding was chosen based upon the assumption to provide no more than two inputs to the adder. Encode the adder input field to allow two or fewer inputs to the adder. What purpose would one input serve?

3.4   Design a new vertical microinstruction format for Figure 3.14 which incorporates inherent constraints to prevent hazards and races as mentioned in the text.

3.5   How does functional encoding differ from resource encoding?

3.6   What are the two minimum functions of a microinstruction?

3.7   List the advantages and disadvantages of encoding.

3.8   In what types of application would vertical microprogramming be chosen over horizontal microprogramming?

3.9   What features of digital machines support the concept of encoding?

3.10 Describe two types of phase control.

3.11 Write a microprogram to perform integer multiplication for unsigned numbers using Figure 3.28. Assume that c_3 and c_4 automatically enable the correct number of operands for each ALU operation.
a) Assume a horizontal format.
b) Assume a vertical format.

3.12 With the digital machine shown in Figure 3.28, design the following organizations (organize the control bits, c_1, c_2, ... into fields):
a) Horizontal
b) Vertical
c) Monophase
d) Polyphase

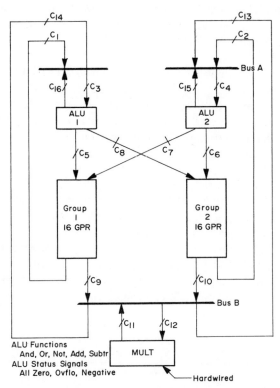

Figure 3.28   Architecture for Problem 3.11 through 3.15

Which encoding philosophy are you choosing, resource or function? Why?

3.13 Suppose that the digital machine of Figure 3.28 is to serve as a floating-point processor and ALU 1 is reserved for exponent operations while ALU 2 is reserved for mantissa operations. Organize the following microinstruction formats:

a) Vertical
b) Horizontal

3.14 If Bus A of Figure 3.28 is now divided into three or four separate buses (instead of two), could you improve upon the solution of Problem 3.13? What division would you make? Why?

3.15 If Bus B of Figure 3.28 is divided into two separate buses, could you improve upon the solution of Problem 3.13? Can the solution of Problem 3.14 be improved?

3.16 A microprogrammable control unit controls a special CPU which has four identical ALU sections connected as shown in Figure 3.29. Organize a microinstruction to implement control for parallel multi-byte arithmetic for addition and subtraction. For example, assume that the macroinstruction for multibyte addition is

$$ADD \; X, \; Y, \; Z$$

where X is the number of bytes in each operand, Y and Z are source operand addresses. Note that X may take on any value from one to four. Assume that

a) The ALU executes $+$, $-$, OR, AND, complement, and clear.
b) Each ALU is 8-bits wide with a carry/borrow bit.
c) ALU_1 has a special micro-order to add "one" to the result.
d) Each ALU executes 2's complement integer arithmetic and is entirely combinatorial logic.

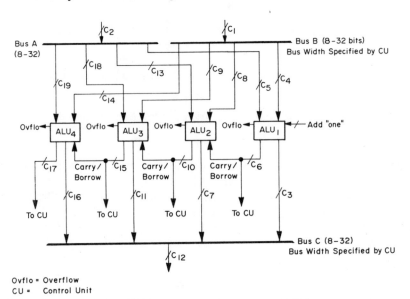

Ovflo = Overflow
CU = Control Unit

Figure 3.29 Central processing unit (CPU)

e) The microprogrammable control unit, CU, has a variable clock period equivalent to one, two, three or four intervals required of a single ALU execution.

f) The CU has, at least, a counter and branch address register and provisions to retrieve information from the macroinstruction and the CPU.

g) Data entering the CPU is formatted beforehand to satisfy the multibyte operation. Hence c_1, c_2, and c_{12} may each actually gate from eight to thirty-two lines.

h) The CU is to monitor overflow.

i) Only the minimum microinstruction execution interval is desired in any byte length macroinstruction.

j) Control gate delays are insignificant compared to ALU path delays.

Do the following for a) horizontal, b) vertical, and c) diagonal formats:

a) Lay out the format. Be descriptive. Specify bit positions for each c_i to provide a readily understandable word.

b) Identify the width of each field.

c) Describe the use of each field and the use of each bit in those fields where such usage is *not* obvious. Specify your encoded field formats.

d) Identify the timing phase structure of your format (i.e., monophase, polyphase, etc.). Show the specific micro-orders activated at each phase.

3.17 In Problem 3.16, the control unit (CU) can test carry or borrow only if the appropriate control gates are enabled (i.e., c_6, c_{10}, c_{15}, c_{17}). Suppose that the signals to the CU, are in front of the control gates c_6, c_{10}, c_{15} and c_{17} instead of where they are now, what changes in the solution of Problem 3.16 would you expect?

3.18 Microprogram Example 1.3 in Chapter 1 is actually the Interdata Mod 4 which uses four word formats depicted below (test and command formats are considered the same) to implement five classes of instruction also described below.

a) What kind of microinstruction organization does this machine employ?

b) Which field or fields redefine other fields?

Description of instruction classes

1. Instructions add, subtract, exclusive-or, and, inclusive-or, and load combine the contents of the source register with the A-register and

Instructions Add, Subtract, Exclusive Or, And, Inclusive Or, And Load

0		2	3	4			7	8			11	12		15
OP Code			0		Destination				Source			Extended Field		

Immediate Instructions, Add, Subtract, Exclusive Or, And, Inclusive Or, And Load

0		2	3	4			7	8						15
OP Code			1		Destination				Data					

Branch Instructions

0			3	4			7	8						15
0	0	0	1		Condition				Branch Address					

Command Instructions

0			3	4										15
0	0	1	1		Command Literal									

Test Instructions

0			3	4										15
0	0	1	0		Test Literal									

(Reprinted Courtesy of Interdata Corp.)

Figure 3.30   Instruction formats

store the result in the destination register. The extended field is used to control actions of carry flipflops, word shifts, etc.

2. Immediate instructions add, subtract, exclusive-or, and, inclusive-or, and load combine the contents of the A-register with the data field of the instruction (bits 8 to 15) and store the result in the destination register.

3. Branch instructions are used to test processor conditions and branch to the proper microinstruction depending on the processor status.

4. Command instructions are used to initiate certain actions in the system. For example, they initiate a memory read or memory write cycle.

5. Test instructions are used to test for certain machine conditions and will set internal flags depending on whether they are true or false.

3.19 Suppose we desire to compare the memory requirements for horizontal and vertical microprograms. Given that p is the average number of micro-operations concurrently executable in horizontal microprograms and

L_v = number of bits in a vertical microinstruction
L_h = number of bits in a horizontal microinstruction
m_v = number of vertical microinstructions in a typical microprogram
m_h = number of horizontal microinstructions in a typical microprogram

find

a) Total number of bits required in the vertical microprogram.

b) Total number of bits required in the horizontal microprogram.

c) Relations for p in terms of L_h and L_v for the cases when both microprograms require identical memory space (words x bits), and when one microprogram requires less space than the other.

REFERENCES

Descriptions of several microprogrammable computers can be found in two books: A. B. Salisbury, *Microprogrammable Computer Architectures,* American Elsevier Publishing Company, Inc., New York, 1976, and A. K. Agrawala and T. G. Rauscher, *Foundations of Microprogramming,* Academic Press, New York, 1976.

An interesting discussion of hard/soft notions in microprogramming is offered by M. J. Flynn, "Microprogramming—Another Look at Internal Computer Control," *Proc. IEEE,* November, 1975.

An in depth treatment of the IBM 360 series machines can be found in S. S. Husson, *Microprogramming: Principles and Practices,* Prentice-Hall, Englewood Cliffs, New Jersey, 1970. In particular, the general design parameter structure for the 360 models is presented in Chapter 6.

Details of the GPC/P machine can be found in Publication No. 4200005A entitled "Product Description-General Purpose Controller/Processor (GPC/P), MOS/LSI System Kit," National Semiconductor, 2900 Semiconductor Drive, Santa Clara, CA 95051. A microcoding manual is also available.

Chapter Four

MINIMIZATION OF ROM WIDTH

4.1 INTRODUCTION

At some point in the design of the microprogrammable control unit, it may be desirable to minimize the storage dimensions of the ROM (i.e., the number of bits, B, or the number of words, W). Such might be the case where the actual microprograms for the control unit simply do not fit in the ROM because the chosen ROM devices are too short or narrow. Occasionally, the actual ROM device is preselected for other reasons. These include the constraints imposed by physical characteristics of the storage devices such as power and thermal requirements or pin count, board size and backplane wiring.[1] Hence, it may be beneficial, if not necessary, to be able to employ techniques whereby the microprograms can be modified either by reducing the width of each microinstruction or by minimizing the number of microinstructions in each microprogram.

Minimization of the dimensions of the ROM belongs to the general problem of optimizing microprograms. But, although we may couple the physical dimensions ($B \times W$) to some cost of implementation, we may likely suffer from a loss of speed and of flexibility. And, even though at first glance the speed of execution of a microprogram may be proportional to the number of microinstructions (which suggests that minimizing the number of microinstructions increases the speed), a speed improvement may not follow in practice. Other factors may prevent any potential gain (e.g., the need for extra peripheral logic which increases path delay).

Minimizing ROM dimensions is only one aspect of optimization. Others include: a) bit-reduction, b) word-reduction, c) state-reduction, and d) heuristic-reduction. Bit-reduction techniques, as the name implies, attempt to reduce the width of the ROM solely by eliminating bits (only after the

---

[1] It is not uncommon to select a particular ROM only because it is already in the company stockroom.

microprogram has been generated). Be advised! One serious penalty is the inflexibility of the final ROM design. Word-reduction techniques rely on a reciprocal relationship between the speed of execution and the number of words. Hence, an optimized microcode results if and only if speed increases as words decrease. Word-reduction techniques are commonly performed at the microinstruction generation phase of compilation. State-reduction techniques, in contrast to the previous techniques, assume that a microprogrammable digital machine can be partitioned into two interconnected finite-state machines (a control part, CP, and an operation part, OP) which are defined by state-transition tables.[2] Here, optimization proceeds by reducing the number of states. Heuristic-reduction techniques assume that the control part can be microprogrammed either with a phrase structured (ps) language or a microinstruction structured (ms) language.[2] Judicious employment of these "language" types in some hierarchy of control storage elements is required. One element operates as a "residual control" in some way subordinate to another element.

This chapter focuses upon the bit-reduction techniques for optimizing microprograms. Initially, we study coding efficiency, bit packing, and function extraction. Coding efficiency is an ad hoc procedure for estimating microcode utilization. Unfortunately, this is insufficient to completely describe microcode utilization because a degree of "randomness in the bit patterns" in the ROM needs to be considered. Bit packing and function extraction are also rudimentary forms of ROM width reduction. These ROM width reduction techniques are mainly graphical methods. We analyze the microcode on a column-wise basis, to search for patterns, symmetry or functions which can be removed from the control storage and replaced by external circuitry. As ad hoc approaches, they are employed, at best, in very short microprograms. When microprograms exceed twenty to thirty lines of code,[3] more effective measures must be taken. Then, a large digital computer implements specialized software designed to optimize microcode.

If speed is important, we may not allow trade-offs between a narrower ROM and increasing path delays in the peripheral hardware (most of the reduction methods require an increase in external hardware peripheral to the ROM). If slower access were the only penalty for employing a narrow ROM, bit-reduction techniques may still be desirable. However, care is required since any bit-reduction will require some encoding of the micro-orders. Hence, the inherent flexibility of a wide microinstruction is lost as more

---

[2] Further discussion of these techniques can be found in Chapter Five.

[3] It is difficult to identify the crossover point. We simply mean that graphic procedures are adequate for short microprograms.

tightly encoded microinstructions appear. In fact, *all* advantages of micro-programming may disappear.

Let us illustrate this with the following example. Assume the following microprogram.

Example 4.1

Microword	Micro-orders
1	$\{m_1, m_2, m_3, m_4, m_5, m_6\}$
2	$\{m_3, m_7, m_8, m_9\}$
3	$\{m_1, m_2, m_8, m_9, m_{10}\}$
4	$\{m_4, m_8, m_{11}\}$
5	$\{m_6, m_8\}$

At one extreme, we could assign a single bit to each micro-order. Then, the number of bits for this case is eleven. This, of course, is extremely inefficient usage of the bit dimension, B. Yet, the advantage is maximum flexibility since no combinatorial logic is employed at the output of the ROM. And, the ROM can be arbitrarily reprogrammed. Suppose, however, that at the other extreme, the microprogram is "maximally encoded". We say that a ROM is maximally encoded when no further reduction in B can occur. Since there are five unique words, the maximal encoding is $B = \lceil \log_2 5 \rceil = 3$.[4] This approach minimizes B at the expense of speed and logic. An additional combinatorial circuit must now be provided to decode the micro-orders for each microinstruction. Even less attractive is the fact that the ROM is used simply to sequence words in the microprogram since each address is fully encoded in the corresponding word. There is no flexibility! The combinatorial circuit restricts the generation of words.

Later in the chapter more formal techniques for bit-reduction will be described. These techniques, much like function extraction and bit packing, necessarily assume the pre-existence of the actual microprogram. The first of these formal techniques (Section 4.6) assumes that a microprogram can be modeled in the framework of switching theory. Here, the notion of "compatibility" is introduced. The second formal technique (Section 4.7) is similar to the first except that the mechanism of "covering" is introduced. The last formal technique (Section 4.8) applies linear programming to the bit-reduction

---

[4] $\lceil A \rceil$ means the smallest integer greater than or equal to A.

problem. Again, all of these formal techniques initially require a micropro-gram specification.[5]

4.2 CODING EFFICIENCY

Coding efficiency is a measure of the degree of randomness of the bits in a ROM. As such, it serves to identify a "utilization" level of the ROM as a con-trol store for microprograms via the pattern behavior of the "1's" and "0's" in the rows and columns for the actual microprogram under investigation. We then view the microprogram from an information theoretic standpoint. That being the case, the bit patterns (or more importantly, the lack thereof) can be measured based upon purely statistical considerations. If upon ex-amination, the bits are found to have no pattern or symmetry, this measure of randomness can be exploited. If this degree of randomness is low, pattern extraction by subsequent external hardware implementation may be possi-ble. However, if the bits are very random, it may be difficult to extract pat-terns which can then be implemented by external logic.

The measure of randomness will be defined as the coding efficiency, CE, of a ROM.[6] Similar to channel capacity concepts in communications systems, we will assign a probability of occurrence of a "1" in a column in the ROM as P_1, and the probability of occurrence of a "0" in a column in the ROM as P_0. The number of bits of information, N, contained in a bit string of length $B \times W$ bits, satisfies:

$$N = \left[P_0 \left[\log_2 \frac{1}{P_0} \right] + P_1 \left[\log_2 \frac{1}{P_1} \right] \right] [B \times W] \qquad (4.1)$$

and the coding efficiency is defined as:

$$CE \triangleq \frac{N}{B \times W} \, 100\% = \left[P_0 \left[\log_2 \frac{1}{P_0} \right] + P_1 \left[\log_2 \frac{1}{P_1} \right] \right]. \qquad (4.2)$$

A graph of (4.2) is shown in Figure 4.1.

---

[5] A more versatile solution is obtained when we can start with the specifications of the macro-instruction set to be emulated. The problem then becomes one of optimally encoding a microin-struction set; that is, to find among all possible microprograms, that microprogram which has the minimum value of $B \times W$. These techniques are introduced in the next chapter.

[6] Clare (see references) was the first to identify this measure. He proposed that CE be a simple upper limit on the amount of information stored in the ROM expressed as a percentage of the maximum amount of information storable in the same number of bits.

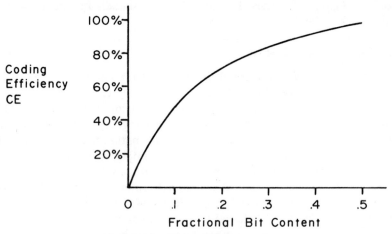

Figure 4.1   Coding efficiency chart

To employ the coding efficiency as a measure, simply count the lesser number of 1's or 0's in each column and divide by the number of available ROM bit positions ($B \times W$). This is the fractional bit content of the ROM. The potential maximum coding efficiency of the ROM can be determined from Figure 4.1. Heuristically, we see that whether we choose the lesser of 1's or 0's in each column is immaterial. Complementing a column leaves the information content unchanged (an inverter in any column output will recomplement the results). Furthermore, the coding efficiency function, itself, is symmetric about $P_i = 1/2$. The number obtained from Figure 4.1 represents the percentage of theoretically maximum coding efficiency for a ROM of some given size. For example, if a fractional bit content of .22 is obtained for some ROM, the ROM possesses a coding efficiency within 75% of the theoretical maximum.

This efficiency measures the degree of randomness in the distribution of bits in the ROM. If, then, a microprogram has maximum efficiency, little can be done to reduce the number of bits. Hence, an exercise to reduce the ROM may not succeed. Efficiencies less than maximum suggest the existence of a pattern in the ROM, although extraction may not be obvious. Unfortunately, coding efficiency simply measures the capacity of a ROM to be minimized but does not give any indication of what can be done to successfully reduce the width.

As an example of ROM coding efficiency, consider the matrix shown in Figure 4.2. This microprogram has six lines of code with six output control

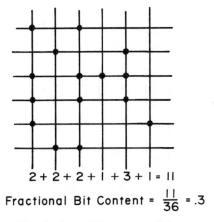

$$2 + 2 + 2 + 1 + 3 + 1 = 11$$

$$\text{Fractional Bit Content} = \frac{11}{36} = .3$$

Figure 4.2   Coding efficiency example

signals. We calculate the coding efficiency by tabulating the number of entries in each column, and choose the lesser of the two entries. In the first column there are two 0's and four 1's, and therefore we choose to count the two 0's instead of the four 1's. The second column has two 1's and four 0's, and in this case we count two 1's. Continuing on through the six columns, the total sum accumulated is eleven. This sum is divided by the total number of bit positions to derive the fractional bit content (e.g., $11/36 = .3$). From Figure 4.1, observe that a fractional bit content of .3 is equivalent to an 88% maximum coding efficiency. This coefficient of 88% tells us that this ROM is coded to within 88% of its theoretically maximum coding efficiency for a 36-bit ROM. The CE by itself is not sufficient to actually extract patterns. There is a blind side to this measure. As mentioned earlier, we should look at the actual bits in the ROM. In Figure 4.2 no apparent visual bit pattern can be observed. Intuitively then, this ROM is sufficiently utilized.

Let us demonstrate a case where, even when coding efficiency is high, the actual ROM utilization is low. Obviously, Figure 4.3 is an ill-defined microprogram. In Figure 4.3a we see identical patterns in each row and column. Yet, the fractional bit content is 1/2 for a theoretically maximum coding efficiency of 100%! This 6×6 ROM can be replaced by a 2×2 ROM as shown in Figure 4.3b. Surely this example is academic. However, it clearly shows that coding efficiency measures must not be blindly applied to microprograms. In fact, coding efficiency may serve only as a clue to further success at minimization.

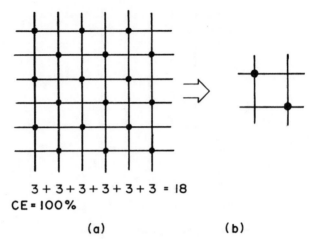

$$3 + 3 + 3 + 3 + 3 + 3 = 18$$
$$CE = 100\%$$

(a)   (b)

Figure 4.3   Ill-defined ROM microprogram

4.3   FUNCTION EXTRACTION AND BIT PACKING

In this section elementary procedures for ROM minimization are presented. These are function extraction or bit packing (proposed originally by Clare). In the former procedure, columns in the ROM are examined for some intrinsic Boolean relationship. For example, if the fourth column in a ROM is identical to the sixth column in the same ROM, this equivalence relationship permits us to eliminate one column from the ROM. Hence, we have reduced the bit dimension, B, of our microprogram by one bit. In the latter procedure, bit packing, the columns are again examined to find individual micro-orders or groups of micro-orders that are individually activated or group-wise activated, respectively. As we will show later, these micro-orders are "non-conflicting". Hence, such micro-orders can be encoded without destroying the microprogram.

The function extraction method focuses on the columns. For instance, columns in the ROM can be examined for coincidence or equivalence, ANDing, ORing, etc. All of these relationships represent Boolean functions of the columns.

Example 4.2: As an example, let us examine Figure 4.4a. Here an eight word microprogram energizes eight micro-orders, m_1, ..., m_8. To apply Boolean group reduction techniques, initially seek the simplest group classification, equivalence. Note that micro-orders m_1 and m_2, whenever energized, are equivalent for every ROM word. Thus, columns 1 and 2, which are outputs for micro-orders m_1 and m_2, belong to an equivalence class. Therefore, one column can be eliminated since they are identical. Our ROM is now reduced by one column. Next, examine columns 3 and 4 which energize micro-orders m_3 and m_4. Column 4 is the Boolean complement of column 3. Just as with columns 1 and 2, take the complement of column 3 and use that for energizing micro-order m_4. In Figure 4.4b combine columns 1 and 2 into one column and combine previous columns 3 and 4 into a new column 2. The ROM is now reduced by two columns.

Having accounted for micro-orders m_1, m_2, m_3, and m_4, examine the remaining columns. Observe that micro-order m_5 is enabled by previous column 5 in Figure 4.4a and can be energized, now, by new column 3 in Figure 4.4b. Also, micro-order m_6 in the initial ROM is energized by a function of columns 1 and 2, namely the Boolean AND of columns 1 and the complement of column 2. Therefore, eliminate column 6 from the previous ROM and use the function of columns 1 and 2 by using the external gate and inverter in Figure 4.4b. Lastly, columns 7 and 8 in the previous ROM cannot be reduced. Therefore, they are included in the new ROM without modification. This group reduction exercise is now complete. The eight column ROM is reduced to five columns.

Of course, bit packing techniques, presently described, represent ad hoc methods to reduce the ROM width. It is certainly possible to automate this reduction technique by a digital computer. However, for short microprograms, which might be found in dedicated machines, this manual process is sufficient.

Recall that as noted earlier, grouping by Boolean function techniques can result in minimizing ROM widths, but only at the expense of increasing peripheral hardware to the ROM. In the case of Figure 4.4b, two inverters and an AND gate were required. This represents only a minor increase in hardware, but it does require that one gate delay be included in the ROM access time for the m_3 micro-order control path and two control gate delays for the m_5 micro-order control path. Hence, the microinstruction access interval has increased for *every* access by two gate delays. We must be careful to realize that these additional gate delays may not be allowed in a given design.

Unfortunately, it is impossible to predict the maximum number of gate delays which may be needed prior to the application of these ad hoc reduction techniques. Consequently, bit packing by Boolean group minimization sometimes leads to an unsatisfactory "engineering" solution. Therefore, before we initiate a reduction exercise, we must be allowed to lengthen the microinstruction access time. Speed degradation is not the only drawback of these methods. Any encoding leads to loss of flexibility in microprogramming

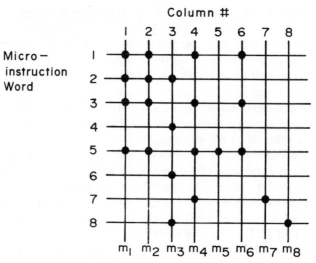

Figure 4.4a   ROM with internal Boolean groups

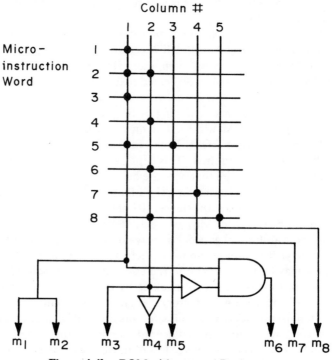

Figure 4.4b   ROM with external Boolean group

itself. Collapsing an 8-bit ROM word to five bits and partially imbedding the control signal information into peripheral hardware obviously inhibits the capability to microprogram a machine. Therefore, we also need to recognize the possibility of a resultant inflexible control unit. Of course, digital machines for dedicated applications are seldom affected by this restriction.

4.4 CONFLICT GROUPS

In some instances, especially in sparsely coded ROM's, there may exist a micro-order, m_i, controlled by column outputs which are seldom activated. Also, suppose throughout an entire microprogram, any time micro-order m_i is energized, no other micro-order is energized. It is possible to take advantage of these special micro-orders which are seldom activated to some extent. But first we must realize that if we wish to isolate these micro-orders which are singly activated, the "isolation" of such micro-orders must be characterized. Isolated micro-orders are those seldom activated. More precisely, we say that a micro-order or groups of micro-orders are nonconflicting if no two are ever activated simultaneously. The bit-reduction process in this section, simply, is to search for *multiple column outputs which are never activated simultaneously.*

Example 4.3 Let us illustrate this concept for the ROM in Figure 4.5. Here the last microinstruction, when retrieved, energizes micro-order m_5 and no other micro-order. Furthermore, when the fifth microinstruction is called, m_5 is energized, again always alone. This property of the m_5 micro-order is classified as nonconflicting with any other micro-order. Can any other micro-orders be found which are singly activated for *any* microinstruction or conflicts with no other micro-order? If so, let us group these mutually exclusive activated micro-orders into one field. Then use decoders at the outputs of these ROM columns to select outputs.

A convenient graphical procedure will now be described to implement the method of examining a ROM layout for conflict groups. We will use Figure 4.5 to illustrate a ROM width reduction by conflict groups. Observe in Figure 4.5 that there are ten micro-orders to be energized, $m_1, \ldots, m_{10}$. By examining simultaneous column outputs or micro-orders, we generate a conflict diagram. This conflict diagram will visually aid us in eventually grouping or encoding the original ROM in order to reduce the ROM width.

Begin with micro-order m_1 in Figure 4.5, and observe that when micro-order m_1 is activated (in microinstruction 1 and microinstruction 3), micro-orders m_6 and m_{10} are simultaneously activated. Therefore, in the conflict diagram of Figure 4.6, draw a line from m_1 to m_6 and from m_1 to m_{10}. This indicates that when m_1 is energized, it is also possible that either m_6 or m_{10}

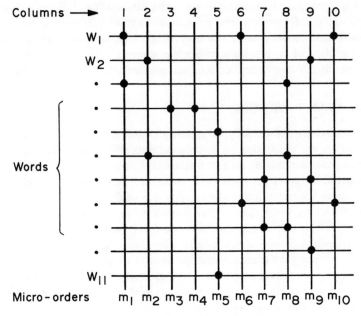

Figure 4.5   ROM with no encoding

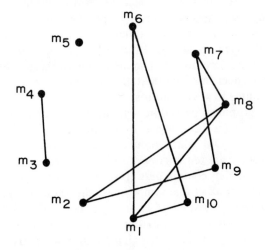

Micro-order Conflicts

Figure 4.6   Conflict diagram for Figure 4.5

may be simultaneously energized. The interpretation of the connecting lines between m_1 and m_6 or m_{10} is that in this microprogram there exist micro-instructions which simultaneously activate m_1 and m_6 or m_{10}. When the first microinstruction is retrieved from the ROM, m_1, m_6, and m_{10} are activated simultaneously. Therefore, m_1, m_6, and m_{10} conflict. Continue down column 1 (equivalent to micro-order m_1) and observe that, in the third microinstruction, micro-order m_8 will also be energized (when m_1 is energized). Hence, micro-order m_1 also conflicts with micro-order m_8. Consequently, in Figure 4.6, draw a connecting line between m_1 and m_8. At this point when micro-order m_1 is energized, it is possible that m_6, m_8, or m_{10} may be energized and thus m_1 conflicts with m_6, m_8, or m_{10}.

Now consider column 2, which represents an output for micro-order m_2. When microinstruction 2 is retrieved, micro-orders m_2 and m_9 are energized. Therefore, m_2 conflicts with m_9 and we draw a line between m_2 and m_9 on Figure 4.6. Furthermore, from microinstruction 6, we see that m_2 also conflicts with m_8. Draw the necessary line on the conflict diagram. Proceed through the ROM for all remaining micro-orders and their conflicts, making the appropriate connecting link (to designate a conflict) between the conflicting micro-orders. Upon exhausting all possibilities for conflicts, we proceed to the conflict diagram in order to group the micro-orders in Figure 4.6 into nonconflicting sets.

Recall that since we desire to find columns of a ROM which never appear simultaneously as outputs (micro-orders), we combine into a set (field) all nonconflicting micro-orders. This grouping procedure is aided by the conflict diagram. Since in Figure 4.5 m_5 is isolated, micro-order m_5 conflicts with no other micro-order. Hence, m_5 is a totally nonconflicting micro-order. The node m_3 conflicts with m_4 and, therefore, m_3 is a singly-conflicting micro-order. The node m_1 conflicts with m_6, m_8, and m_{10} and is triply-conflicting. In this conflict diagram, three conflicts also represent the maximal conflict of any micro-order.

We define an n-maximal conflict micro-order as follows:

Definition 4.1:   A micro-order, m_i, is an n-maximal conflicting micro-order when its activation requires activation of one or more micro-orders from a set of n different micro-orders in the microprogram.

Another property of conflict diagrams is the property of compatibility of micro-orders. We say that *micro-order m_i is compatible with micro-order m_j if $m_i \in W_k$ implies $m_j \notin W_k$ for all k where W_k is the kth word in our microprogram.* Later we will collect compatible micro-orders into compatible classes in which *a compatibility class, C_L, of micro-orders is a class whose members are pairwise compatible.* Observe that m_5 does not conflict with any micro-order and, therefore, is compatible with every micro-order. The node m_1 conflicts with m_6, m_8, and m_{10}, but m_1 does not conflict with m_2. Therefore, m_1 and m_2 are two compatible micro-orders and (m_1, m_2) represents a compatible class. Also, since m_1 conflicts with three micro-orders, we say that m_1 is a three-maximal conflict micro-order.

4.5 CONFLICT PARTITION ALGORITHMS

A convenient algorithm, the Conflict Partition Algorithm, for searching through conflict sets to obtain compatible sets for encoding bits is now described. Let us outline the method shown in the flowchart of Figure 4.7. The algorithm makes use of the conflict diagram. The first step is to search through the conflict diagram for the set or sets which have the greatest number of conflicts and to isolate all such sets. We want to separate these sets into groups which cannot be used as inputs to the same decoder (note that this relationship is opposite to that of compatibility!). These partitioned sets are called disjoint sets. The next step is to group remaining sets into compatibility sets. Eventually, such sets will serve as inputs to decoders. Finally, check to see that all micro-orders have been assigned, returning to the first step, or completing the ROM width reduction by encoding these sets into fields.

Let us illustrate this algorithm for the ROM of Figure 4.5. Begin by grouping disjoint n-maximal conflict sets where n is the largest conflict micro-order to be found. In Figure 4.5, let us start with m_1, a three-maximal conflict. Micro-order m_2 is a two-maximal conflict which is compatible with m_1, m_3 is a one-maximal conflict micro-order, and m_5 is compatible with all micro-orders.

Now we examine the diagram finding all lesser conflicting micro-orders which are compatible with the previous entries in our set. These micro-orders are assigned to the compatible set. The process is continued until we have searched through all candidate micro-orders.

The next step in our algorithm is to determine whether the number of elements in that set in one less than a power of two (hardware decoders ordinarily decode by even powers of two). Include a NOP in every set.

In the disjoint grouping, $\{m_1, m_2, m_3, m_5, m_7\}$, the NOP is included as a micro-order for a maximum number of six elements in this set. Choose a one-out-of-eight decoder since eight possible choices need only three inputs. Therefore, the five column ROM, namely m_1, m_2, m_3, m_5, m_7, can be reduced to three columns. Next, check to see if n is equal to 1. If it is not, proceed through the conflict diagram again observing those micro-orders which have not been incorporated in a previous set. Again, begin with the

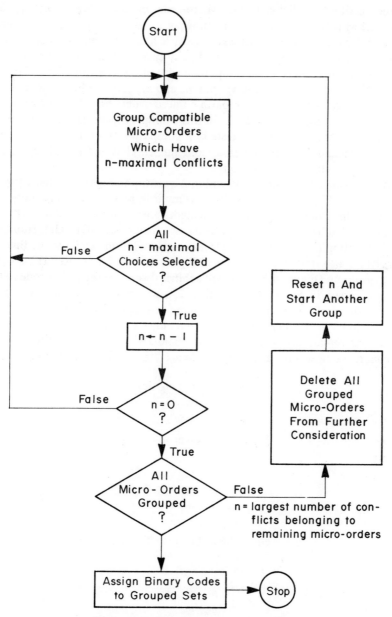

Figure 4.7   Conflict partition algorithm
(A computer program is found in Appendix A)

three-maximal conflict elements. Micro-order m_8 conflicts with m_7, m_2, and m_1. Arbitrarily choose m_8 as a member of a new set. Since no other three-maximal conflict micro-order exists (which has not been assigned to some previous disjoint group), now include any two-maximal micro-orders compatible with m_8. Since m_9 is compatible with m_8, it is a candidate. Continuing in this same fashion, observe that m_4 and m_6 can also be included in this set. Again determine if all compatible micro-orders have been found at the current n-maximal conflict level. In this example m_{10} remains. However, all other micro-orders have been tested for compatibility with m_{10}. Hence, m_{10} will be assigned to a separate group and our search is now complete. Finally, we encode each compatible group.

Application of the Conflict Partition Algorithm to Figure 4.5 generates the set shown in Figure 4.8a. We call this compatibility set 1. Compatibility set 1 includes three fields: one with five elements, one with four, and one with one element. Note that each of these fields also includes a NOP. Unfortunately, with this simple algorithm, there is no unique solution. To illustrate this, the algorithm also finds the partitions of Figure 4.8b and 4.8c. Returning to the first grouping (Figure 4.8a), we will arbitrarily choose set 1 to encode fields. This is shown in Figure 4.9. For field 1A, we assign the coding 000 to the NOP, 001 to micro-order m_1, 010 to micro-order m_2, etc. For field 1A, using a three-to-eight decoder, we have utilized only six outputs, hence, two output selections remain unused. Likewise for field 1B, again with a three-to-eight decoder, we need only five outputs, hence, three will remain unused. The

$$m_1, \; m_2, \; m_3, \; m_5, \; m_7$$
$$m_4, \; m_6, \; m_8, \; m_9$$
$$m_{10}$$

Figure 4.8a   Compatibility set 1

$$m_4, \; m_5, \; m_6, \; m_8, \; m_9$$
$$m_1, \; m_2, \; m_3$$
$$m_7, \; m_{10},$$

Figure 4.8b   Compatibility set 2

$$m_2, \; m_4, \; m_5, \; m_7, \; m_{10}$$
$$m_1, \; m_3, \; m_9$$
$$m_6, \; m_8$$

Figure 4.8c   Compatibility set 3

Field 1A		Field 1B		Field 1C	
000	NOP	000	NOP	1	m_{10}
001	m_1	001	m_8	0	NOP
010	m_2	010	m_9		
011	m_3	011	m_4		
100	m_7	100	m_6		
101	m_5				

Figure 4.9   Encoding field assignment for Example 4.3
(Figure 4.5) with compatibility set 1 (Figure 4.8a)

final encoded ROM with the decoder outputs for the chosen conflict diagram and compatibility set 1 is depicted in Figure 4.10.

We have reduced the ROM from a 10-bit width to a 7-bit width and reconfigured the ROM to agree with the field decoding assignments of Figure 4.9. It is good practice to verify the final design. For instance, the micro-order m_1 is assigned a code of 001 (see Figure 4.9). The micro-order m_2 is assigned the code 010. From the original ROM, Figure 4.5, note that micro-order m_2 needs to be energized during microinstruction 2 and microinstruction 6. In Figure 4.10, then, the encoded ROM uses a code of 010 in row 2 and row 6. Therefore, when microinstructions 2 and 6 are energized, the output decoder will energize micro-order m_2, and only m_2. Continue to encode the new ROM (Figure 4.10) by specifying the bit code per the field assignments, 1A, 1B, and 1C, of Figure 4.9.

Let us repeat the procedure for decoder 2. Begin with microinstruction 5 as shown in Figure 4.10 as an encircled area with no bits. Therefore, when microinstruction 5 is energized, no outputs should appear from decoder 2 since it only decodes field 1B consisting of m_4, m_6, m_8, m_9, and NOP. Returning to the original microprogram of Figure 4.5, we see that the fifth microinstruction does not energize any micro-orders in the field (m_4, m_6, m_8, m_9). The fifth microinstruction is now correct. Also, whenever micro-order m_6 is called in the original microprogram, it is only energized in microinstruction 1 and microinstruction 8. From Figure 4.9, our encoding shows that micro-order m_6 requires a 100. Therefore, we insert 100 in lines 1 and 8 in field 1B. Figure 4.10 is the completely encoded ROM utilizing two decoders to collapse the original columns from ten to seven.

The conflict group approach represents another ad hoc method for ROM reduction, which is useful for short microprograms. The algorithm that we use, unfortunately, does not necessarily generate a uniquely encoded set of compatible micro-orders, as already demonstrated in Figure 4.8. We should

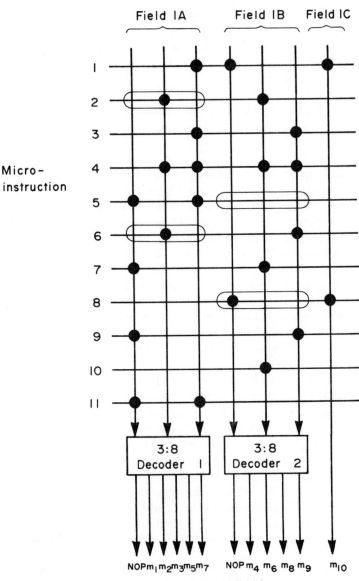

Figure 4.10   Encoded ROM

also observe that it is possible to combine both function extraction and conflict grouping in the bit-reduction exercise. For the current example, observe that micro-orders m_3 and m_4 in the original ROM are identically activated for all microinstructions. At the very beginning we could have reduced m_3 and m_4 to one line before invoking the conflict grouping procedure. This was also true for micro-orders m_6 and m_{10}.

Even for a dedicated application, the subsequent necessity to change only 1 bit of the original microprogram can cause a total redesign effort and (possibly) completely destroy the reduction.

4.6 A COMPATIBILITY CLASS ALGORITHM

Suppose, now, that instead of pursuing the bit-reduction problem by isolating the conflict groups, as proposed earlier, we choose to invoke an exhaustive search through the microprogram words for micro-orders that are compatible. But now we want to use the smallest number of decoders. In this section, we will examine an iterative algorithm proposed by Schwartz which essentially partitions the micro-orders into a minimal number of groups. Basically, the procedure begins by finding the word, W_j, which has the largest number of micro-orders, m_j. As we shall soon see, the minimal number of groups can be no less than m_j. Of course, in the worst case, if there are B bits in the original word width, the maximal number of groups cannot exceed B. Returning to W_j, let us assign a group designation, G_i, to each micro-order. Now proceed through the remaining words one at a time to assign micro-orders to the previous groups if they are pairwise compatible or else introduce a new group for each incompatible micro-order. Micro-order assignment to the groups is made according to the following set of rules:

Rule 1. All micro-orders in the same word must be placed in different groups.

Rule 2. Previously assigned micro-orders found in the current word must not have been combined into the same group. Any new micro-order in the current word must be assigned to groups not in prior use in the word.

Note that this algorithm must exhaustively evaluate all micro-order candidates for possible pairwise compatibility. For instance, if, after examining the first six words, we find violations of the compatibility property (rule 1) between two micro-orders in the seventh word (because of a previous group assignment of these two micro-orders), we must then return to the previously examined words to reassign the micro-orders so as to insure compatibility of the two micro-orders in the seventh word. We see this clearly in Figure 4.11. Suppose that m_1 and m_2 have been assigned to G_1. Unfortunately, upon examination of W_6 we see that m_1 and m_2 are incompatible (rules 1 and 2). Hence, we must reassign m_1 and m_2 to different groups (rule 1). Assign m_2 to G_2. Also, m_3 in W_6 cannot be assigned to G_1 or G_2 (rules 1 and 2).[7] It is precisely these situations which seldom permit us to iterate only once through the entire ROM. This, of course, is a drawback for manual reduction but less so for automated means. Schwartz demonstrates that it is theoretically possible to obtain the minimum number of groups.[8] However, this minimal number of groups *does not guarantee* that the minimal width of the ROM has also been achieved. A counterexample is Example 4.1, which we saw earlier in this chapter. Here, a minimum group solution is:

$$(m_1), (m_2, m_7), (m_3, m_{10}, m_{11}), (m_4, m_9), (m_5, m_8), (m_6).$$

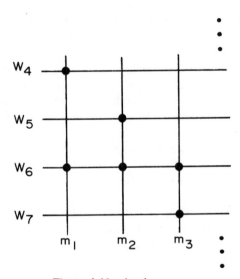

Figure 4.11 A microprogram

---

[7] If W_4 through W_7 were the only words in our microprogram, we would immediately start with W_6 (it has the most bits). Then, three groups would be designated one bit to each group.

[8] A minimal number of groups is desirable when the least number of decoders is to be utilized in the hardware implementation.

Note that these six groups will require a ROM with ten bits (all groups, except the first and the last, require two bits to encode the subsequent fields). However, suppose we choose the following grouping:

$$(m_1), (m_2), (m_3), (m_4, m_7, m_{10}), (m_5), (m_6, m_9, m_{11}), (m_8).$$

The seven groups require a 9-bit wide ROM! (All groups require one bit, except groups 4 and 6 which each require two bits.)

For completeness, let us stepwise apply the algorithm to the ROM below. In the first step, we begin with the word with the largest number of micro-orders. Since W_1 has the maximum number of micro-orders, we will assign one micro-order to each of six groups as shown in Figure 4.12.

	G_1	G_2	G_3	G_4	G_5	G_6
Step 1	(m_1)	(m_2)	(m_3)	(m_4)	(m_5)	(m_6)
Step 2	(m_1)	(m_2, m_7)	(m_3, m_9)	(m_4, m_8)	(m_5)	(m_6)
Step 3	(m_1)	(m_2, m_7)	(m_3, m_9)	(m_4, m_8)	(m_5, m_{10})	(m_6)
Step 4			(m_3, m_9, m_{11})	(m_4)	(m_5, m_8)	(m_6, m_{10})
Step 5	... no change ...					

Figure 4.12   Compatibility class exercise

We then proceed to W_2 and observe that m_7, m_8, and m_9 are activated. Hence, rule 1 requires us to place each of these micro-orders in different groups. The micro-order m_3 is already assigned to G_3 and m_7, m_8, and m_9 must be separated. Assign m_7 to G_2 since it is compatible with m_2. Likewise, we will assign m_8 to G_4 and m_9 to G_3. For W_3, m_1 and m_2 have already been assigned but rule 2 prevents the assigning of m_8, m_9, or m_{10} to any groups which contain m_1 and m_2. We ignore m_8 and m_9 since they are already

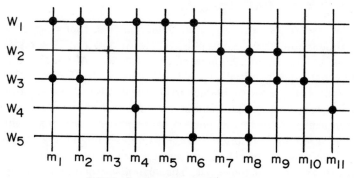

ROM microprogram in Example 4.1

assigned, and m_{10} will be assigned to G_5 (G_4 is not permissible since rule 2 prohibits this assignment of m_{10}). In W_4, m_{11} cannot be assigned to G_4 (by rules 1 and 2). Furthermore, in W_4 we see, for the first time, that m_8 and m_4 are not compatible (by rule 1)! Hence, we must return to the step which made the m_8 assignment and reassign m_8 (as well as any other micro-orders, if necessary). Reassign m_8 to G_5. However, in W_3 we need to reassign m_{10} (since m_8, m_9, and m_{10} must be separated). Assign m_{10} to G_6. Now, upon return to W_4, only m_{11} remains unassigned. Choose G_3. For W_5, all micro-orders have now been assigned. Hence, this exercise is complete and the groups are as shown below:

G_1	G_2	G_3	G_4	G_5	G_6
(m_1)	(m_2, m_7)	(m_3, m_9, m_{11})	(m_4)	(m_5, m_8)	(m_6, m_{10}).

Notice, again, that this minimal set, although only six groups in number, is different from our previous set yet still requires ten bits in the ROM. Unique solutions are not readily obtained.

Although these rules will partition the micro-orders into a minimal set of groups, it is necessary to recognize that this partitioning occurs by exhaustive enumeration in iterative fashion. For large microprograms this is hardly satisfactory. Worse yet, even for our simple example, we have demonstrated that more than one iteration through the microprogram will occur. Had there been more words or more densely coded words, the problem would certainly have been magnified. If minimal grouping is not necessary, could we identify inherent properties of relative positions of bits in a microprogram? Furthermore, could we invoke less exhaustive techniques to minimize the bit dimension? In the next section, we introduce the notion of a "cover" table which partially improves on the Schwartz procedure.

4.7   COVER ALGORITHMS

In the last section we examined a bit-reduction algorithm which insures that the minimum number of *groups* of bits is always obtained. As a result, such a technique generates a minimum number of decoders. Although this is useful, we still cannot specify initially the size of each decoder (for example, two-to-four decoders or three-to-eight decoders). Recall, also, that this bit-reduction method does not insure that the minimum number of bits in the ROM itself has been achieved. In this section we will examine a technique which *does guarantee a minimal bit solution* in the ROM (although it does not solve the minimal decoder problem). Also, our present technique will provide for alternative solutions, if they exist. The current method assumes, as before, that the ROM words are to be considered as sets of micro-orders.

$$W_1 = (m_{11}, m_{12}, \ldots, m_{1n})$$

$$W_2 = (m_{21}, m_{22}, \ldots, m_{2n})$$

$$\vdots$$

$$W_i = (m_{i1}, m_{i2}, \ldots, m_{in})$$

$$\vdots$$

$$W_L = (m_{L1}, m_{L2}, \ldots, m_{Ln}).$$

Each m_{ij} represents a single micro-order in the ith word and jth bit position.[9] As before, we will use the concept of compatibility classes. Recall that a compatibility relationship among micro-orders is defined as follows:

Definition 4.2:   Two micro-orders, m_{ij} and m_{pq}, are *compatible* if $i \neq p$ for all j, q.

Definition 4.3:   A compatibility class (CC) of micro-orders is a class C_i whose members are pairwise compatible.

If we then form a set, Δ_i, of compatibility classes such that

$$\Delta_i = (C_{i_1}, C_{i_2}, \ldots, C_{i_n})$$

where every micro-order, m_{ij}, in our microprogram is in at least one CC of Δ_i, we have generated a set of compatibility classes which "covers" every micro-order. This is, we have a set of CC's in which every micro-order is activated at least once.

Definition 4.4:   A micro-order is *covered* by a set of compatibility classes if that micro-order is in at least one compatibility class in the set.

Covering algorithms then solve the problem of finding a collection of CC's, Δ_i, such that (a) every micro-order, m_{ij}, is covered by Δ_i, and (b) the cost, B, in bits is minimal where

$$B = \sum_{p=1}^{n} \lceil \log_2(\#C_{i_p} + 1) \rceil ,$$

---

[9] m_{ij} is a "1" if the jth micro-order in the ith microinstruction is selected.

and $\#C_{i_p}$ denotes the number[10] of elements in the pth group of the ith class. Finding solutions to the covering problem assumes that we can encode micro-orders into groups in such a way that no two micro-orders appearing together in the same ROM words are encoded in the same group. These groups, at present, bear no direct relationship to the CC's we will determine for each microprogram. However, the CC's will be used at intermediate stages of the cover algorithm to identify candidate groups for encoding. Because we have various possibilities for CC's in any microprogram, we possess some flexibility in the solution while generating a solution for the ROM width which may be minimal.

Several investigators have proposed covering algorithms, all of which are based on models developed in the framework of switching theory. Briefly, such models assume that the problem is formulated as a matrix of elements (in our case, micro-orders) which are coverable by some set of rules while insuring that the cover has no solutions which are repeated or "redundant".[11]

Grasselli and Montanari have shown that a minimal solution is possible in either of the following cases: (a) the collection of C_i where C_i is non-maximal and $\#C_{i_p} = 2^h - 1$, $h = 1, 2, \ldots$, or (b) the collection of C_i where C_i is maximal and $\#C_{i_p} \neq 2^k$, $k = 1, 2, \ldots$, for all p groups. These two classes of C_i are denoted as *prime* CC's and are sufficient classes for a minimal solution where maximality of each C_i is defined as follows:

Definition 4.5: A *maximal compatibility class* (MCC) of micro-orders is a compatibility class to which no further micro-order can be included without violating the pairwise compatibility condition for all micro-orders in the compatibility class.

The covering algorithm assumes that we can construct a cover table by writing $m_1, m_2, \ldots, m_k$ (our micro-orders) in a row and by entering C_i below m_j if $m_j \in C_i$, and $C_i \in$ MCC's. Then each such column is, in fact, a collection of those MCC's that can cover a specific micro-order. We denote this table as a *cover table*, quite analogous to a cover table used in the minimization of switching functions.[12] Our problem then reduces to finding a minimal cover for any of the above compatibility classes. Since the table has a column corresponding to every prime class, the cost of row i is equivalent to the cost of the corresponding class, C_i. As such, the bit-reduction solution becomes one in which we select rows in the cover table so that the total cost is

[10] A "1" is added to each $\#C_{i_p}$ in order to include the NOP micro-order.
[11] A formal definition follows later.
[12] Discussion of switching functions in beyond the scope of this book.

minimized and each column is covered (hence, each micro-order is also covered).

One major drawback of this method is that microprograms tend to generate cover tables with an unreasonably large number of rows and few columns. This is manually awkward.[13] It is true that we can apply integer programming to the set covering problem; however, such methods tend to be computationally inefficient because the size of the tables is usually quite large. If, then, we could delete information from the cover table which is superfluous or redundant in some sense, we may be able to reduce the size of the original cover table to a manageable size. Such an approach is feasible. We will demonstrate it by solving the bit-reduction problem with the covering algorithm of Grasselli and Montanari.

Consider the microprogram in Example 4.1. The set of MCC's corresponding to the microprogram is shown in Table 4.1 and the corresponding cover table is shown in Table 4.2. The properties of cover tables which are quite useful for analysis within the algorithm are now described. Recall that we want to delete redundant information from the table. First, observe that MCC's may appear alone in some columns. Such MCC's are called *globally*

Table 4.1   Maximal Compatibility Classes

$C_1 = (m_1, m_7, m_{11})$	$C_6 = (m_5, m_7, m_{10}, m_{11})$
$C_2 = (m_2, m_7, m_{11})$	$C_7 = (m_5, m_8)$
$C_3 = (m_3, m_{10}, m_{11})$	$C_8 = (m_5, m_9, m_{11})$
$C_4 = (m_4, m_7, m_{10})$	$C_9 = (m_6, m_7, m_{10}, m_{11})$
$C_5 = (m_4, m_9)$	$C_{10} = (m_6, m_9, m_{11})$

Table 4.2   Cover Table

Micro-Order	m_1	m_2	m_3	m_4	m_5	m_6	m_7	m_8	m_9	m_{10}	m_{11}
	C_1	C_2	C_3	C_4	C_6	C_9	C_1	C_7	C_5	C_3	C_1
Maximal				C_5	C_7	C_{10}	C_2		C_8	C_4	C_2
Compatibility					C_8		C_4		C_{10}	C_6	C_3
Class							C_6			C_9	C_6
							C_9				C_8
											C_9
											C_{10}

---

[13] In switching theory, these set covering problems refer to seeking "prime" implicants. Even there, minimal solutions are not directly obtained from the cover table.

essential, and micro-orders which head these columns in the cover table are called *globally distinguished* micro-orders. In Table 4.2 the set of MCC's (C_1, C_2, C_3, C_7) is globally essential and the set of micro-orders (m_1, m_2, m_3, m_8) is globally distinguished. The second property of cover tables (which we formally define) is concerned with the "solution" of a cover table.

Definition 4.6:   An *irredundant solution* or simply, a *solution, I_j*, of a cover table is a set of MCC's which covers all micro-orders in the microprogram. Further, if any MCC in the solution is deleted, at least one micro-order is not covered.

The second property of a cover table is simply that a solution is minimal if the cost B in bits is minimum. By the properties of cover tables and by the solution of a cover table, we assert the following theorem (due to Das, et. al.):

Theorem 4.1:   Let C_m be a globally essential MCC in a column headed by micro-order m_i. Then C_m or any subclass of C_m containing m_i *must* appear in all irredundant solutions of the cover table.

This theorem provides us with the mechanism to reduce the cover table to a more manageable size. It is our first clue to improving the search procedure.

It is also possible to encounter columns (called dominant columns) in a cover table which are identical to or are proper subsets of other columns. That is, solutions of a cover table tend to be strongly influenced by the dominant columns. Dominant columns with fewer numbers of MCC's will belong in the final cover table solution. Hence, we can show that (again, due to Das et. al.):

Theorem 4.2:   A solution to a cover table can be found in the reduced cover table obtained by deleting all columns which contain globally essential MCC's.

If we apply Theorem 4.2 to Table 4.2, we see that C_1, C_2, C_3, and C_7 are globally essential. Deleting all columns which contain any of these MCC's results in the reduced cover table shown in Table 4.3. Notice that Table 4.3 is much smaller than Table 4.2. Consequently, we can apply conventional procedures[14] to find all irredundant solutions to a smaller cover table. Although this is only a partial solution to the total microprogram, we need simply

---

[14] These conventional procedures are identical to the procedures for finding all irredundant prime implicant covers of switching functions.

Table 4.3 Reduced Cover Table

Micro-Order	m_4	m_6	m_9
Maximal	C_4	C_9	C_5
Compatibility	C_5	C_{10}	C_8
Class			C_{10}

recognize that *the complete solution can be obtained by combining this partial solution with the globally essential MCC's.* For the reduced cover table, we see that (1) C_4C_{10}, (2) $C_4C_8C_9$, (3) C_5C_{10}, and (4) C_5C_9 are partial solutions. Therefore, we obtain complete solutions by combining the globally essential MCC's with the partial solutions. In our example, (1) $C_1C_2C_3C_4C_7C_{10}$, (2) $C_1C_2C_3C_4C_7C_8C_9$, (3) $C_1C_2C_3C_5C_7C_{10}$, and (4) $C_1C_2C_3C_5C_7C_9$ are complete solutions.

Any irredundant solution can be used to obtain an encoded set of micro-orders which will reduce the number of bits in the ROM. Suppose we choose the first solution, $C_1C_2C_3C_4C_7C_{10}$. Then the following procedure is carried out. A table is constructed much like the original cover table except that, now, we will allow only classes from a single I_j to form this *solution cover table*.

Definition 4.7: A *solution cover table* is a cover table constructed with MCC's which belong to the particular solution.

Conveniently, our solution cover table has all the properties of any cover table. The solution cover table for our I_j chosen above is depicted in Table 4.4, and we see that all table entries have been selected from the set, $C_1C_2C_3C_4C_7C_{10}$, which represents the solution of concern.

Since we expect to establish a similar procedure for our solution cover table as we did for the cover table, we should determine which properties of the solution cover table (similar to those found in the cover table) we could use. Thus, similar to the cover table, our solution cover table may have column entries that appear alone in addition to the globally essential MCC's. Such MCC's in the solution cover table are *locally essential* MCC's in the table and the corresponding micro-orders are *locally distinguished* micro-orders. The solution cover table is important because its entries readily indicate which particular MCC (or its subclass) *must* be retained in the complete solution in order to cover all the micro-orders in our microprogram.

From Table 4.4, we see that m_1 can be covered solely by C_1. Thus, we *must* include C_1. Since $C_2C_3C_4C_7C_{10}$ cover m_2, m_3, m_4, m_5, m_6, m_8, and m_9, we

Table 4.4   Solution Cover Table for $I_j = (C_1 C_2 C_3 C_4 C_7 C_{10})$

Micro-Order	m_1	m_2	m_3	m_4	m_5	m_6	m_7	m_8	m_9	m_{10}	m_{11}
Maximal	C_1	C_2	C_3	C_4	C_7	C_{10}	C_1	C_7	C_{10}	C_3	C_1
Compatibility							C_2			C_4	C_2
Class							C_4				C_3
											C_{10}

must include these MCC's. Hence, $C_1 C_2 C_3 C_4 C_7 C_{10}$ must be retained. This is our original irredundant solution. We should expect to find columns which have a single MCC for every element of our irredundant solution! This observation is less important (but it does provide a self-check on the validity of our solution cover table) than the observation that those columns in the solution cover table which have multiple MCC's can be further reduced! In our example, micro-orders m_7, m_{10}, and m_{11} are such micro-orders. If we can now find all possible ways of covering m_7, m_{10}, and m_{11}, we can construct a reduced solution cover table for them and apply our previously observed properties for reduced cover tables to finally arrive at complete solutions for all I_j. Since C_1, C_2, C_3, C_4, and C_{10} cover m_7, m_{10}, and m_{11}, we construct such a table as shown in Table 4.5 corresponding to the solution cover table as shown in Table 4.4.

From our reduced solution cover table we again seek all irredundant solutions. For Table 4.5 they are readily found as : (1) $C_1 C_3$, (2) $C_1 C_4$, (3) $C_2 C_3$, (4) $C_2 C_4$, (5) $C_3 C_4$, and (6) $C_4 C_{10}$. Thus, m_7, m_{10}, and m_{11} can be covered by C_1 and C_3 or by C_1 and C_4 and so on. If we then choose to cover m_7, m_{10}, and m_{11} by C_4 and C_{10}, they may now be deleted from all other MCC's. With this in mind, we derive the irredundant solution for our original microprogram (Example 4.1) with the following encoded fields:

C_1	C_2	C_3	C_7	C_4	C_{10}
(m_1)	(m_2)	(m_3)	(m_5, m_8)	(m_4, m_7, m_{10})	(m_6, m_9, m_{11})

and this is our solution assuming that (a) we cover m_7, m_{10}, and m_{11} with MCC's C_4 and C_{10}, and (b) our irredundant solution can be found from the MCC set $(C_1 C_2 C_3 C_4 C_7 C_{10})$. Each field can be determined as follows by referring to Table 4.4. The micro-orders (m_1), (m_2), and (m_3) are covered by C_1, C_2, and C_3, respectively. Similarly, (m_4, m_7, m_{10}) can be covered solely by C_4, and (m_6, m_9, m_{11}) can be covered solely by C_{10}. This leaves (m_5, m_8) which obviously can be covered by C_7.

Table 4.5   Reduced Solution Cover Table for Table 4.4

Micro-Order	m_7	m_{10}	m_{11}
Maximal	C_1	C_3	C_1
Compatibility	C_2	C_4	C_2
Class	C_4		C_3
			C_{10}

To obtain these fields, we concentrated on the irredundant solutions to the reduced solution cover table (Table 4.5). We then chose one set (namely, C_4 and C_{10}) to cover the micro-orders in the solution cover table (Table 4.4) which are coverable by more than one MCC. The remaining micro-orders (m_1, m_2, m_3, m_5, m_8) which could not be covered by this set (in Table 4.4) must then be covered by the remaining MCC's (C_1, C_2, C_3, C_7). Those micro-orders (m_4, m_6, m_9) which are coverable by the irredundant solution (C_4 and C_{10}) and which are locally distinguished are combined into the fields whose other micro-orders are also coverable by the irredundant solution but which are not locally distinguished (m_4, a locally distinguished micro-order, is combined with m_7 and m_{10} which are not locally distinguished but which are at least coverable by the same MCC, namely C_4).

Let us summarize the covering algorithm technique. First, identify all MCC's and use these MCC's and only these MCC's to generate a cover table which tells us how each micro-order can be covered but which does not yet indicate which MCC should be used in the solution. Search through the cover table to find columns with globally essential MCC's, columns with identical sets of MCC's, and columns which dominate other columns. A new table or reduced cover table is generated from the original cover table by deleting these columns. Next, generate irredundant solutions for the reduced cover table. The reduction in the size of the cover table helps us to apply minimization techniques. Now, combine these irredundant solutions with the globally essential MCC's to arrive at sets of complete solutions. A computer program is provided in Appendix B.

These complete irredundant sets are not, in general, minimal. If we do not care, at this point we generate the encoded fields in our microprogram by using any one of these complete irredundant solutions to select the cover for each micro-order from the cover table and our bit-reduction exercise is complete. If, however, we wish to find a minimal solution, we continue to use each complete irredundant solution to generate a solution cover table. Again, we apply the same procedures to reduce the solution cover table. By now we have identified a complete solution for the reduced solution cover table and the solution cover table. With this solution, we return to the solution cover table to assign an MCC to each micro-order. Subsequently, we generate the encoded set of fields for that particular irredundant solution. In order to insure that a solution is minimal, we need simply to repeat the process for all irredundant solutions to the solution cover table (we need not return to the cover table) and choose the minimal solution.

4.8   A LINEAR PROGRAMMING SOLUTION TO MINIMIZING ROM WIDTH

Up to now we have been performing bit-reduction with techniques solely employing cover tables with compatibility relationships between classes. We have seen that the cover tables may become large even for the simplest microprograms. Even if they are reducible by the methods previously shown, the reduction process is not simple. Also, our solutions were restricted to prime classes. If prime classes are not suitable, we can establish further properties of compatibility classes to obtain more general solutions. In this section we introduce the additional properties of classes which are useful in a more general setting. The first property of compatibility classes refers to the cardinality (number of elements in) of the class.

Definition 4.8:   A compatibility class, C_i, of micro-orders is a *principal* class if the cardinality of $C_i \neq 2^j$ where j is a positive integer.

Principal classes, like MCC's, can be used to obtain a minimal solution as seen by the proof of the following theorem:

Theorem 4.3:   The minimal solution to the bit-reduction of a microprogram can be obtained from a set of principal classes if at least one principal class exists.

Proof:

1. Let $\Delta = (C_1, C_2, \ldots, C_n)$ be a minimal solution.
2. If there exists at least one class, $C_i \in \Delta$, which is not a principal class, then $\#C_i = 2^k$ and $\lceil \log_2(\#C_i + 1) \rceil = k + 1$.
3. Hence, $\#C_i = \#C_i{}' + \#C_i{}''$ such that $\#C_i{}' = 2^k - 1$ and $\#C_i{}'' = 1$.
4. But $\lceil \log_2(\#C_i{}' + 1) \rceil + \lceil \log_2(\#C_i{}'' + 1) \rceil = \lceil \log_2(2^k) \rceil + \lceil \log_2 2 \rceil$
5. Hence, any class in Δ which is not a principal class can be dissected into two classes which are principal without increasing the cost.
6. Hence, the solution is still minimal.

Q.E.D.

Another property of compatibility classes which is quite useful is the notion of *intersection*. We will use this property also to establish a minimal solution.

Definition 4.9:   Two compatibility classes, C_i and C_j, intersect if and only if they have one or more micro-orders in common.

Theorem 4.4:   The minimal solution can be obtained from a set of compatibility classes such that the intersection between any two classes is zero.

Proof:

1. Let $\Delta = (C_1, C_2, \ldots)$ be a minimal solution with two intersecting classes, C_i and C_j, with $M_{i,j}$ elements in common between them.
2. The cost of encoding the set (C_i, C_j) is then $B = \lceil \log_2(\#C_i + 1) \rceil + \lceil \log_2 (\#C_j + 1) \rceil$.
3. Let $\#C_{j,i}$ be the set of micro-orders in C_j exclusive of $M_{i,j}$.
4. Let $\#C_{i,j}$ be the set of micro-orders in C_i exclusive of $M_{i,j}$.
5. Then C_i, C_j can be partitioned into two classes, $(C_i, C_{j,i})$ and $(C_j, C_{i,j})$, such that the two classes are compatible, non-intersecting, and cover all micro-orders covered by (C_i, C_j).
6. But the cost of each class is
   $B' = \lceil \log_2(\#C_i + 1) \rceil + \lceil \log_2(\#C_{j,i} + 1) \rceil$
   $B'' = \lceil \log_2(\#C_j + 1) \rceil + \lceil \log_2(\#C_{i,j} + 1) \rceil$.
7. And $B > B' + B''$.
8. Hence, any intersecting classes can be partitioned into non-intersecting classes with no increase in cost.
9. Therefore, a minimal solution is obtainable with non-intersecting compatible classes.

Q.E.D.

Although non-intersection is an important property, we will need to include a property of classes which specifies another technique for partitioning micro-order classes. This is the notion of incompatibility.

Definition 4.10:   An *incompatibility* class is a class of micro-orders $(m_1, m_2, \ldots)$ such that no pairwise compatibility exists between any m_i, m_j in the class.

Definition 4.11:   A *maximally incompatible class*, MIC, is a class of micro-orders in a microprogram such that adding any additional micro-order to the class violates pairwise incompatibility of some member.

Note that, by definition, all micro-orders in the same word are incompatible and the word with the largest number of micro-orders is a MIC. For instance, the set $(m_1, m_2, m_3, m_4, m_5, m_6)$ in W_1 of Example 4.1 is a MIC since the addition of any other micro-order to this class automatically becomes pairwise compatible. If we attempt to include m_7, for example, in our MIC, we can easily show that m_7 is pairwise compatible with every m_i in the MIC except m_3 (since in W_2 we find both m_3 and m_7 which makes m_3 incompatible with m_7). Likewise, if we introduce m_8 in the MIC, m_8 is compatible with m_5 (m_8 is incompatible with m_3 by W_2, with m_1 and m_2 by W_3, and with m_4 by W_4).

The purpose of identifying the MIC's is to provide a test on the lower bound, B_{LB}, of the cost function or bit dimension. In fact, the total number of non-intersecting classes *can never be less* than the number of elements in the largest MIC. We can apply the previous theorems and properties of incompatible classes to find the minimal solution. Jayasri and Basu have already determined the lowest bound for various conditions on the classes. The conditions have been obtained by applying linear programming in the following setting. First, we use a relationship between the total number of micro-orders, N, and the number of classes, a_i, containing i micro-orders.

$$\sum_{i=1}^{n} ia_i = N \tag{4.1}$$

where

$$i \neq 2^j, j = 1, 2, \ldots, (\lceil \log_2 n \rceil - 1)$$

Secondly, we observe that the cardinality of the classes always exceeds the cardinality of elements in the largest MIC, i.e., M (because of the non-intersection property), hence,

$$\sum_{i=1}^{n} a_i \geq M \tag{4.2}$$

for the same conditions on i as above.

In the linear programming formulation, a cost function must be selected which can be minimized. As a natural choice, we employ the cost of the bit dimension given by

$$B = \sum_{i=1}^{n} \lceil \log_2(i + 1) \rceil a_i. \tag{4.3}$$

Lastly, in the formulation we introduce a slack variable, a_t, into the inequality of (4.2); consequently, the formulation for the linear programming technique will utilize (4.1) through (4.4).

$$\sum_{i=1}^{n} a_i - a_t = M \tag{4.4}$$

If we then minimize the cost function, B, subject to the constraints of (4.1) and (4.4), we obtain the lowest bound for the bit dimension. Results are tabulated in Table 4.6 where only principal classes are considered basically with sets of non-intersecting compatibility classes which include all the N micro-orders.

We briefly describe the method with this formulation for the condition $nM \geq N$ and refer the reader to the appropriate reference for greater details.

Step 1. Assume some initial basic feasible solution by introducing two artificial variables, a_x and a_y, in eq. (4.1), respectively. Choose $a_x = a_n$.

Step 2. Replace a_y with a_1.

Step 3. The solution is minimal if $r \geq (n - 1)/(p - 1)$ where
$p = \lceil \log_2(n + 1) \rceil$
$\log_2(K + 1) = p - 1$
$r = n - K$.

Step 4. If $r < (n - 1)/(p - 1)$, and $KM \geq N$, replace a_n with a_K. The solution is minimal.

Step 5. If $KM < N$, replace a_1 with a_K and the solution is minimal.

Recognize that in the linear programming formulation, the minimal solution consists of, at most, two variables. In terms of the types of compatibility classes, the type which has the largest number of elements will be called a "major class". And, for example, if $nM \geq N$, $r \geq (n - 1)/(p - 1)$, a_n is the cardinality of major classes. An important conclusion (as shown by Jayasri and Basu) is that for a given problem, the final solution can never include a larger number of major classes than the results of Table 4.6.

The procedure for establishing the lowest bound in any problem does not directly indicate the steps we need to take to encode the fields. However, we can identify the simple procedure in which to obtain the number of fields and the number of elements in each field. This is specified by each a_i as we see in the following application to Example 4.1.

Table 4.6 Minimal Solutions for Different Relationships
Among n, M, N, r, K, and p

Condition	Solution
1. $nM \geq N$	
a) $r \geq \dfrac{n-1}{p-1}$	$a_1 = \dfrac{nM-N}{n-1}$, $a_n = \dfrac{N-M}{n-1}$, B_{LB}
	$= a_1 + \lceil \log_2(n+1) \rceil\, a_n$
b) $r < \dfrac{n-1}{p-1}$ and $KM \geq N$	$a_1 = \dfrac{KM-N}{K-1}$, $a_K = \dfrac{N-M}{K-1}$, B_{LB}
	$= a_1 + \lceil \log_2(K+1) \rceil\, a_K$
c) $r < \dfrac{n-1}{p-1}$ and $KM < N$	$a_K = \dfrac{nM-N}{n-K}$, $a_n = \dfrac{N-KM}{n-K}$, B_{LB}
	$= \lceil \log_2(K+1) \rceil\, a_K + \lceil \log_2(n+1) \rceil a_n$
2. $nM < N$	
a) $r \geq \dfrac{n}{p}$	$a_n = \dfrac{N}{n}$, $a_t = \dfrac{N-nM}{n}$, $B_{LB} = \lceil \log_2(n+1) \rceil\, a_n$
b) $r < \dfrac{n}{p}$	$a_K = \dfrac{N}{K}$, $a_t = \dfrac{N-KM}{K}$, $B_{LB} = \lceil \log_2(K+1) \rceil\, a_K$

Y = Number of micro-orders in the largest MCC.
n = Y if the largest MCC is a principal class and $Y-1$ if the largest MCC is a nonprincipal class.
M = Number of elements in the largest MIC.
N = Total number of micro-orders for any given problem.
a_i = Number of classes containing i micro-orders each, for $i = 1, 2, \ldots, n$.
$r = n - K$
$K = \lceil \text{antilog}_2(p-1) \rceil - 1$
$p = \lceil \log_2(n+1) \rceil$

Example 4.4   For this problem $Y = 4$ and the largest MCC is not a principal class. Substituting for the necessary variables in Table 4.6, we see that:

$$n = Y - 1 = 3 \qquad p = 2$$
$$M = 6 \qquad\qquad K = 1$$
$$N = 11 \qquad\qquad r = n - k = 2$$

These variables indicate that we are to use row 1a of the table. Hence, substituting for n, M, and N in the expressions for the minimal solution, we find:

$$a_3 = 2.5 \qquad a_1 = 3.5 \qquad B_{LB} = 8.5$$

Since our solution must assume integer values, we employ an integer factorization procedure for all a_i. In our case,

$$a_3 = I_n + F_n = 2 + .5$$
$$a_1 = I_1 + F_1 = 3 + .5$$

Jayasri and Basu show that a_3 and a_1 must always be rounded down, hence,

$$a_3 = 2 \qquad a_1 = 3$$

The remaining variable to be determined is a_2 and can be found by noting that $a_m \leq nF_n + F_1$. Also, to maintain no increase in cost, the cardinality of a_m is one (by applying (4.1) and (4.2)). [*Note. This integer factorization procedure applies only to the case, $nM \geq N$ and $r \geq (n - 1)/(p - 1)$.*]

Now we have obtained the cardinality of each MCC and the number of total MCC's from which to select our encoded fields. Recall that a_3 represents sets of MCC's with three elements, a_2, ... with two elements, and so on. When we scan the maximal compatibility class tables (see Table 4.1) we find that the two sets (m_4, m_7, m_{10}) and (m_6, m_9, m_{11}) suffice for a_3. (Remember that $a_3 = 2$ means that we must select two MCC's which each have three elements. Furthermore, we must choose only non-intersecting classes.) Note also that we can only select (m_5, m_8) for a_2. Since $a_1 = 3$, we now must find three sets in the remaining micro-orders which include only one element. Consequently, we automatically choose (m_1), (m_2), and (m_3). Our minimal solution becomes:

$$\underbrace{(m_1)(m_2)(m_3)}_{a_1} \quad \underbrace{(m_5, m_8)}_{a_2} \quad \underbrace{(m_4, m_7, m_{10})(m_6, m_9, m_{11})}_{a_3}$$

Let us summarize the procedure. First, we determine if the largest MCC is a principal class. If so, we apply the conditions for $nM < N$ in Table 4.6. If not, use the condition for $nM > N$ in the table. Next, we substitute for n, M, N to obtain the minimal solution in rational form which we, in turn, reduce to integral values by the methods previously described. Finally, we inspect the MCC table of the microprogram to find suitable non-intersecting classes for each a_i. Such classes then offer candidate selections for encoded fields. The reader should observe that we have alternative solutions. For instance, in the example, had there existed more than two non-intersecting MCC's with three elements each, a different set of encoded fields could have been selected.

One drawback of this linear programming solution is that although the number of sets and the cardinality of each set are obtained, the final search through the MCC table may not find suitable non-intersecting classes for this solution. Since such a grouping may not exist in a given problem, the optimal grouping must be further partitioned. However, any minimal solution can be found by restricting the search to principal classes (Theorem 4.3) and by satisfying (4.1) and (4.4). Of course, the cost increases by "1" for each additional partition. These additional partitioning steps are terminated when this new grouping of micro-orders successfully includes all micro-orders in the microprogram. In large microprograms, some trial and error steps may be experienced before a minimal solution can be obtained. Jayasri and Basu demonstrate their technique on a microprogram with thirty-one words and twenty-five micro-orders which were field encoded into ten fields ($a_1 = 7$, $a_4 = 1$, $a_7 = 2$) for a total cost of sixteen. Here the word width is reducible by nearly 30%. Even though trial and error steps may be required at any stage of the selection process, the exact grouping of micro-orders to be obtained is known. Consequently, the search need only be confined to these groups.

SUMMARY

In this chapter we present some techniques for reducing the width of a ROM based purely on the bit positions in the ROM, making no considerations for the actual micro-orders to be controlled. This differs somewhat from the previous chapter in that here we are encoding on the microprogram itself with no regard to the functional activity being controlled at any given time. We are motivated by the necessity to reduce the width of a ROM at the expense of increased hardware in the terms of logic for Boolean group methods and decoders for the conflict group method. In either event, we realize that we pay a penalty of increased gate delays in the interval from the microinstruction access to the final control gate destination. As we employ these methods to reduce the ROM width, we are building structure into our ROM which now decreases the microprogramming flexibility of that ROM. For instance, if we were to "write" a different ROM microprogram into an encoded ROM, as in Figure 4.10, we will be constrained by decoder 1 and decoder 2. Although it may be possible to reprogram our ROM, in all likelihood the decoders will have to change. This structure then restricts the otherwise total flexibility of our ROM-centered design. A more versatile solution to microprogram optimization is obtained when we can begin with the specifications of the macroinstruction set. The problem then becomes an optimal selection of microinstructions such that $B \times W$ is minimized. This approach forms the basis of microprogram optimization in the next chapter.

PROBLEMS

4.1   What is the maximum code efficiency of the ROM below?

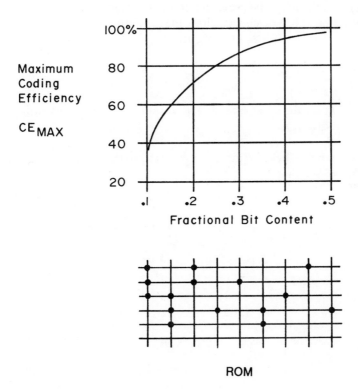

ROM

4.2   Reduce the width of the following ROM.

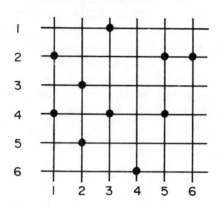

4.3   Given the following Boolean functions, which functions cannot be used to group ROM columns with external hardware?

AND	NAND
OR	N O R
IOR	XOR

4.4   What are the advantages and disadvantages of the bit packing methods of this chapter?

4.5   Is coding efficiency sufficient to describe the effective utilization of a microprogram?

4.6   Using the following ROM's, encode the outputs with conflict diagrams. Calculate the coding efficiency before and after.

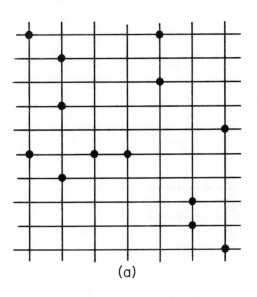

(a)

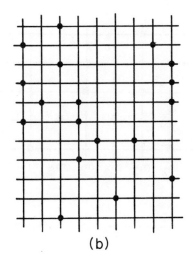

(b)

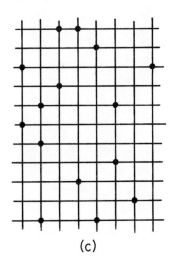

(c)

4.7   What is a conflict group?

4.8   The encoding reduction algorithm of Figure 4.7 requires that we start grouping the sets which conflict with the most elements. Suppose that we started with sets which conflict with the least elements. Discuss any problems introduced in this way.

4.9   Assuming some cost per decoder and a cost per bit, determine a formula to compare direct encoded schemes. What factors have been ignored here?

4.10 Apply the compatibility class algorithm of Section 4.6 to obtain a minimal number of groups for each of the following microprograms.

a)

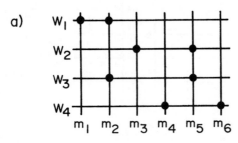

b)

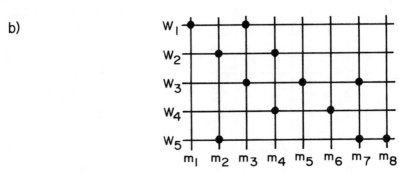

c)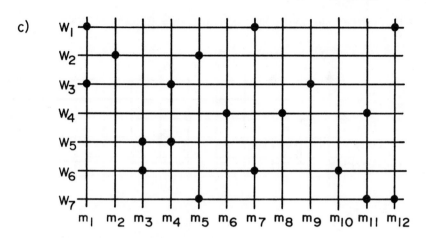

4.11 Prove Theorem 4.1.

4.12 Prove Theorem 4.2.

4.13 In Example 4.1, use the method of Section 4.7 to generate encoded fields for the microprogram assuming that the irredundant solution $C_1C_2C_3C_4C_7C_{10}$ for the cover table is used with the following irredundant solutions for the reduced solution cover table.

a) C_1C_3
b) C_1C_4
c) C_2C_3
d) C_2C_4
e) C_3C_4

4.14 In Example 4.1, use the method of Section 4.7 to generate encoded fields for the microprogram assuming that the following irredundant solutions are used.

a) $C_1C_2C_3C_4C_7C_8C_9$
b) $C_1C_2C_3C_5C_7C_{10}$
c) $C_1C_2C_3C_5C_7C_9$

4.15 For the following ROM microprograms, find the MCC's.

a)

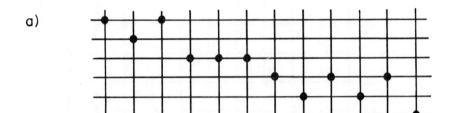

b)

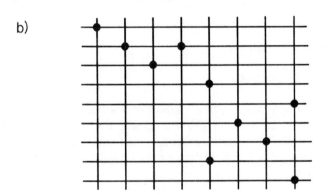

c)

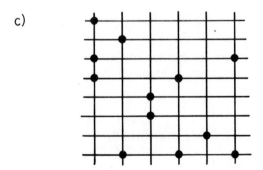

4.16 In Problem 15, find the MIC's for each microprogram.

4.17 In Problem 15, generate the following for each microprogram:

a) cover table
b) reduced cover table
c) solution cover table
d) reduced solution cover table.

4.18 In Problem 15, list the non-intersecting MCC's.

4.19 In Section 4.7, some effort can be saved in searching through all ir-redundant solutions if we use the following theorem.

Theorem 4.5: Let C_1 and C_2 be any two MCC's in a solution, α_1, of a cover table which contain m_1 and m_2 micro-orders, respectively, and let k_1 and k_2 be the number of (globally or locally) distinguished micro-orders in C_1 and C_2, respectively.

If the $m_1 - k_1$ and $m_2 - k_2$ nondistinguished micro-orders in C_1 and C_2 are identical, then in solution α_1, there exist solutions of the non-distinguished micro-orders as $C_1 C_r$ and $C_2 C_r$ where C_r represents a set of MCC's and both of these solutions lead to identical cost reduction from α_1 provided that

$$\lceil \log_2(k_1 + t + 1) \rceil = \lceil \log_2(k_2 + t + 1) \rceil,$$

where $t \le m_1 - k_1$. Prove the theorem.

4.20 What is the minimal cost of implementation for the example discussed in Section 4.8.

4.21 The integer factorization method of Section 4.8 assumes the conditions $nm \ge N$ and $r \ge (n - 1)/(p - 1)$. Obtain the rules for integer factorization for the remaining conditions in Table 4.6.

4.22 A compatibility class, C_i, is defined as a Spanning Compatibility Class (SCC) if

i) $C_i = 2^K$, $K = 1, 2, \ldots$
ii) C_i spans the set of ROM words, i.e., every ROM word contains one micro-order of C_i

Prove that the cost of a SCC with 2^K micro-orders is K.

4.23 Prove that every SCC is a MCC.

4.24 Find the set of SCC's for Example 4.1.

4.25 Generate a minimal solution for Example 4.1 using SCC's.

4.26 Show that any incompatible class which cannot be covered by any other incompatible class is an MIC.

4.27 Show that every ROM word which is not a subset of any other ROM word is an MIC.

REFERENCES

The ad hoc techniques for ROM minimization are further described by C. R. Clare, *Designing Logic Systems Using State Machines,* McGraw-Hill, New York, 1972.

A discussion of the compatibility class algorithm is provided by S. J. Schwartz, "An Algorithm for Minimizing Read-Only Memories for Machine Control," *IEEE 10th Annual Symposium on Switching and Automata Theory,* 1968, pp. 28–33.

Greater details of the covering algorithm are discussed by A. Grasselli and V. Montanari, "On the Minimization of Read-Only Memories in Microprogrammed Digital Computers," *IEEE Trans. on Computers,* November, 1970, pp. 1111–1114. In addition, the method with a reduced solution cover table with alternative approaches to the covering problem is presented by S. R. Das, D. K. Banerji, and A. Chattopadhyay, "On Control Memory Minimization in Microprogrammed Digital Computers," *IEEE Trans. on Computers,* September, 1973, pp. 845–847.

A survey of techniques for microprogram optimization can be found in T. Agerwala, "Microprogram Optimization: A Survey," *IEEE Trans. on Computers,* October, 1976, pp. 962–973.

Additional remarks on the linear programming method applied to bit-reduction algorithms can be found in T. Jayasri and D. Basu, "An Approach to Organizing Microinstructions Which Minimizes the Width of Control Store Words," *IEEE Trans. on Computers,* May, 1976, pp. 514–521.

For further information on variables in linear programming, see G. Hadley. *Linear Programming.* London: Addison Wesley, 1965.

Chapter Five

FIRMWARE ENGINEERING

5.1 INTRODUCTION

For small digital machines, hand-coded microinstructions are typically sufficient. This is especially true if such machines require few microinstructions. In this event, the process of hand-coding could even resolve issues pertaining to optimization of the microprogram (for instance, minimal number of microinstructions or maximal usage of concurrent operations). And as seen previously, should a minimal bit dimension on the control store be desired, the techniques of the preceding chapter can be effective. However, the bit-reduction methods previously considered depend on the pre-existence of a microprogram. Optimization in that setting is simply a matter of reducing the word width. The length of the microprogram is not considered. Unfortunately, bit-reduction techniques tend to restrict the inherent flexibility of the eventual microprogrammable capability of the machine. Thus, the objectives of bit-reduction are limited.

A more global viewpoint assumes that the control store including its microprogram can be optimized in some sense. This umbrella concept is called firmware engineering. *Firmware engineering is the practice of identifying beneficial attributes of parallel execution, selecting physical components in the control store, and maximizing machine throughput without loss of economy* (*in time and space*). This broader understanding of microprogram optimization must assume that we can engineer prior to the generation stage of the actual microcode.

Broader goals of optimization are more important in firmware engineering. They depend upon

a) Requirements of execution time versus real time,
b) Production costs (software and hardware)
c) Life cycle costs (product maintenance).

These concerns motivate us to develop the tools presented in Chapter 5.

Firmware engineering minimizes execution time and/or physical control storage space. Since these goals can be conflicting, engineering trade-offs will always be made. In the real world, memory devices continue to plummet in price. Hence, on a relative basis, the saving of one less chip may not encourage us to commit several engineering man-hours to the task. Replication is a major determining factor. Such trade-offs are dominant in the engineering approach taken by the designers of the control store in the M68000. As a result, chip redesign becomes an iterative, evolving process with trade-offs optimally made along the way.

Suppose that a truly optimized machine is desired, even before the microcode is available. What, then, should we consider as significant parameters? Two suitable parameters are *the minimal number of microinstructions required of the eventual microprogram and the maximal amount of concurrency implemented by any microinstruction*. Besides reducing the length of a control store, the first parameter may also reduce the total execution time of a microprogram. Of course, this assumes that each microinstruction represents one unit cycle at the microprogram level and that every microinstruction requires, at most, one unit cycle. The second parameter may, indirectly, minimize execution time (since parallel operation is invoked wherever possible) but, equally important, concurrency enforces greater usage of machine dependent features. Hence, although microprogram optimization may employ machine-independent notions, for practical matters, the optimization should be performed for the target machine (the machine upon which the microprogram will eventually run). Hence, the second parameter allows us to consider the machine-dependent features necessary for maximal concurrency. Obviously, employment of both parameters in microprogram optimization is beneficial if the original user program has been improved (e.g., by reducing the computation time) without introducing possible logic flaws.

Of course, as before, we must begin with some "user" input. However, unlike the previous chapter, our à priori information need not be a detailed control store microprogram. In some instances, a description of a set of desired sequential tasks may suffice. For example, this may be a vertical microprogram which is eventually to become a horizontal microprogram (assuming concurrency is possible and desired). In other instances, the à priori information may be a machine program in which the sequential tasks are realized by a program of machine instructions (e.g., assembly language programs). Both of these "initial programs" are only remotely useful to those required of bit minimization. In Chapter 4, the detailed microcode, imbedded in the control store, was assigned to specific locations (microinstruction words). In the present chapter, the optimization is initiated before the actual microcode is generated. This is because the microprogrammer expects to capitalize on the generality of the description of the initial sequential tasks, and intends to search through the task assignments themselves for machine dependent properties as well as task dependent properties. Only then does he or she begin to minimize the length of the eventual microprogram and maximize the concurrency of the microcode.

To do so, certain "models" or abstractions of a typical microprogram are desirable. The first model assumes that microprograms are segments of sequentially executable microcode. *The segments are called blocks.* Segments which contain no branch microinstructions are called *subblocks*. Hence, subblocks can be found between all branch microinstructions. For many of the microprogram optimization techniques, subblocks will serve as the underpinnings. The second model views a microprogram as a graphical entity, composed of nodes and arcs. *Nodes* represent micro-orders and *arcs* represent some relational aspect between the micro-orders, typically the dependency of data between nodes (micro-orders). As will be seen later, blocks relate to these graphs in a specific manner. A third model assumes that some timing relationship can be specified in the model. Hence, either blocks or graphs can be partitioned according to some measure of "anticipation of data" or data type for each microcode (in the blocks) or each node in the graphs.

These three models stress the relational aspect of tasks in the original program regardless of whether it is a vertical microprogram or an assembly language program. They are employed as word-reduction techniques. Alternately, microprogram optimization can be considered with respect to the implemented machine structure. In this setting two other concepts are evident, the first of which is optimization by state-reduction. Here, the microprogrammable machine is analyzed in terms of two interacting finite-state machines: a control part (CP) and an operation part (OP). Each can be described by a state-transition table. Since the machines interact, CP reduction is feasible by classical state-reduction techniques. The OP is generally a finite Moore automaton while the CP may be either a finite Mealy or Moore automaton. Microprogram optimization, then, attempts to reduce the number of states of the CP automaton.

Yet, another type of microprogram optimization is possible. For the CP of the microprogrammable machine, the microprogram can be defined by means of either a phrase structured (ps) language or a microinstruction structured (ms) language. Rules for generating phrases and microinstructions are employed keeping in mind that each defines part of the CP. The phrase structure embodies the notion of cause and effect (which in microprogrammable machines can be related to the branch enable bits in a microinstruction and the condition or status flags of the machine). The structure of the ms language depends on the actual branching of microinstructions.

Hence, optimization proceeds by minimizing dimensions of the CP (cause and effect relations) and reducing the maximum number of branches. These methods belong to the class of heuristic-reduction techniques for microprogram optimization.

This class also includes optimal partitioning of micro-orders by assuming that control information contains static as well as dynamic commands. Information which is static remains unchanged for several microinstructions. Dynamic commands change frequently. Consequently, static commands can be deleted from microinstructions and placed in "set-up" registers (much like the staticizers of the IBM 360). As a result, two control storage units can be employed in some hierarchical fashion to efficiently store static information (seldomly changing) and dynamic information (frequently changing). Optimization proceeds by minimizing the combinations of particular fields of microinstructions and their respective set-up registers.

Of the three optimization techniques, word-reduction, state-reduction, and heuristic-reduction, only the first is covered in this book. Word-reduction has been most thoroughly studied. State-reduction and heuristic-reduction, although alternative approaches to microprogram optimization, have either seen little use or have appeared only recently. The Nanodata QM-1 and Motorola 68000 are recent implementations. An interesting case history for the 68000 is included in Section 9 of this chapter. Hence, the practicality of both reduction techniques has yet to be established. In fact, the power of state-reduction, while effective for small machines with few states, still remains elusive for machines with many states, which unfortunately includes almost all current computers (even a microprocessor has hundreds of states).

At first glance, optimizing a microprogram appears to parallel optimizing any program at any level. Consequently, we might conjecture that it may be possible to employ any optimizing compiler to compile one microprogram into another. Compilers generate code in an algorithmic fashion. Why not simultaneously optimize microcode while generating flawless functional routines regardless of the program sequences involved? It seems plausible that modification of the algorithm may be possible in the compilation stage to automate the verification as well as the optimization of programs. Could not the same rules apply to microprograms? The reader is cautioned here. Kleir and Ramamoorthy have investigated such techniques and these are presented next. The material serves beneficially to introduce some concepts early, while simultaneously contrasting the differences between conventional program optimization (assembly language programs, etc.) and microprogram optimization. Here, the pitfalls of employing existing compiler optimization techniques (redundant and negated actions, code motion, etc.) to microprograms are identified. The set of techniques, although only partially complete, sufficiently serves to contrast the process of microprogram optimization.

5.2   MICROPROGRAM OPTIMIZATION VIA COMPILATION

One alternative to hand-coded microprograms is to employ microprogram compilers. If then, automatic translation of microcode is possible, an optimization phase similar to that found in current compilers may be effective in improving the performance of microprograms. Furthermore, as increased interest in expanding the applications of microprograms develops, large microprograms may become commonplace. Hence, hand-coding may even be fatal! Although compilers do not guarantee the best programs (in the sense that the least computational effort is expended on a task), any reduction of computation time or computer resources may be desirable. Optimization may then be warranted if the recoverable execution time of the final program exceeds the time spent in optimizing the original program.

Let us now look at the behavior of conventional compilers. Recall that the essential task of any compiler is the production of logically flawless code. But flawless code is not necessarily efficient code. Even if compilers operate in an algorithmic mode, inefficiencies may result. For example, a reliable compiler may generate code to test the input of a logarithmic evaluation to insure that negative arguments are never allowed. Yet, if an absolute value operation precedes the logarithmic evaluation, the nonnegative test is superfluous. Consequently, less object code would be required (since the sign test is wasteful). However, a compiler operating in strict algorithmic fashion would miss this opportunity to delete the test. So, in practice, it is desirable to scan, oftentimes manually, the object code produced as a "quasi-optimization" pass to detect useless code in such special instances.

At least for compilers which generate object code from source code which are called *macrocompilers* (in contrast to *microcompilers* of this section which compile microcode), some inefficiency is possible. First, object code, once compiled, typically goes through development and maintenance phases. Consequently, unless we are diligent, these modifications may introduce superfluous code. Second, more often than not, code is written in "tutorial" fashion to facilitate maintenance and aid understanding of the subparts of a program later on. Yet, such an organization does not necessarily lend itself to expeditious computation. Third, during the debug phase of program development, the manner of execution sequence is commonly designed to facilitate control and sampling of intermediate values. This results in redundant code. Lastly, compiled programs which rely on a system library convey certain ideas to a user. For instance, the user seldom knows the internal structure of a library routine. Hence, a typical user tends to ignore the inherent checks (as in the sign test above) in a routine, and may even, unknowingly, duplicate the task with his or her own user test.

Since macrocompilers are subject to these anomalies, microcompilers should be made capable of capitalizing on such opportunity to improve program performance. The optimization phase of a compiler, regardless of which code level is being compiled, should perform four basic steps: *a) segmentation and analysis of the flow characteristics in the program, b) removal of nonessential operations, c) rescheduling execution to improve speed, and d) maximization of concurrency in machine resources*.

The last three steps are obviously beneficial. However, they can proceed only after some intermediate text is generated. The purpose of the intermediate text is to facilitate inspection and subsequent manipulation of the microcode beyond that which would be made possible by a single sequential listing of microinstructions. Consequently, the intermediate text should convey sufficient detail to allow the generation of the final microinstructions. In translating the original code to the final microprogram, the text should be able to support the "optimization" phase (permit code motion and/or reduction). This latter feature depends on our intrinsic capacity to analyze the interaction of various program subparts via some environmental analysis (i.e., consider the data dependency features of the task as well as the architectural parameters of the actual machine).

The strategy assumes that existing macrocompiler optimization techniques may be effectively applied to microcompilation. Here the two main goals are: a) *removal of nonessential operations* via isolation of negated and/or redundant code and b) *code motion* to minimize frequently encountered code population. Negated code generates results never used anywhere. As an example, some retrieved library functions may be only partially used even though computation must proceed through the entire function. Redundant code occurs when results are predictable and currently available from previous identical code executions.

Generation of an intermediate text is actually a mapping process from high-level code to various tools or descriptions. For example, one tool used in the process is a directed linear graph or *program graph* which represents the tasks by micro-orders in flow chart format with *nodes* corresponding to micro-orders and *arcs* corresponding to possible successor nodes much like Figure 5.1. Here node 1, the *entry* node, has a specifically assigned micro-order. The program graph also indicates that the translation makes nodes 2, 4, and 6 possible *successor* nodes to node 1. Likewise, node 1 is a *predecessor*

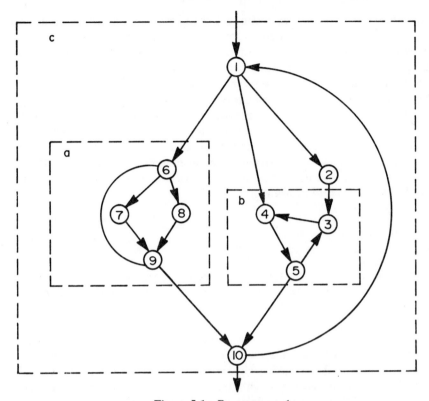

Figure 5.1   Program graph

node to nodes 2, 4, and 6. Node 10, the *exit* node, also has node 1 as a successor.

To facilitate the environmental analysis, the program graph is partitioned into regions. For this example, three regions, a, b, and c, are shown. (Note that nodes 1 and 10 are entry and exit nodes for region c.) One important asset of this graphical description is the ability to readily identify *articulation* nodes or nodes upon which all paths (each *path* is an ordered list of nodes that corresponds to some execution sequence) must traverse. Obviously, these nodes can neither be deleted nor migrated out of the region during the optimization phase. Nodes 1 and 10 are articulation nodes for region c.

Another tool in the intermediate text is a list of *mobility* pointers for each node. A *forward* mobility pointer points to the first successor node at which either a data conflict (current micro-order generates an output required by a subsequent micro-order as an input) or a resource conflict (current and subsequent micro-order use the same primitive machine element) appears. A *backward* mobility pointer points to the last predecessor node at which either a data or resource conflict appears. Now the mobility pointers combined with the program graph provide useful information for optimization via code motion. Optimization by eliminating redundant and/or negated code is simply a matter of carefully translating the micro-orders from the original program. Detection of concurrent operations is also made evident by the intermediate text. For instance, since each node is assigned a mobility range, nodes can be migrated up or down the program graph, inside the mobility range, to facilitate concurrent operation. Two micro-orders can be executed in parallel if the following conditions are met:

Condition 1. The output of one micro-order is not used as an input to the other and vice-versa.

Condition 2. No resource conflict exists between the two micro-orders.

The optimization procedures of this section represent the earliest attempt to transfer macrocompiler optimization techniques to microcompilation. Unfortunately, major unresolved issues still remain. For example, no means exist to handle microprogram branches. The region partitions (a, b, and c) of Figure 5.1 are a start, but a rigorous treatment remains to be done. Also, further difficulties are encountered when indexing and indirect addressing are required. Lastly, the original program must be constrained to exclude self-modifying code (programs which alter the instruction stream during execution). Some of these issues are partially resolved by a more rigorous definition of the graphical model itself. The remaining sections describe such efforts.

5.3 BLOCKS, SUBBLOCKS, AND DEPENDENCY GRAPHS

In the previous section, some optimization concepts in compilation were introduced which at first appeared to have direct application to the generation of optimal microprograms. However, after further study we found that the intermediate text, serving as the test bed for analysis, needed further definition. For example, the program graph, although replicating the desired sequential set of tasks, did not readily portray the relationships between micro-orders and the data flow throughout the machine. In this section we will introduce the necessary definitions upon which to formulate word-reduction techniques for microprogram optimization.

For now, we will assume that the microprogrammable control unit exerts control on two basic resources: 1) *storage resources,* and 2) *data path resources*. A storage resource is capable of holding or latching its contents for one or more processor cycles (e.g., memory cells, registers, indicators, flags, flipflops). A data path resource is simply a processing device through which data passes (e.g., gates and buses). In some cases, data transformation is possible (e.g., ALU's). In either case, a data path resource is without memory (that is, a combinatorial circuit). Both of these resources, storage or data, may be employed in a functional unit which is defined as follows:

Definition 5.1:   A *functional unit* is a hardware device which transforms input data or control signals into output data or control signals.

This is, of course, a very general description of a functional unit. Our purpose is to demonstrate that we need not be restricted solely to the primitive operations. However, in order to effectively employ graphical models for microprograms, a precise description of the primitive operations is necessary. Therefore, we define a micro-operation as:

Definition 5.2:   A *micro-operation* is an expression with one, and only one, micro-order and its operands.

A micro-operation is not merely a micro-order. A micro-order describes some primitive function in the machine which may not necessarily include the operands. As we shall observe momentarily, the data flow requirements of the tasks need to be included during our analysis in order to identify which micro-operations can be combined into concurrently executable steps. We do so by defining a necessary relationship between micro-operations.

Definition 5.3:   A *resource conflict* is a relationship between two or more micro-operations whereby they contend for the same resource.

Obviously, a *transfer* conflict is a resource conflict in contention for a register bus, while a *function* conflict is a resource conflict in contention for a functional unit.

At the beginning of this text, we casually stated that a microprogram is a collection of microinstructions necessary for some specific task. Later, we saw that a microprogram with a horizontal format will differ from that with a vertical format. Likewise, our current optimization procedures must consider which format is assumed because the placement of micro-operations to a given microinstruction will depend on the format. If a horizontal format is available, we are really saying that machine concurrency is possible. Hence, at least for the optimization phase, we would like to maximize this capability.

In this case, an initial microprogram (before optimization) is likely to appear rather vertical. At the outcome of the optimization, if successful, the microprogram will appear more horizontal. Naturally, this transformation from vertical to horizontal depends on the available machine resources as well as the initial program.

Suppose that the initial program can be identified by a block (perhaps even sequential locations in control memory) defined as follows:

Definition 5.4:   A *block* is a subset of a microprogram consisting of either a maximally strongly connected segment of micro-operations or a maximal segment of micro-operations which does not belong to any maximally strongly connected segment.

A strongly connected segment of a microprogram is a segment which allows for numerous paths through the segment. A maximally strongly connected segment simply means that any path through the segment is possible by virtue of the branching specifications of the particular segment. The connectedness property of a block is equivalent to the connectedness property of the program graph of the previous section.

In the formulation of the program graph, we arbitrarily introduced the notion of a region. A region is strongly connected if the subgraph[1] in the region possesses the property that any node can be reached from any other node by traversing only arcs within the subgraph. (A path is an ordered list of nodes that corresponds to some execution sequence.) Parallels can now be drawn between the program graph and the block. Like the program graph, the block has a connectedness property (by virtue of the branching capacity of the microprogram). The block is also an ordered list of micro-operations which also corresponds to some execution sequence. Obviously, a loop in both the program graph and block is a path in which the last node (or exit from the list) and the first node (or entry to the list) are the same.

For the moment, assume that the optimization is performed on microprogram blocks which are loop-free. Such blocks, which can be found between branch microinstructions, are appropriately called subblocks and are defined as follows:

Definition 5.5:   A *subblock* is a subset of a block consisting of a maximum loop-free segment of micro-operations with a unique entry point and a unique exit point. At most, one branching micro-operation is permissible and only as the last micro-operation in the segment.

Obviously, each subblock is a maximum sequential segment of micro-operations in which either all or none are executed. We will optimize on these subblocks. In fact, we will generate microinstructions (one or more) for each

---

[1] A subgraph is a portion of the program graph. The graph in region a of Figure 5.1 is a subgraph of the program graph in region c.

subblock which maximize the allowable concurrency of the machine (hopefully reducing the number of words). Given the notion of a subblock, we must introduce another important relationship between micro-operations. In particular, we define the data-dependency relationship.

Definition 5.6:   In the same subblock, one micro-operation is *directly data-dependent* on another micro-operation if the former either relies on the data produced by the latter or destroys the data needed by the latter.

Data-dependency is a useful relationship. We can begin to imbed machine characteristics (our "environment") into the analysis. To do so, we must introduce the dependency graph.

Definition 5.7:   A *dependency graph, G,* is a connected, acyclic digraph[2] which represents the data-dependency information for all micro-operations of a subblock.

Each and every node of a dependency graph is uniquely assigned to one micro-operation. Arcs indicate which micro-operations are directly data-dependent on other micro-operations. Any node is directly data-dependent on its immediate predecessor. Hence, each node is data-independent on any node for which it is neither a predecessor nor successor.

For example, Figure 5.2 depicts both a cyclic (Figure 5.2a) and an acyclic (Figure 5.2b) digraph. The cyclic digraph is also strongly connected, although not maximally connected (there is no path *from* node 4 *to* node 2). In either digraph, node 1 is an entry node and node 4 is an exit node. If Figure 5.2b is also a data-dependency graph for some subblock, then node 3 is data-dependent on nodes 1 and 2, and node 4 is data-dependent on nodes 2 and 3. Node 1 in Figure 5.2b is data-independent. Of course, the cyclic digraph is of little use in further study since it is not loop-free. By definition, Figure 5.2a cannot be a dependency graph!

5.4   DATA-AVAILABLE AND COMPLETE MICROINSTRUCTIONS

Data-dependency graphs illustrate the data-dependency relationships between micro-operations for any subblock. More importantly, the graphs can be used to establish an optimal grouping of micro-operations (perhaps one in which the least number of microinstructions are required for a particular subblock). However, to insure that the collection of microinstructions will

---

[2] An acyclic digraph is a graph of nodes and arcs which contains no loops. Every arc has a direction indicated by an arrow.

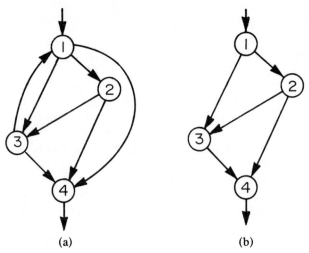

(a)   (b)

Figure 5.2   Digraphs

correctly perform the original tasks, we need to include another property of micro-operations, data availability.

Definition 5.8:   A *data-available* micro-operation is a micro-operation where all micro-operations on which it is directly data-dependent have been assigned to microinstructions.

For example, in Figure 5.2b, node 4 is a data-available micro-operation if nodes 2 and 3 have been assigned to one or more microinstructions. Obviously, a data-available set is a collection of data-available micro-operations. Microinstructions are collections of micro-operations; however, this observation is insufficient to describe microinstructions to be used for optimization purposes. For instance, we need to determine the validity of each collection. Validity depends on conflicts. If a resource conflict exists between two micro-operations in the same microinstruction, such a microinstruction is "invalid". We therefore define microinstruction and complete microinstruction as follows:

Definition 5.9:   A *microinstruction* is a set of data-independent micro-operations with no resource conflicts.

Definition 5.10:   A *complete microinstruction* is a microinstruction to which no additional micro-operations of the data-available set in a subblock can be added due to resource conflicts.

5.5 PARTITIONS ON DATA-DEPENDENCY GRAPHS

Now we are ready to assign micro-operations to microinstructions in a sub-block or a data-dependency graph. To do so, observe that a subblock or dependency graph can be divided into levels or time-frames. A time-frame or level is equivalent to a clock cycle in a control unit. The notion of partitions will be used.

Definition 5.11: A *partition* of a subblock or data-dependency graph, G, is an assignment of the micro-operations or nodes to different levels or time-frames such that each micro-operation is assigned to a unique level.

Figure 5.3 depicts a data-dependency graph with four levels. The partition for this graph is an assignment of node 1 to level 1, nodes 2 and 3 to level 2, nodes 4 and 5 to level 3, and node 6 to level 4. This implies that the micro-instruction partition for the respective subblock portrayed by Figure 5.3 has micro-operation 1 assigned to a microinstruction in L_1, micro-operations 2 and 3 assigned to another microinstruction in L_2, and so on. The partition is *valid* if it does not violate any dependency requirements. These microinstructions are also executed in sequence starting with the microinstruction in L_1, followed by the microinstruction in L_2, and so on.

The key to optimizing a microprogram depends upon the ease with which we can partition the data-dependency graph. Although the partition for Figure 5.3 is unique (hence, no further optimization is possible), such is not the case for Figure 5.4. If micro-operation 6 does not conflict with micro-operations 4 and 5, we can "migrate" node 6 to level 3. This eliminates level 4. Consequently, the original partition which had six microinstructions now reduces to five microinstructions. However, node 6 cannot migrate to level 5, as the reader can justify.

There are two partitions of special significance.

Definition 5.12: The *earliest precedence partition, E,* assigns each micro-operation to the earliest time-frame or level prior to which all micro-operations on which it is data-dependent could be executed.

Definition 5.13: The *latest precedence partition, L,* assigns each micro-operation to the latest time-frame possible without exceeding the number of time-frames in the longest path in the dependency graph.

Each data-dependency graph has both an E and an L partition. For small dependency graphs (few nodes), the precedence partitions can be found directly. However, for large dependency graphs, we will employ a tool, the connectivity matrix, to conveniently find E and L.

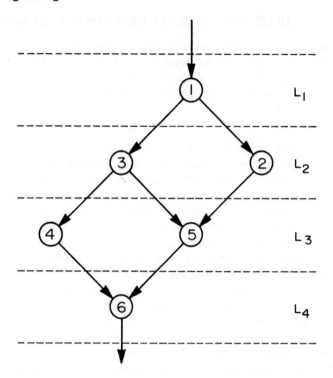

Micro - operation executed

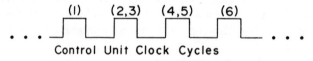

Control Unit Clock Cycles

Figure 5.3   Data-dependency graph with level assignment

Given a data-dependency graph, G, we define a *connectivity matrix, M*, whose rows and columns are equivalent to the nodes of G assigned in ascending order. Each element, M_{ij} [3] in M is a "1" if, and only if, the graph has an arc from the ith node to the jth node; otherwise M_{ij} is "0". For example, the data-dependency graph of Figure 5.5 has the connectivity matrix, M, shown in Figure 5.6. Here, M_{12} is "1" because an arc exists *from* node 1 *to* node 2. M_{13} also is "1" because an arc exists *from* node 1 *to* node 3. Note that column 1 and row 14 have no "1"'s since node 1 and node 14 are entry and exit

---

[3] M_{ij} is the element in the ith row and jth column of the connectivity matrix.

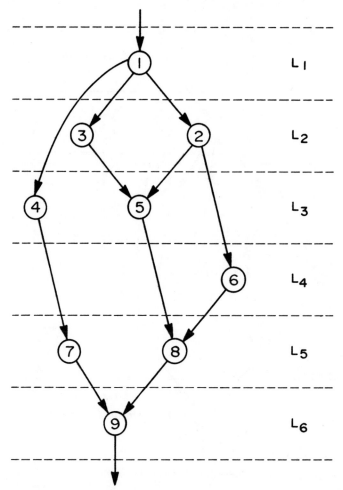

Figure 5.4 Data-dependency graph with multiple level assignments

nodes, respectively. The connecting matrix helps us to find the E or L parti-tion.

The E-precedence partition or $\{E_1, E_2, \ldots, E_n\}$ is obtained from the con-nectivity matrix for the data-dependency graph as follows. Those nodes cor-responding to columns which have all zeroes are assigned to E_1. For Figure 5.6, $E_1 = (1)$. Now all rows and columns corresponding to nodes in E_1 are deleted from further consideration. In this reduced matrix, those nodes which have all zeroes in their columns are assigned to E_2. For Figure 5.6,

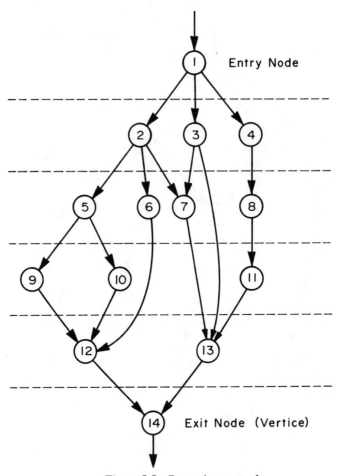

Figure 5.5 Dependency graph

$E_2 = (2, 3, 4)$. Then rows and columns 2, 3, and 4 are deleted from further consideration. (Note that row 1 and column 1 are already deleted.) The previous step is repeated, assigning to E_3 the nodes which have all zeroes in their columns, resulting in $E_3 = (5, 6, 7, 8)$, and these columns and rows are deleted. This process is continued until rows and columns are deleted. For the data-dependency graph of Figure 5.5, the E-precedence partition becomes:

$$E = \{E_1, E_2, E_3, E_4, E_5, E_6\}$$

$$= \{(1), (2, 3, 4), (5, 6, 7, 8), (9, 10, 11), (12, 13), (14)\}.$$

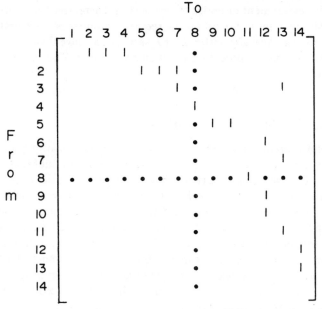

Figure 5.6 Connectivity matrix, M, for Figure 5.5 ("0" Entries omitted for clarity)

The L-precedence partition is obtained by performing the above procedure on the transpose of the matrix. Hence, for Figure 5.5, the L-precedence partition becomes:

$$L = \{L_1, L_2, L_3, L_4, L_5, L_6\}$$

$$= \{(1), (2, 4), (3, 5, 8), (6, 7, 9, 10, 11), (12, 13), (14)\}.$$

By application of graph theoretic principles to data-dependency graphs, we obtain the following important properties:

Property 1: The cardinality of E is identical to L for the same data-dependency graph.

Property 2: If $E = \{E_1, E_2, \ldots, E_n\}$ and $L = \{L_1, L_2, \ldots, L_n\}$ are E and L partitions of a data-dependency graph, then $E_i \cap L_i \neq 0$ for all $1 \leq i \leq n$.

Recall that our ultimate goal is to migrate nodes upwards or downwards in the data-dependency graph such that fewer microinstructions result. However, rarely will E or L directly enumerate the final number of microinstructions because in any practical situation resource conflicts will appear. This may require assignment of nodes to new levels! Therefore, the cardinality of E or L is simply a lower bound on the required number of microinstructions for any subblock. Actually, either E or L serves as a convenient starting point for introducing the machine dependent characteristics. This is the subject of the next section.

5.6 THE COMPACTION PROBLEM

If we employ graphical models for a subblock, our optimization problem is to obtain a minimum valid microinstruction partition on the subblock of micro-operations. In practice, this partition is an assignment of micro-operations to microinstructions which fully exploits the inherent concurrency of the digital machine. Or in other words, we want to employ all resources concurrently without any resource conflicts. In a general sense, we can establish a lower bound on the number of levels in a valid microinstruction partition. Let n be the number of micro-operations in a subblock, r the number of resources, and L the length of the longest path in the data-dependency graph. Hence, a "tentative" *lower bound, m,* can be defined where $m = \max(L, \lceil n/r \rceil)$. This bound is somewhat optimistic because we have taken a very naive viewpoint on assigning micro-operations. For example, we have not considered many practical matters which surface in the real world (such as races and hazards). Obviously, the previous result must be cautiously applied in any real machine. An *upper bound* is more certain. It is equivalent to the total number of micro-operations in the subblock since all individual micro-operations can be executed sequentially (no resource conflicts can exist). In an actual machine, the optimum execution time (equivalent to some microinstruction partition) lies between the upper and lower bound. Resource conflicts determine this bound.

5.7 COMPACTION OF HORIZONTAL MICROPROGRAMS

Earlier, we introduced a graph model for microprograms and suggested possible alternatives towards implementing an optimization scheme. One overriding consideration in each alternative was the ability to detect resource conflicts. Compaction of horizontal microprograms magnifies this problem. In particular, two properties of horizontal microinstructions defy compaction in the conventional programming sense. They are:

1. Concurrency of micro-operations
2. Allocation of microprogram resources.

Consequently, although an optimization in a conventional program may exercise a parallel detection scheme,[4] this scheme alone is insufficient to fully exploit maximal concurrency. Subsequently, to compact a horizontal microprogram we must include *both* a parallel detection technique and a resource allocation scheme. Firmware engineering takes on this added dimension.

As before, we will use the graph model to represent ordering and execution of individual micro-operations from our vertically coded source microprogram. Likewise, only subblocks are used (segmentation of the microprogram is made at control branches and each branchless segment is treated independently). Let us again *assign individual nodes to one unit time of execution* (*one control unit clock cycle*). This is important because the improvements obtained by this optimization scheme can be easily measured by the reduction in execution time. The E and L partitions are also used as preliminary partitions.

Our problem is to generate a horizontal microprogram from some vertical coded program.[5] Subsets of micro-operations will now be grouped to indicate the earliest and latest times during which those micro-operations may be executed without increasing the minimum execution time of the graph. However, unlike before, within each subset, micro-operations will be further subdivided as a function of the resource type required by each micro-operation. Let P represent a precedence partition and T_i represent the ith microinstruction in a vertical microprogram. For a partition with Z levels and a graph with n micro-operations, P becomes:

$$P = \{[P_1], [P_2], \ldots, [P_Z]\}$$

$$= \{[T_1]_1, [\ldots, T_i, T_j, \ldots]_2, \ldots, [T_n]_Z\}. \qquad (5.1)$$

Assume that K available resource types exist. Regroup each subset of the partition, P, to account for resource type utilization. P now becomes:

$$P = \{[(T_1)_i]_1, \qquad [(\ldots, T_0, T_q, \ldots)_j, \ldots,$$
$$(\ldots, T_m, \ldots)_k]_2, \ldots, [(T_n)_k]_Z\} \qquad (5.2)$$

where $[\ldots]_Z$ implies the subset of micro-operations executable at the Zth time-frame, $(\ldots)_k$ is the subset of micro-operations employing the kth resource type, and T_q is the qth micro-operation.

---

[4] A parallel detection scheme attempts to search through a set of sequential tasks to determine which, if any, can be executed in parallel.

[5] In fact, any sequential listing of tasks will suffice at the beginning.

The inclusion of the resource requirement subscripts for P can be reformulated into a resource requirement matrix, R, as depicted in Figure 5.7. Each row is assigned to one and only one micro-operation (equivalent to a node in the data-dependency graph) and each column is assigned to one and only one resource type. An entry at R_{ij} indicates that micro-operation i (i.e., execution of the ith vertically oriented microinstruction) utilizes resource j.

Example 5.1:   Given the data-dependency graph of Figure 5.8, a possible partition, P, is:

$$P = \{[1]_1, [2, 3, 4]_2, [5]_3\}. \qquad (5.3)$$

Micro-operation 1 is activated at time-frame 1. Micro-operations 2, 3, and 4 are activated at time-frame 2, and micro-operation 5 is activated at time-frame 3. At present, P does not indicate which resources are required by each micro-operation. Assume that the resource requirement matrix, R, of Figure 5.7 applies to the data-dependency graph. We rewrite P as follows:

Micro-operations Types 2 and 4

$$P = \{[(1)_1]_1, [\overbrace{(2, 4)}_1, (3)_2]_2, [(5)_2]_3\} \qquad (5.4)$$

Time-frame 2

Resource Type 1

By rewriting P to include the resource requirements, a resource conflict between micro-operations 2 and 4 in microinstruction 2 is made evident. Consequently, the present partition is not valid unless multiple sources of resource 1 are available.

When the demand for a resource type exceeds the availability of the resource, conflicts arise and some micro-operations must be *delayed*. If D_{ij} represents the requirement (demand) of micro-operation j for resource i, then n concurrently executable micro-operations require D_i sources, where

$$D_i = \sum_{j=1}^{n} D_{ij}. \qquad (5.5)$$

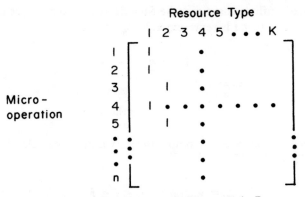

Figure 5.7   Resource requirement matrix R

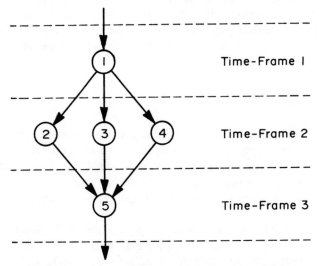

Figure 5.8   Data-dependency graph for Example 5.1

Furthermore, if A_i represents the number of available resources of type i, the number of micro-operations to be delayed becomes:

$$\text{mo}_D = \begin{cases} D_i - A_i, & \text{for } D_i > A_i \\ \\ 0, & \text{otherwise.} \end{cases} \qquad (5.6)$$

Since resource conflicts cost time, the time delay due to resource conflict at level j for resource type i is represented by δ_{ij} where:

$$\delta_{ij} = \begin{cases} \left[\dfrac{D_i - A_i}{A_i} \right] & D_i > A_i \\[2ex] 0 & , \text{ otherwise.} \end{cases} \qquad (5.7)$$

The total time, Δ_j, at level j is simply the maximum time delay for all conflicts at level j or:

$$\Delta_j = \max\{\delta_{ij}\}, \quad 1 \le i \le K \qquad (5.8)$$

where K is the number of resource types. The parameter Δ_j measures the increase in microprogram execution time beyond the minimum specified by either the E or L partition. But this only considers the conflicts at the jth level. For the entire data-dependency graph (all levels or time-frames under consideration), an upper bound on the total execution time which includes resource conflicts becomes:

$$\text{UBT} = L + \sum_j \Delta_j \qquad (5.9)$$

where L is the number of partitions in the latest precedence partition of the data-dependency graph. Unless we encounter some extremely anomalous behavior such as in the microprogram control unit, UBT represents the maximum upper (or pessimistic) bound on execution time for a vertically organized microprogram which is to be horizontally reformatted.

Example 5.2:   Given the dependency graph of Figure 5.9a, suppose T_2, T_3, T_4, and T_7 (nodes 2, 3, 4, and 7) all require the same resource type while only two units of that type are available. Also, suppose that T_6 and T_8 each require different resources than T_2, T_3, T_4 and T_7 (no conflict). From the previous discussion, UBT $= 2 + 2 = 4$. But, we also see that T_2 and T_3 can be assigned to level 3′ in conjunction with T_6. One new level (3′) rather than two has been introduced.

Tsuchiya and Gonzalez identify a set of rules for node migration in the event of resource conflict. These apply to the two main issues:

1. If a micro-operation is to be delayed, which of the candidate micro-operations should be delayed?

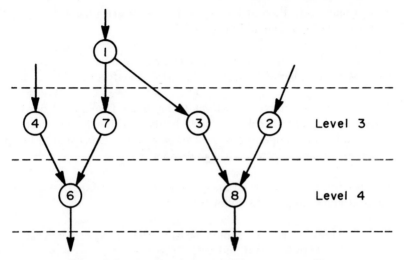

Figure 5.9a Level assignment with resource conflicts

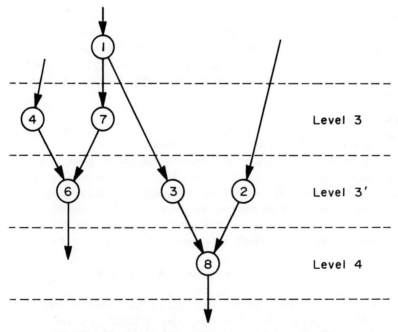

Figure 5.9b Level assignment without resource conflicts

2. If a micro-operation at level $(j + 1)$ is to be executed at level j, which micro-operations should be selected?

They suggest that further migration of contending micro-operations should depend on the number of common successors. An effective rule is as follows:

Rule 1: The first micro-operations to be delayed (migrated downwards from level j to level $(j + 1)$) should be those with only one successor. If additional micro-operations need to be delayed, delay should be specified as a function of common successors.

Upwards migration depends on the predecessor relationships of micro-operations, and might employ the following rule:

Rule 2: Micro-operations should be advanced (migrated upwards from level $(j + 1)$ to level j) if and only if they are not predecessors of micro-operations already delayed to level j.

Notice that from Example 5.2, when T_2 and T_3 were delayed, T_6 rather than T_8 was migrated into level $3'$. In fact, observe that T_6 is chosen as a candidate from the E partition. Selecting T_8 is equivalent to proposing to execute a micro-operation one time unit earlier than that indicated by its position in the L partition (which is impossible). In essence, after we have satisfied the precedence conditions, we migrate a micro-operation up (or advance it) only when no resource contention will result with a micro-operation which has just been delayed to that level.

Example 5.3:   (Horizontal Code Compaction)

Suppose that we are given the microprogram graph shown in Figure 5.10 and our objective is to reduce the execution time of our microprogram after machine resource conflicts have been considered. At present, the microprogram graph does not reflect the resource conflicts. Furthermore, let us assume that each node is an individual micro-operation. The particular machine of interest is partially described by the resource vector:

$$[R_0, R_1, \ldots, R_{15}, \text{Add, Logic, Shift, Bus}].$$

Besides sixteen general-purpose registers, the machine contains an adder, shift, ALU (logic) and bus. For our purposes, these resources are the only resources we have available for each node in the graph. The resource usage

Level

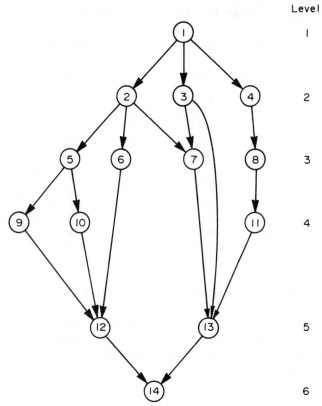

Figure 5.10   A program graph for a microprogram

for the microprogram is listed in Table 5.1. With the microprogram graph and the resourse usage table, we are ready to proceed with the optimization.

The first step is to generate the latest precedence partition, except that now we will tag each microinstruction with the resource required from the usage table. The L partition generated in this fashion clearly indicates the conflicts at each level. Our modified L partition becomes:

$$L_1 = [(1)_{R0}]$$
$$L_2 = [(2)_{B,R1}, (4)_{L,R4}]$$
$$L_3 = [(3)_{B,R2}, (5)_{R5}, (5, 8)_L, (8)_{R7}] \qquad (5.10)$$
$$L_4 = [(6, 9)_S, (6, 10)_{R7}, (7)_{R6}, (9)_{R4}, (7, 10, 11)_A, (11)_{R8}]$$
$$L_5 = [(12)_{S,R7}, (13)_{L,R8}]$$
$$L_6 = [(14)_{L,R8}].$$

Table 5.1   Resource Usage Table

Node	Source	Data-Path	Destination
1	(clear)		R_0
2	R_1, R_0	B	R_1
3	R_2, R_0	B	R_2
4	R_3, R_4	L	R_4
5	R_1, R_4	L	R_5
6	R_1, R_5	S	R_7
7	R_1, R_2	A	R_6
8	R_0, R_4	L	R_7
9	R_5	S	R_4
10	R_4, R_5	A	R_7
11	R_7, R_3	A	R_8
12	R_7	S	R_7
13	R_6, R_8	L	R_8
14	R_7, R_8	L	R_8

Now examine each level separately for resource conflicts. If no conflict exists at a level, each micro-operation in that level is potentially capable of being included in one microinstruction. Where conflicts exist at any level, micro-operations must be moved to another level. Such motion simply translates into additional time delays. The conflicts, δ_{ij}, for the ith resource at the jth level are as follows:

$$
\begin{aligned}
&\delta_{R0,1} = 0 \\
&\delta_{B,2} = 0, \ \delta_{R1,2} = 0, \ \delta_{L,2} = 0, \ \delta_{R4,2} = 0 \\
&\delta_{B,3} = 0, \ \delta_{R2,3} = 0, \ \delta_{R5,3} = 0, \ \delta_{L,3} = 1, \ \delta_{R7,3} = 0 \\
&\delta_{A,4} = 2
\end{aligned}
\tag{5.11}
$$

Now we can obtain the total execution time for the microprogram when resource requirements are included:

$$
\text{UBT} = L + \sum_{j=1}^{6} \Delta_j
$$

$$
= 6 + \Delta_3 + \Delta_4 = 6 + 1 + 2 = 9
\tag{5.12}
$$

At this point, if each micro-operation requires one unit clock cycle, then in the worst case, the microprogram is executable in nine clock cycles. The effect of the delays on the microprogram graph introduced by the resource conflicts is represented in Figure 5.11. Three additional levels are provided, 3′,

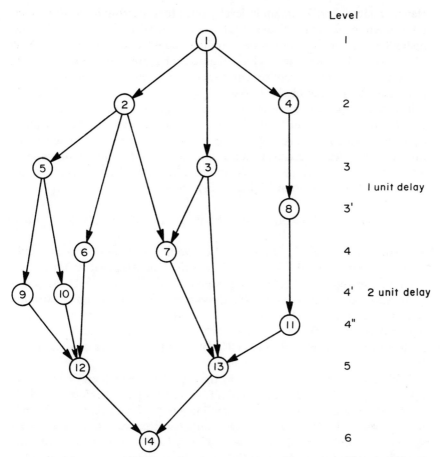

Level

I

2

3

I unit delay

3'

4

4'   2 unit delay

4"

5

6

Figure 5.11   The program graph (Figure 5.10) modified for resource conflicts

4', and 4" for nodes 8, 9 and 10, and 11. Node 8 is moved to a later level
because it conflicts with node 5. We choose to migrate node 8 because it has
fewer successors than node 5. Most likely, node 8 will have a lesser impact on
subsequent node migration than node 5.

Level 4 also has resource conflicts. Nodes 6 and 9 contend for the shifter,
S. Nodes 6 and 10 contend for R_7 while nodes 7, 10, and 11 all contend for
the adder. Obviously, some nodes must migrate lower. In fact, because some
contending nodes conflict in more than one way (6 contends with 9 and 10),
we may expect to introduce more than one level of delay. Just as with level 3,
we commit to level 4 those nodes which do not conflict with each other.

Hence, nodes 6 and 7 remain in level 4 since they are simultaneously executable micro-operations. Nodes 9, 10, and 11 need to be examined. Since
nodes 9 and 10 do not conflict we introduce nodes 9 and 10 to level 4 '. Node
11 now must be placed in level 4". Figure 5.11 represents the worst we can
do, if we ignore the inherent concurrency of our machine. But our objective is
to reduce the number of clock cycles.

The next step is to determine which nodes (micro-operations), if any, can
now be moved to earlier levels. In this step we generate the earliest precedence partition. This partition will now guide us in the choice of node migration to earlier levels. Keep in mind that we would like to eliminate levels
altogether so long as precedence is observed and resource conflicts are
prevented. The E partition for Figure 5.10 becomes:

$$E = \{[1], [2, 3, 4], [5, 6, 7, 8], [9, 10, 11], [12, 13], [14]\}. \qquad (5.13)$$

We return to Figure 5.11 and proceed to examine each level. Nodes 2 and 4
cannot migrate to level 1 since the E partition specifies that nodes 2 and 4
cannot move above level 2. However, nodes 6 and 7 in Figure 5.11 can potentially move to a higher level without violating the E partition constraints.
Node 6 cannot move to level 3 ' since it uses R_7, a conflict with node 8. But,
node 6 does not conflict with nodes 3 or 5, and hence can be moved to level 3.
Node 7 can also be moved to level 3 '. Observe that we have now eliminated
level 4.

There are other nodes indicated by the E partition which may be migrated
upwards. Nodes 9 and 10 in Figure 5.11, tentatively placed at level 4 ', can be
migrated upwards. As we test each candidate node, we see that node 9 can be
moved to level 4. Node 10, however, conflicts with node 7 (both use the adder). Our attempt to eliminate level 4' has failed. In fact, all remaining
migration tests fail and our optimization is complete. The final graph is
depicted in Figure 5.12. Note that our program graph is equivalent to a
dependency graph.

5.8 DETECTION OF PARALLELISM IN MICROPROGRAMS

Detection of parallelism in microprograms or *microparallelism* is the first
step to generating parallel sets of micro-orders from a sequential form of
microprogram. The sequential form of microprogram might take on the appearance of a straight line microprogram as shown in Figure 5.13 which
depicts the flow of control. Parallelism detection algorithms should accept
this initial form of input, detect the potential parallelism among micro-
orders, and finally generate a set of parallel micro-orders which performs the

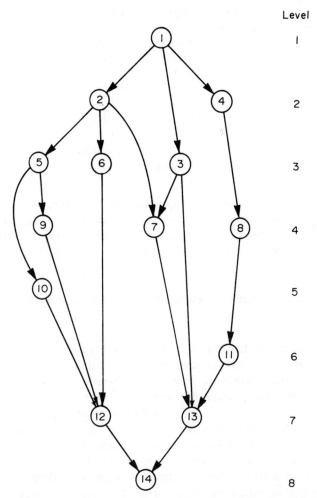

Figure 5.12   The final program graph with optimized partitions

equivalent task of the original straight line microprogram (SLM). An optimal set consists of the smallest number of microinstructions necessary to perform the task specified in the SLM.

Definition 5.14:   A *Straight Line Microprogram* or SLM is a sequential microprogram, S, equal to $\langle m_1, m_2, \ldots, m_t \rangle$ with a single entry point, m_1, and a single exit point, m_t, and with no branch decisions in between the entry and exit points.

(1) AIL ← ACCl; $[\Pi_1]$
(2) AIR ← 0; $[\Pi_1]$
(3) AO ← AIL + AIR;   [ADDER, Π_2]
(4) AO ← shl(AO);   [SHIFTER, Π_3]
(5) ACCl ← AO; $[\Pi_3]$
(6) AIL ← −1; $[\Pi_1]$
(7) AIR ← GR3; $[\Pi_1]$
(8) AO ← AIL + AIR;   [ADDER, Π_2]
(9) GR3 ← AO; $[\Pi_3]$

(Reprinted courtesy of ACM Computing Surveys)

Figure 5.13   A straight-line microprogram

Our procedure is to use the sequential listing and hardware dependent properties of the machine to determine which micro-orders can be placed in the same microinstruction to reduce the sequential tasks to a minimal form. We say that a pair of micro-orders in an SLM is parallel ($m_k \parallel m_j$) if and only if

(1) they are resource conflict-free during execution and (2) specified data dependencies in the SLM are preserved.

If m_i precedes m_j in the SLM, $m_i \parallel m_j$ because they can be placed in the same microinstruction without violating the two rules above.

One important hardware factor to determine parallel micro-orders depends on the phase relationship within each microinstruction. A detection scheme for a monophase microinstruction will differ considerably from that of a polyphase microinstruction. Algorithms in both cases have been developed by several investigators. In the example of Figure 5.13 not that each micro-order was assigned a time validity from among Π_1, Π_2, Π_3, a three phase format. The following algorithm from Dasgupta and Tartar generates an output sequence of parallel sets. The algorithm works with a general polyphase format and is one of the many local optimization algorithms which deal strictly with an SLM.

Algorithm 1:   Detection of Parallel MOs in an SLM

Input: An SLM = $\langle m_1 m_2 \ldots m_t \rangle$.
Comment: "Current MO" refers to the input element being examined. The

sequence of parallel sets $P = \langle P_1, P_2, \ldots, P_i \rangle$ obtained at any given time, is the "current parallel set sequence" in which P is the "earliest parallel set" and P_i the "latest parallel set." The basic idea of the algorithm is to place the jth input MO (for $j = 1, 2, \ldots, t$) in the earliest possible parallel set such that 1) there are no resource conflicts, 2) the data dependencies in the input SLM are preserved, and 3) the resulting current parallel set sequence is the smallest for the MOs thus far processed.

(1) $P_1 \leftarrow \{m_1\}$;
(2) **If** there are no more MOs in the input string
   then STOP **fi**;
(3) **If** current MO m_j is a branch MO
   then If $m_j \parallel m_k$ for all m_k in the latest parallel set P_i,
   then $P_i \leftarrow P_i \, U\{m_j\}$
   else $P_{i+1} \leftarrow \{m_j\}$; $i \leftarrow i + 1$ **fi**;
   goto (2) **fi**;
(4) **If** there exists some m_k in the latest parallel set P_i such that m_k must execute before m_j
   then $P_{i+1} \leftarrow \{m_j\}$; $i \leftarrow i + 1$;
   goto (2) **fi**;
(5) **If** $m_k \parallel m_j$ for all $m_k \in P_i$ but m_j cannot precede m_k
   then $P_i \leftarrow P_i \, U \{m_j\}$;
   goto (2) **fi**;
(6) **If** there exists some P_k preceding P_i in the current parallel set sequence such that for all $m_p \in P_k$, $m_p \parallel m_j$ but m_j cannot precede P_k
   then $P_k \leftarrow P_k \, U \{m_j\}$;
   goto (2) **fi**;
(7) **If** there exists no parallel set in P in which m_j can be placed, but m_j can precede P
   then $P_{i+1} \leftarrow P_i$; $P_i \leftarrow P_{i-1}$; $\ldots$; $P_2 \leftarrow P_1$; $P_1 \leftarrow \{m_j\}$;
   $i \leftarrow i + 1$;
   goto (2) **fi**;
(8) **If** there exists no parallel set in P in which m_j can be placed and m_j cannot precede P
   then $P_{i+1} \leftarrow \{m_j\}$; $i \leftarrow i + 1$;
   goto (2) **fi**;

Algorithm 1 is a linear algorithm. Micro-orders are added in some order to an initially empty list of microinstructions. Then the algorithm attempts to add another micro-order to the existing microinstruction. Only if it fails is a new microinstruction created. The search begins with a data dependency analysis, finds the earliest microinstruction eligible for placing a micro-order without generating a resource conflict, and terminates when all micro-orders have been placed.

One important property of this algorithm is its "first-come, first-placed" nature. This affects the algorithm's performance to *the* extent that the optimal solution is not always obtained.

Example 5.4:   A Parallel Set Sequence. (Reprinted Courtesy of ACM Computing Surveys)

When we apply the above algorithm to the straight line microprogram of Figure 5.13, we obtain the current parallel set sequence shown in Figure 5.14. When we perform the first iteration according to the algorithm, we obtain micro-order 1 in the parallel set, P_1. After the second iteration, we find that micro-orders 1 and 2 can be placed in the same current parallel set, P_1. After the third iteration, we find micro-orders 1, 2, and 3 combined in the current parallel set, P_1. It is not until step 5 that we find that micro-order 5 cannot be combined with micro-orders 1, 2, 3, and 4. At that point we begin to generate a new parallel set, P_2. After nine iterations we have exhausted all micro-orders and have obtained three parallel sets, P_1, P_2, and P_3, which indicates that only three microinstructions are required to execute the same task performed by the SLM. Hence we have reduced the nine step SLM to a three step sequence of three microinstructions.

5.9   THE PRACTICE OF FIRMWARE ENGINEERING

This section[6] describes the experiences of designing a two level control structure of the MC68000 processor with special attention to the constraints which LSI technology imposes on processor implementation. There are four such constraints: circuit size, circuit speed, interconnection complexity and package pin count. The implications of these constraints on the structure of a microprocessor control unit and its microcode are explored. The actual practice in firmware engineering is described.

In the two level control structure each macroinstruction is emulated by a sequence of microinstructions. The microinstructions are narrow, consisting primarily of pointers to nanoinstructions. (Microinstructions also contain information about branching in the micro sequence.) The nanoinstructions are wide, providing fairly direct, decoded control of the execution unit. Nanoinstructions, in general, can be placed randomly in the nano store since few sequential accesses to nanoinstructions are required. Also few copies of each unique nanoinstruction need be stored.

---

[6]This section is an adaptation of material developed by Nick Tredennick, IBM Corp.

Iteration	Current Parallel Set Sequence
1	$P_1 = (1)$
2	$P_1 = (1, 2)$
3	$P_1 = (1, 2, 3)$
4	$P_1 = (1, 2, 3, 4)$
5	$P_1 = (1, 2, 3, 4), P_2 = (5)$
6	$P_1 = (1, 2, 3, 4), P_2 = (5, 6)$
7	$P_1 = (1, 2, 3, 4), P_2 = (5, 6, 7)$
8	$P_1 = (1, 2, 3, 4), P_2 = (5, 6, 7), P_3 = (8)$
9	$P_1 = (1, 2, 3, 4), P_2 = (5, 6, 7), P_3 = (8, 9)$

(Reprinted courtesy of ACM Computing Surveys)

Figure 5.14   Output produced by algorithm 1 for the SLM in Figure 5.13

An extension of the two level concept is made in the Nanodata QM-1. In that machine a microinstruction can specify a *sequence* of nanoinstructions. This approach was *not* taken in the MC68000 for two reasons. First, the initial microprograms showed that micro sequences tend to be very short (one, two, or three microinstructions), so sequential nanoinstructions cannot be used to advantage. Second, unless some facility for nano branches is implemented, multiple copies of some nanoinstructions must be kept in nano store.

Traditional implementation of the MC68000 control section using a single Control Store with internal state sequencing information was investigated. It was found to be impractical because the control store was too large for a single chip implementation. Methods for reduction of the total control store area required were considered. It was determined that necessary control store area could be substantially reduced through the use of a two level control store structure. The structure selected for the MC68000 control unit is shown in Figure 5.15.

In a two level structure, the first level (micro control store) contains sequences of control word addresses for the lower level (nano control store). Dynamic operation is illustrated in Figure 5.16 (bus activity for an indexed address, register to memory 32 bit add). The Instruction Decode provides the starting address for a single macroinstruction routine. The micro control store provides a sequence of addresses into the nano control store. The nano control store contains an arbitrarily ordered set of almost unique machine state control words. The practicality of this structure for space reduction rests on two mutually dependent assumptions.

First, the number of different control states actually implemented is a small fraction of the number of possible control states. For example, a reasonably horizontal control word for the MC68000 Execution Unit contains 68

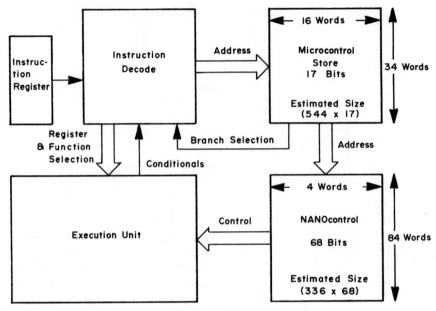

Figure 5.15   MC68000 control structure

bits, implying a possible 2^{68} different control words. Most of the possible control states are not meaningful for macroinstruction execution. The implementation of the complete set of macroinstruction sequences for the MC68000 processor requires only about 200 to 300 ($<2^9$) unique nano words. This set of nano words is a very small fraction of the set of possible states. Nano words are uniquely specified by 10 bits of address. As a result, words in the micro control store address sequences need only allocate 10 bits for each nano control store address.

Second, there must be some redundant use of the necessary control words to realize a reduction in control store area. If there were a one-to-one correspondence between nano control store addresses in the micro control store and control words in the nano control store, then the nano address in the microinstruction could be replaced by the contents of the addressed nanoinstruction and the address bits eliminated. If, however, there are more addresses in the instruction sequences than there are unique control words, a reduction in total control store size may be possible. (The nano control store could be viewed as merely an orderly method for translating maximally encoded state information to a significantly more horizontal format.)

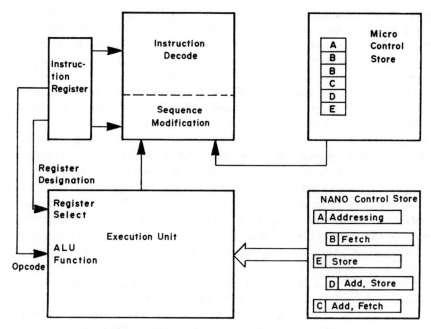

Figure 5.16   MC68000 control unit dynamic operation

Within a specific subfield of a nano word the control bits are encoded into the minimum bits necessary to provide the required subfunction states subject to the constraint that the decode to individual control lines involve no more than approximately two logic levels. Some space is necessary between the nano control store output and the Execution Unit control points for: (1) alignment of the control store outputs with their respective control points, (2) mixing macro static information with the micro dynamic information, and (3) combining certain timing information with appropriate control point variables. Within this space it is possible to provide minimal decoding at very little cost in additional areas while the signal encoding in the nano control store saves considerable nano word width and, hence, total storage space required. In the MC68000 control unit, the nano word width is 68 bits, while the Execution Unit contains about 180 control points.

The decision to implement the MC68000 control unit using a two level storage structure was based on minimizing control store area. Although necessary control store area was significantly reduced, introduction of the two level concept created several problems. One problem with a two level control store is that access to a memory is not instantaneous and in a two level structure the accesses must be sequential. The alternative, combinatorial decoding, does not proceed in zero time either, which partially compensates for the extra memory access. Further compensation for the extra access time requires complex control timing techniques such as instruction prefetch, access overlap, and multiple word accesses.

Another problem associated with a two level structure is the delay associated with conditional branching. Viewed in a strictly sequential fashion, a condition set in the Execution Unit must affect the selected micro control store address sequence which, in turn, affects the nano word selected. The nano word selected ultimately causes actions which can be dependent upon the value of the tested combination. Techniques used to minimize the sequential nature of this type of delay include physical organization of words within both control store levels and simultaneous access to more than a single control store word. For example, an access to a row of nano store (containing multiple nano words) can be initiated early in a cycle, with subsequent single-word selection. Also, in many cases, probable outcome of a conditional branch favors one branch more than another. In such an instance, it may be possible or even desirable to prefetch instruction words associated with the most likely branch condition. The best example of the usefulness of this idea is its application to a decrement and branch-not-zero type instruction. Branching is heavily favored and a prefetch at the destination location can greatly minimize execution delays associated with looping.

If common microinstruction routines, such as the address calculation routines, are to be shared among several macroinstructions, then mechanisms must be provided which facilitate functional branches for both entering and leaving the common routines. Care must be taken to avoid delays associated with functional branches in a two level store, especially when the common routines are short (making it more difficult to overlap accesses to different routines in different control stores).

The capability to perform *direct branches in the micro control store* allows various macroinstruction sequences to share common ending routines. It also permits more flexibility in organizing the micro routine sequences within the control store address space. Branching mechanisms occur very commonly. In the MC68000 micro control store, the average microinstruction sequence encounters some type of branch at about one out of every two nano addresses. Implementation of efficient branching mechanisms is critical for providing fast execution times with a microprogrammed structure.

Example 5.5:   In this example, the control store size reduction with a two level control store is compared to one level stores.

Assume:

n = number of individually-controlled switches in an execution unit (width of the horizontal control word)

k = total number of control states required to implement all instructions

p = proportion of unique control states to total number of control states

Single Level Control Store—In a simplified model of a single level control store there are k microinstructions, each containing a control state (n bits) and a next microinstruction address ($\lceil \log_2 k \rceil$ bits). See Figure 5.17.
Total size of single level control store:

$$S_1 = k(n + \lceil \log_2 k \rceil) \tag{5.14}$$

Two Level Control Store—A simplified model of a two level control store has a microcontrol store of k microinstructions with a nano address ($\lceil \log_2 v \rceil$ bits) and a next microinstruction address ($\lceil \log_2 k \rceil$ bits). The nano control store has $v(=pk)$ nanoinstructions, each containing a control state (n bits), as shown in Figure 5.18.

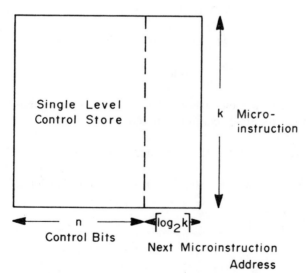

Figure 5.17   Model of a single level control store

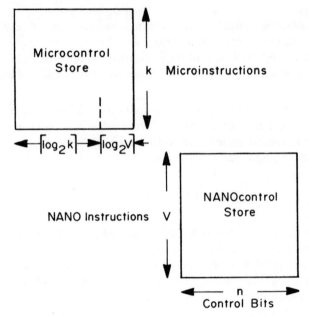

Figure 5.18   Model of a two level control store

The total size of two level control store is

$$S_2 = k(\lceil \log_2 v \rceil) + \lceil \log_2 k \rceil) + nv \tag{5.15}$$

$$\text{where } v = pk. \tag{5.16}$$

Control Store Size Comparison—The two level store requires fewer control store bits than the single control store if $S_2 < S_1$. Using

(5.14), (5.15) and (5.16) gives:

$$k(\lceil \log_2 pk \rceil + \lceil \log_2 k \rceil) + npk < k(n + \lceil \log_2 k \rceil). \tag{5.17}$$

Simplifying (5.17) gives:

$$\lceil \log_2 k \rceil + \lceil \log_2 p \rceil + np < n \tag{5.18}$$

Solving for n and k in (5.18) gives the result that the two level store is smaller than the single level control store if

$$n > \frac{\lceil \log_2 k \rceil + \lceil \log_2 p \rceil}{1 - p} \tag{5.19}$$

or

$$k < \frac{1}{p} 2^{n(1-p)} \tag{5.20}$$

In typical microprogrammed machines, n (the width of the horizontal control word) varies from 20 to 360, and k varies from 50 to 4000. Typical values for p are not known.

In the MC68000 microprocessor

$$n \simeq 70$$
$$k \simeq 650$$
$$p \simeq .4$$
$$S_1 = k(n + \lceil \log_2 k \rceil)$$
$$\quad = 52400$$
$$S_2 = k(\lceil \log_2 v \rceil + \lceil \log_2 k \rceil) + nv$$
$$\quad = 30550$$

$$\frac{S_2}{S_1} = .58$$

$$\Delta S = S_1 - S_2 = 21850 \text{ bits}$$

5.10   OPTIMIZATION IN USER-MICROPROGRAMMABLE (GENERAL-PURPOSE) MACHINES

Up to now the optimization techniques discussed in Chapter Four and in the present chapter focus on microprogrammed (dedicated) machines. Little of these existing techniques can be applied to the optimization of user-microprogrammable (general-purpose) machines. Obviously one important factor which must be taken into account both with the design of the writable control store in a user-microprogrammable machine as well as the optimization of the microcode is that the designer can never be fully aware of all of the user applications. Previous to this section in the text, such imprecise knowledge has not been considered. In microprogrammed machines, a ROM organization can be determined *after* the microprogram has been specified. We enjoy no such luxury in user-microprogrammable machines. Thus our assumptions and objectives underlying these types of applications must be altered considerably. ROM's are generally employed by the manufacturer to implement specific machine architecture. However, the user works with a writable control store which enables the implementation of different architectures. It is seldom possible to predict what a user will do. Hence, although optimal microprograms are an integral part of the total control store design in microprogrammed machines, this is definitely not the case for user-microprogrammable machines. In this setting, firmware engineering takes on new dimensions.

We need to treat the optimization process of writable control storage differently than that of the ROM. We need to carefully examine all intended applications of user-microprogrammable machines. Of course, the kernel of the control store or that part of the microprogram which must always reside in the machine is subject to the same optimization techniques we have seen thus far. However, user-microprogrammable machines assume that the capability exists to alter the apparent architecture of the machine itself. If this apparent architecture can change, a user expects the machine to implement different machine language codes. Therefore, the first possible source of optimization would be to effectively increase the potential of implementing various codes.

Second, not all users are expert microprogrammers. Hence, the writable control store may implement highly encoded microinstructions while attempting to resemble a familiar machine language. Now the original designer strives to achieve as much hidden parallelism in the encoding as possible by optimizing the available concurrency. A third desirable form of optimization is to provide microprogrammable support for potentially parallel micro-orders as much as possible. This of course places the optimization task upon the capable user.

The cycle time of the control store relative to the main memory is an important consideration for the user-microprogrammer. In fact, if control store is extremely fast, the user may desire to implement more functions in firmware rather than in software. The original designer must consider attributes of the writable control store which optimally implement the user-desired functions. In summary, the factors which then contribute to the potential optimization include:

a) the desired degree of parallelism in the microinstruction,
b) the various apparent structures of the machine microarchitectures, and
c) the desired level of encoding or flexibility in micro-order organization.
   Control designers should be aware of these factors in user-microprogrammable machines.

SUMMARY

Optimizing a microprogram is more than reducing the number of bits in a ROM. In fact, mere word-reduction does not guarantee an optimized microprogram. More importantly, an optimized microprogram executes the desired tasks in a more efficient manner, possibly faster. Second, the microprogram utilizes the machine more effectively. For a machine with the capability to execute parallel tasks, an optimized microprogram will maximize concurrent operation.

At the beginning of this chapter, optimizing notions common to conventional compiling were analyzed. Application to microcompilation was then identified. A program graph was defined and later refined. The dependency graph, a useful tool for including machine dependency, was examined. Finally, dependency graphs, coupled with resource conflict matrices, were used to demonstrate optimization of sequential tasks into horizontal microcode.

In this chapter we have discussed the detection of parallel micro-orders in the generation of parallel sequences. This is quite different from the code optimization proposed by Kleir and Ramamoorthy in the first section of this chapter. In that case we were more concerned with code *transformation* such as elimination of redundant code or useless tasks. Parallelism detection is more like processor scheduling. We are concerned with the *ordering* of a given code.

The principles of microprogram optimization presented in Chapters 4 and 5 introduce the new discipline of firmware engineering. In Chapter 4, we presume the existence of the microprogram. The primary objective is to minimize real estate in control memory. Yet, a true engineering approach recognizes that memory comes in quantized units called ROM's and RAM's, each containing a finite dimension of bits versus words (B $\times$ W). That being the case, we would like to know at the beginning whether our minimization will succeed. Hence, Table 4.6 is quite useful.

In Chapter 5 our minimization process is motivated by the need to optimize far more than just the memory space dimensions. We want to optimize the total function of the control store unit. This engineering approach requires that we look at alternate representations. Abstractions such as data dependency graphs, connectivity matrices, and environment dependent factors (resource conflicts and concurrency) are vital design tools. Such tools are and should be amenable to automation by computer and not human implementation. We have taken this approach.

Many abstract notions for optimizing microcode have been presented in these chapters. Yet, nothing compares with the lessons in life. Section 5.9 is a snapshot of one real world experience. This experience in firmware engineering is valuable, beyond measure.

PROBLEMS

5.1.   Define a program graph.

5.2.   Why is it necessary to optimize microcode in a block?

5.3.   What are the essential differences between a program graph and a dependency graph if any?

5.4.   Is every digraph a dependency graph? Explain.

5.5.   Given a connectivity matrix, M, show that the earliest precedence partition of M is identical to the latest precedence partition of the transpose of M.

5.6.   Prove that the lower bound on the number of microinstructions is the number of nodes in the longest path in the data-dependency graph.

5.7.   Given a connectivity matrix, M, show that more than one dependency graph may be found.

5.8.   Given the program graph in Figure 5.19 and the resource usage table of Example 5.3 in the text,

   a. Generate the latest precedence partition, L.
   b. Generate the earliest precedence partition, E.
   c. Generate the connectivity matrix.
   d. Optimize this program graph as described in Section 5.7.

5.9.   Generate the connectivity matrix for each of the dependency graphs of Figure 5.20.

5.10. Generate the earliest precedence partitions for Problem 5.9.

5.11. Generate the latest precedence partitions for Problem 5.9.

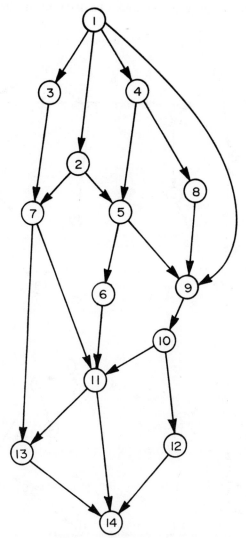

Figure 5.19   A program graph

5.12. Essential nodes in a dependency graph are those nodes which belong in the set $(E_i \cap L_i)$. For example, if $E = [(1), (2, 3), (5)]$ and $L = [(1), (2), (3, 5)]$ then node 2 is an essential node. Given any dependency graph, how can the essential nodes be determined without generating E and L?

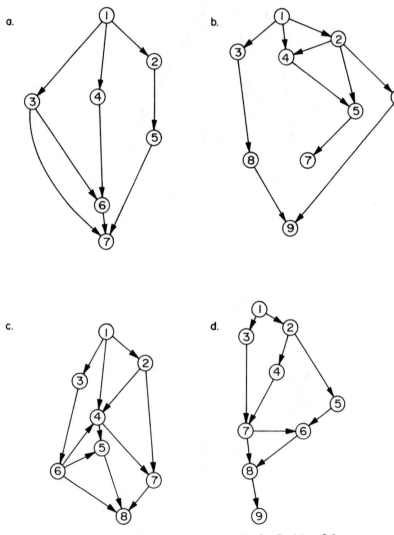

Figure 5.20   Dependency graphs for Problem 5.9

REFERENCES

Optimization of microprograms through compilation is only one alternative to optimizing microcode. Other alternatives are described in R. L. Kleir and C. V. Ramamoorthy, "Optimization Strategies for Microprograms," *IEEE Trans. Computers*, Vol. C-20, No. 7, July, 1971, pp. 783-793.

Some applications of horizontal microprogram optimization techniques are described in M. Tsuchiya and M. J. Gonzalez, "Toward Optimization of Horizontal Microprograms," *IEEE Trans. Computers*, Vol. C-25, No. 10, October, 1976, pp. 992-999.

The formal topic of state-reduction for microprogram optimization is covered in three papers by V. M. Glushkov: "Automata Theory and Structural Design Problems of Digital Machines," *Kibernetika*, Vol. 1, No. 1, 1965, pp. 3-11; "Automata Theory and Formal Microprogram Transformations," *Kibernetika*, Vol. 1, No. 5, 1965, pp. 1-9; and "Minimization of Microprograms and Algorithm Schemes," *Kibernetika*, Vol. 2, No. 5, 1966, pp. 1-3.

Formal notions on heuristic-reduction techniques are described in A. T. Mischenko, "The Formal Synthesis of An Automaton by a Microprogram I," *Kibernetika*, Vol. 4, No. 3, 1968, pp. 24-31; and "The Formal Synthesis of an Automaton by a Microprogram II," *Kibernetika*, Vol. 4, No. 5, 1968, pp. 21-27.

Application of graph theoretic principles to E and L partitions was established by C. V. Ramamoorthy, "A Structural Theory of Machine Diagnosis," in *1967 Spring Joint Comput. Conf. AFIPS Conf. Proc.*, Vol. 30, Washington, D.C.: Thompson, 1967, pp. 743-746.

A more recent discussion of heuristic-reduction techniques can be found in M. J. Flynn and R. F. Rosin, "Microprogramming: An Introduction and a Viewpoint," *IEEE Trans. Computers*, Vol. C-20, No. 7, July, 1971, pp. 727-731.

There are several techniques that can be used to detect and generate parallel microorders. For additional SLM analysis, see S. Dasgupta and J. Tartar, "The Identification of Maximal Parallelism in Straight-Line Microprograms," *IEEE Trans. Computers*, Vol. C-25, No. 10, October, 1976, pp. 986-992; L. W. Jackson and S. Dasgupta, "The Identification of Parallel Micro-Operations," *Inf. Process. Lett.*, Vol. 2, March, 1974, pp. 180-184; and S. S. Yau, A. C. Schowe, and M. Tsuchiya, "On Storage Optimization for Horizontal Microprograms," *Proc. 7th Annual Workshop on Microprogramming*, 1974, ACM, IEEE, New York, pp. 98-106. Dasgupta and Jackson's algorithms operate with a general polyphase scheme. The Yau et. al., algorithm generates a minimal sequence of parallel sets and is exponential in t or the size of the SLM. All of these algorithms determine a local optimization on the SLM.

Chapter Six

A FIRMWARE ENGINEERING DEVELOPMENT TOOL

6.1 INTRODUCTION

In this chapter we examine an alternate approach to microprogram design using *A*lgorithmic *S*tate *M*achine (ASM) concepts normally encountered in the design of logic state machines. ASM designs employ flow chart procedures. Microprogramming can be quite similar to a flow charting design procedure. In fact, many of the documentation schema are simply flow charts (see, for instance, the CAS documentation). Defining the sequential steps in a typical microprogram is similar, then, to drawing a flow chart with appropriate conditional and unconditional branches (for decision blocks) and assigning microinstructions to the blocks. This chapter introduces this firmware engineering tool as a procedural design technique which couples the hardware sequencing implementation directly to firmware design.

Microprogramming with ASM procedures is analogous to flow charting in programming. Given a set of tasks for a digital machine, the designer maps out a set of steps (states) for sequential execution of steps (in our case, microorders) in the machine. Appropriate hardwired logic is introduced to control sequencing and branching. This control sequencing activity is then prescribed within some ROM with support hardware for branching. In a typical ASM design exercise, a flow chart is generated for the tasks. Machine states are assigned and respective control logic is identified. Finally, a state minimization exercise is accomplished if ROM size is of concern. This latter exercise is similar to the bit and word reduction schemes for microprogramming which we examined earlier.

Clare has proposed several sequencing structures for ROM-centered designs, principally, by the ASM techniques. Each ASM chart has a specific hardware structure. In this chapter we will examine link path addressable, state qualifier, assumed addresses, and variable format addressable structures. As we shall see shortly, these structures are similar, if not identical, to microprogram next address sequence schemes described previously. For instance, the link path addressable structure is an implicit addressing scheme, while the variable format addressable structure of this chapter is a simple version of variable mode format sequencing schemes. *The purpose for ASM design procedures is to establish a documentation methodology which both hardware and software engineers can readily utilize during the conceptual design stages of microprogrammable machines.*

The hardware engineer is very much interested in the sequencing behavior of microprograms because he or she needs to develop a reliable control unit. Hence, he/she studies the "flow" of steps necessary to execute a task, and later decides upon the necessary size of the ROM, latches, decoders, and other peripheral logic. Also, of concern is the wiring and pin count of devices (organization of the physical implementation).

The software engineer (in our case, the microprogrammer) specifies the set of micro-orders for each subtask (an algorithm) in order to execute the major tasks requires in his application. The tasks may initially be vaguely specified. Hence, he/she needs to generate a sequential "flow" of subtasks (again, in our setting, eventually describable by micro-orders) in logical fashion. The ASM documentation, which will serve both the hardware and software engineer, is conveniently represented by a flow chart. This common medium of documentation is attractive to both types of engineer.

6.2   PROCEDURAL RULES

Certain rules apply to the flow chart procedure in ASM design. *First, only three chart symbols are required: an unconditional output block, a condition block, and a conditional output block as in Figure 6.1. Second, the flow chart must unambiguously represent the intended algorithm.* Since we will eventually assign states to our subtasks, we will need to insure that the transition from one state to another is unambiguously specified (only one machine state is permitted at any moment). This is equivalent to the constraint that only one path is traversed at any given moment. We will eventually identify a state for each microinstruction in our microprogram. Hence, sequencing through a microprogram must be clearly defined (regardless of conditional or unconditional branches). As part of the design process, we specify micro-orders to the symbols in our ASM chart as in Figure 6.2. Micro-orders can be assigned to either unconditional output blocks or conditional output blocks. However, micro-orders for conditional output blocks are activated only after the immediately preceding conditions in the condition block are satisfied.

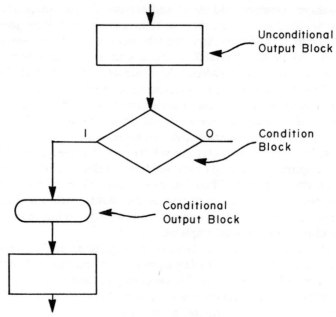

Figure 6.1   ASM symbols

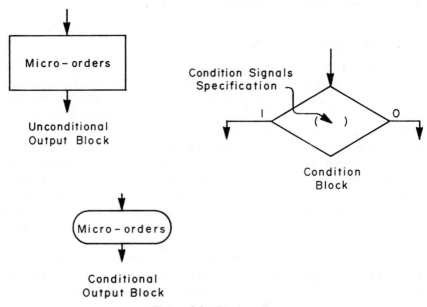

Figure 6.2   Block coding

The third rule for an ASM chart requires us to partition the chart in order to identify "state times" for microinstruction execution. We do so by enclosing appropriate "zones" in each chart, such that one and only one state is permissible in any "zone" and exits from each state are clearly and unambiguously defined for each "zone". For instance, the enclosures for Figure 6.3 are valid, while the enclosures for Figure 6.4 are not. Here, the exit from state "i" is ambiguous since we are not sure whether state "j" or state "k" is encountered next. Ultimately, each enclosure will specify a microinstruction in a microprogram. Obviously, the enclosure assignment of Figure 6.4 cannot be logically represented in our eventual microprogram. Of course, there are other invalid assignments. These consist mainly of combinations of the above invalid assignments.

Given these simple rules, we now proceed with the various structures for addressing via ASM charts. Our first ASM chart assignment assumes that the sequencing architecture is comprised of two arrays (much like Wilkes' original configuration for the "C" and "S" matrices). Although the control information ("C" and "S") may be found in a ROM, for our first scheme it is more likely to be implemented by other types of devices.

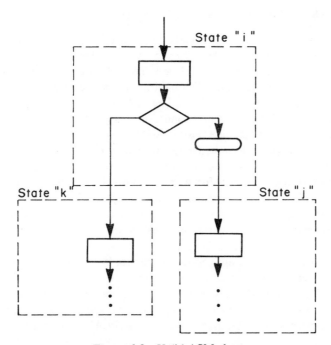

Figure 6.3   Valid ASM chart

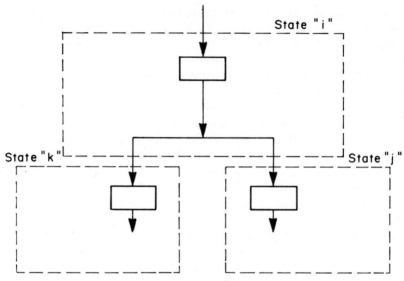

Figure 6.4 Invalid ASM chart

6.3 LINK PATH ADDRESSABLE SEQUENCING

The *l*ink *p*ath *a*ddressable (LPA) structure for microprogram control utilizes an implicit next address sequencing scheme. No address counter is necessary and, therefore, one is seldom employed. The LPA structure relies on a set of state inputs and on a set of conditional inputs (for instance, from the carry or adder overflow signals in the CPU). The next address is obtained by logically combining these state inputs and conditional inputs. The set of state inputs is equivalent to a machine state assignment.

Naturally it is possible to heuristically specify machine states. However, if fewer states are desirable, a state minimization exercise should also be performed. Of course, methods for state assignment must be employed so as to avoid physical races and hazards. It is also desirable to actually use the smallest physical implementation for the LPA structure. A minimal number of logical devices is always attractive. Here, state minimization can also be effective.

The LPA structure is depicted in Figure 6.5. We see that it is analogous to a simple microprogram controller. The structure does differ in the following sense. Although a ROM may be used to store both a link path field, $A_0, A_1,$ ..., A_n, and a control field, $c_0, c_1, \ldots$, we commonly employ another physical device, a *p*rogrammable *l*ogic *a*rray (PLA). Our scheme is not fully

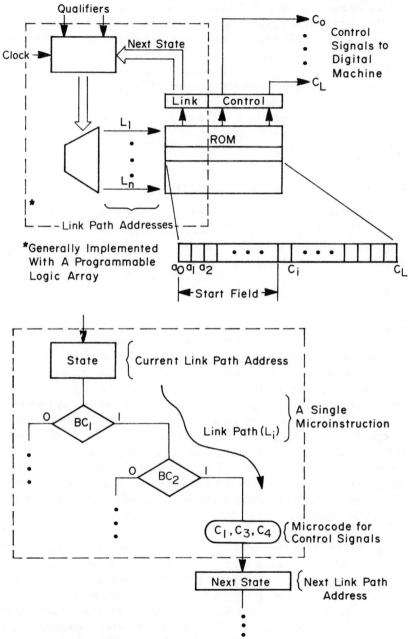

Figure 6.5 Single microinstruction link path addressable sequence

explicit because the link path field only indirectly generates the next address. The link path field is logically combined with state and conditional inputs to determine the next address. *The key to this implementation is the placement of one microinstruction per link path.* As shown in Figure 6.5, the L_i link path is shown with two conditional branch decisions, BC_1 and BC_2, in the path and with a single microinstruction energizing control lines c_1, c_3, and c_4. It is important to realize that each machine state is equivalent to a microinstruction. Finally, since each link path field is utilized as a state assignment, and the address is not explicit, we appropriately relabel our address field, A, as a state field, S.

6.4 PROPERTIES OF LPA STRUCTURES

There are important properties of LPA control structures that we will now discuss. The major property of LPA control is the assignment of one microinstruction for each link path. This is a basic constraint of the hardware implementation. The second property relates to the physical timing behavior of the hardware. This property is concerned with the phase structure of an LPA chart. Two phase structures are possible. A *monophase* ASM structure is one in which one and only one conditional output block exists per exit link path in any given ASM state, as shown in Figure 6.6. Here we see that all conditional micro-orders in Figure 6.6a follow all decision blocks in states X and Y. The *polyphase* structure in Figure 6.6b assigns two or more conditional micro-orders in link paths L_1 and L_2 of state X and state Y.

Sequential access of control signals is a matter of relative placement of the micro-orders in each link path. This placement is governed, not only by the conditions needed for each micro-order (to be executed), but also by the timing specification of our implementation. For a microprogrammable machine with a monophase timing structure, we will find the polyphase LPA structure extremely awkward, if not impossible, to implement. Therefore, we must insure that our micro-order placement is compatible with the timing structure of our physical implementation. A careless choice may incur a subtle penalty in execution cycle timing. This occurs when we need to execute a micro-order well in advance of the next machine state yet carelessly place it "late" in the link path. For greater flexibility, we would use a polyphase machine with a polyphase ASM chart when such timing considerations are important. Note that we can determine the longest clock cycle required in our design by merely searching through the chart for the longest link path.

A third property of the LPA control structure is that each word contains only two fields. One field is the link field which, when combined with the conditions, forms the next address. When the next address does not require a

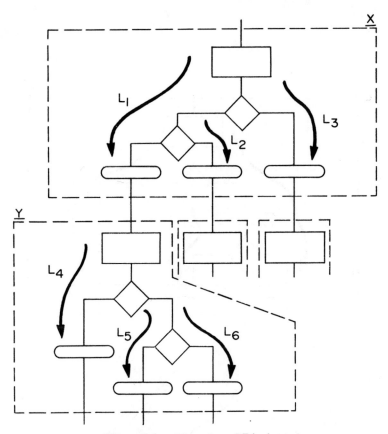

Figure 6.6a   Monophase LPA chart

conditional branch test, we utilize the conditions in a "don't care" sense. The other field of each word is the control field. This field is also classified as the conditional micro-order field, conditioned by the set of branch decisions required in each link path.

Example 6.1:   To further illustrate the properties of LPA structures, we now examine a simple microprogram of a short segment of an ASM chart with four lines of microcode in Figure 6.7. Again we see that each link path, L_1, L_2, L_3, L_4, is equivalent to a single microinstruction. L_1 contains the c_2, c_3, c_6 micro-orders, has two conditional branch decisions and terminates in the next state, 001. In this example, our state assignment $S = S_1 S_2 S_3$ starts with

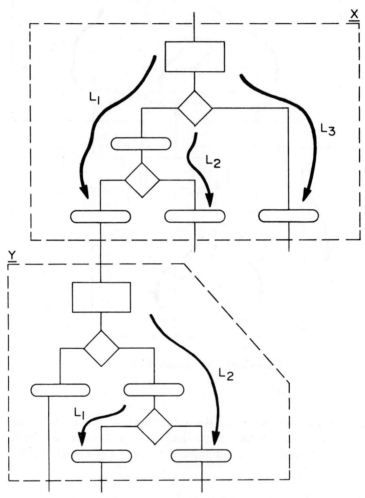

Figure 6.6b   Polyphase LPA chart

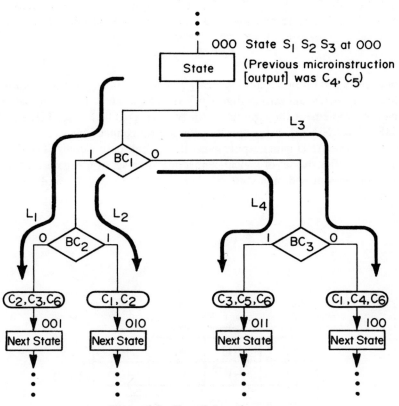

Figure 6.7   Four link path sequence

000. L_2 links next state 010, L_3 links 100, and L_4 links 011. Therefore, our current state, 000, links with one of four next states.

To complete the design, we need to generate a state dependency map. A state dependency map is simply a Karnaugh map of the conditions with the link paths as map variables. The map, of course, is used for simple state minimization (with don't cares) analogous to those found in Karnaugh map techniques. Our state dependency map for this example is shown in Figure 6.8. Note that each link path in Figure 6.7 requires a set of conditions, BC_1, BC_2, BC_3. These are now specified on the map in Figure 6.8. For example,

$$L_1 = S \cdot BC_1 \cdot \overline{BC_2}$$

requires a test on two conditions, BC_1 and $\overline{BC_2}$. Lastly, we will assemble the four link path sequences of Figure 6.7 as in Figure 6.9. In our simple example, we implement the structure with two arrays called AND-TIE and OR-TIE. The AND-TIE array specifies the logical connections to a set of AND gates. These AND gate outputs generate the link path signals. The OR-TIE array specifies the set of logical connections to a set of OR gates. These OR gate outputs provide the state machine signals, S_1, S_2, S_3, and the micro-orders, m_1, ..., m_6. These arrays are depicted in Figure 6.10 for Example 6.1.

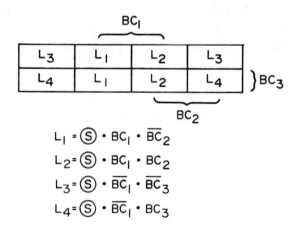

Figure 6.8   Dependency map for link path from state S

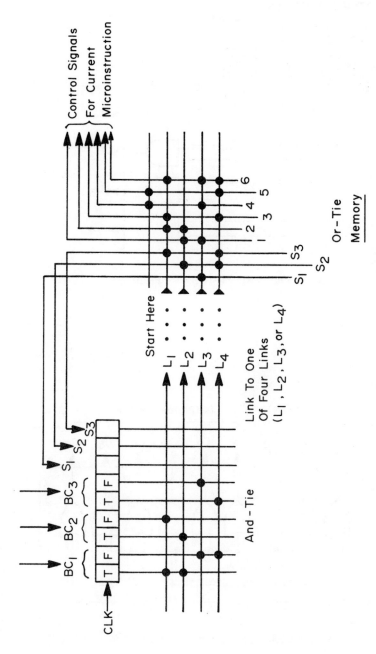

Figure 6.9 Link path address array

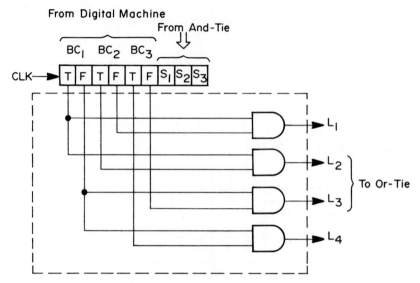

Figure 6.10a   AND-TIE array for Figure 6.9

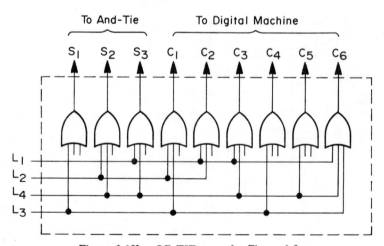

Figure 6.10b   OR-TIE array for Figure 6.9

6.5 PROGRAMMABLE LOGIC ARRAYS (PLA)

The LPA control scheme can be implemented with an AND-TIE and an OR-TIE array as discussed above. For a large digital machine, it would be prohibitive to design these arrays with discrete random logic. Instead, we commonly employ a PLA. In this section, we will examine PLA's in great detail with several examples. This important physical device warrants discussion now, even though you, the reader, may find its inclusion awkward. The PLA is simply two arrays of elementary logic circuits shown in Figure 6.11. The circuit:

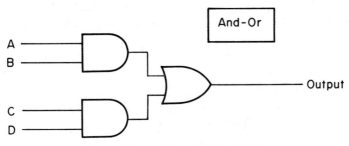

Figure 6.11   A simple PLA circuit

generates the structured two-level Boolean function for a sum of products:

$$\text{OUTPUT} = (AB + CD)$$

or a product of sums:

$$\text{OUTPUT} = ([A + B] \cdot [C + D]).$$

For instance, we implement the following simple sum of products as in Figure 6.12, and the Karnaugh map of Figure 6.13a would be realized as shown in Figure 6.13b.

The Signetics 82S100 is typical of the commercially available PLA's (see Figure 6.14) which are *field programmable* (FPLA). Thus, the designer has the option of programming the chip at his discretion. The characteristics of this device are shown in Table 6.1.

The 82S100 (Tri-State Outputs) and the 82S101 (Open Collector Outputs) are bipolar programmable logic arrays containing forty-eight product terms (AND terms) and eight sum terms (OR terms). Each OR term controls an output function which can be programmed either true active-High (Fp) or

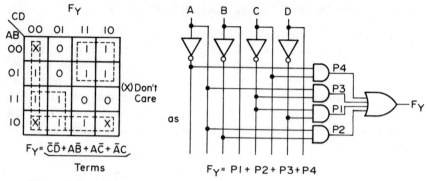

Figure 6.12a K map

Figure 6.12b PLA solution

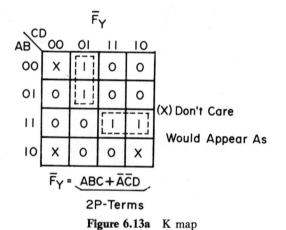

$$\bar{F}_Y = ABC + \bar{A}CD$$

2P-Terms

Figure 6.13a K map

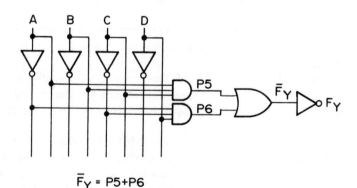

$$\bar{F}_Y = P5 + P6$$

Figure 6.13b PLA solution

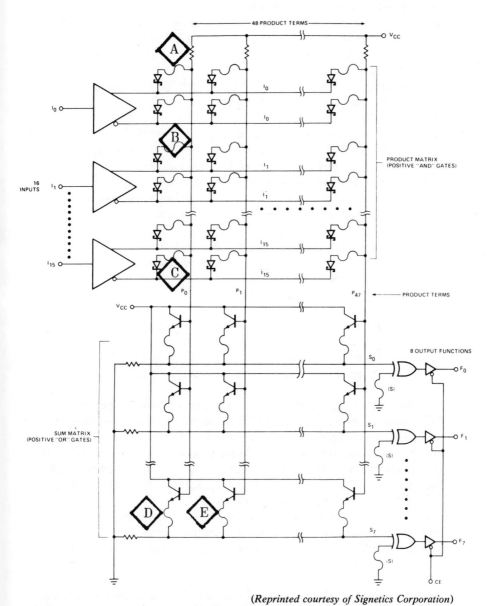

(*Reprinted courtesy of Signetics Corporation*)

Figure 6.14   Signetics bipolar field programmable logic array—82S100, 82S101—
block diagram

true active-Low ($\overline{\text{Fp}}$). The true state of each output function is activated by any logical combination of sixteen input variables or their complements, up to forty-eight terms. Both devices are field programmable, which means that custom patterns are immediately available by following a fusing procedure outlined by the manufacturer.

The 82S100 and 82S101 are fully TTL compatible and include chip-enable control for expansion of input variables and output inhibit. They feature either Open Collector or Tri-State Outputs for ease of expansion of product terms and application in bus-organized systems. Typical applications include those specified in Table 6.2. Internally, the 82S100 FPLA appears as a forty-eight column by sixteen row array of fuseable links for the AND-TIE array and forty-eight column by eight row array of fuseable links for the OR-TIE array. There are sixteen inputs, $I_0, \ldots, I_{15}$, and eight outputs, $F_0, F_1, \ldots, F_7$. The forty-eight product terms, P_n, are generated[1] by:

$$P_n = \Pi_0^{15} (k_m I_m + j_m \overline{I}_m); \quad \begin{array}{l} k = 0, 1, X \text{ (Don't Care)} \\ n = 0, 1, 2, \ldots, 47. \end{array}$$

The outputs, F_r, are implemented by:

$$F_r = f(\Sigma_0^{47} t_n P_n); \qquad r \equiv p = 0, 1, 2, \ldots, 7$$
where:
Unprogrammed state: $\quad j_m = k_m = 0; t_n = 1$
Programmed state: $\quad j_m = \overline{k_m} \quad ; t_n = 0, 1.$

Note that k_m and j_m are equational coefficients that represent the fuseable links. Since k_m and j_m are links which tie the true and complemented outputs of the mth internal gate, at least one link must be programmed as opened to insure no malfunction to the gate. In the programmed state, $j_m \neq k_m$. With this device, the manufacturer provides a programming worksheet similar to Figure 6.15. The designer specifies a programmed chip by inserting a "1", "0", or "X" in the appropriate block.

In reality, the PLA is a functional subset of memory systems because it has no latches or memory states. The most common usage for PLA's is as programmable address selectors in a memory system. Such a requirement might

---

[1] The symbol Π_0^{15} represents product terms, each of which contains no more than 16 variables. The symbol Σ_0^{47} represents 48 sum terms. For example $P_0 = I_0 I_1 \overline{I}_{15}$ means that all fuseable links in the first column of Figure 6.14 for the P_0 term are blown except at points A, B, and C. $F_7 = P_0 + P_1$ means that all fuseable links in the last row of Figure 6.14 for the F_7 output are blown except at points D and E.

Table 6.1   Signetics 82S100 Specifications

Field Programmable (Nickel-Chromium Links)
Input Variables—16
Output Functions—8
Product Terms—48
Address Access Time—50 ns. Maximum
Power Dissipation—600 mW, Typical
Input Loading—(-100μA) Maximum
Output Option:
   Tri-State Outputs—82S100
   Open Collector Outputs—82S101
Output Disable Function:
   Tri-State—Hi-Z
   Open Collector—Hi
Ceramic Dip

Table 6.2   PLA Applications

Replacement of Large Read-Only Memory and Random Logic
Code Conversion
Peripheral Controllers
Look-Up and Decision Tables
Microprogramming
Address Mapping
Character Generators
Sequential Controllers

$P_n \overset{?}{=} f(I_m)$	Input State	Program Table Entry	Fuse Command
Yes	I_m	Ⓗ	Fuse $\overline{I_m}$ link
	$\overline{I_m}$	Ⓛ	Fuse I_m link
No	Dont Care	⊖	Fuse both

(Reprinted courtesy of Signetics Corporation)
Figure 6.15   Signetics FPLA programming form

be found in the decoding of the instruction register "OPCODE" field in a digital computer as in Figure 6.16 and Figure 6.17 where future machines might utilize different instructions. PLA's are very effective when the op code designations tend to change from design to design while the hardware (ALU, I/O, MEM) is fixed. This may also occur when several high-level languages are to be implemented on the same machine. Figure 6.16 depicts one particular configuration for a PLA. A microinstruction decode for some high-level language is listed and a candidate PLA assignment is shown. Bits eight through fifteen of an IR and a FLAG are used as inputs to the PLA. The outputs of the PLA are control signals, ALU SELECT, ALU MODE, and CARRY IN. From the table, we see that an OR instruction is executed when an op code of 51_H is encountered. This instruction requires activation of the $ALUSEL_3$, $ALUSEL_2$, $ALUSEL_1$, and $ALUSEL_0$ control lines and is equivalent to a 15_{10} code in the ALU SELECT column of the table. Although it is not obvious if a redesign would require a different code other than 15_{10}, a reprogrammed PLA could be utilized and direct replacement of a device would suffice. This flexibility is especially desirable when software regeneration costs become prohibitively high.

Another use for a PLA can be found in the subroutine address map and branch logic. In the design of microprogrammed computers, considerable design flexibility is obtained when complete freedom in allocating microprogram subroutines throughout microcontrol store is permitted. The utilization of variable formats in the Instruction Register op code field is now possible.

	PLA INPUTS	PLA OUTPUTS		
INSTRUCTION	OPCODE	ALU SELECT	ALU MODE	CARRY IN
MOVE	1X	12	0	0
ADD	2X	7	1	0
SUBTRACT	3X	13	1	1
AND	50	2	0	0
OR	51	15	0	0
BRANCH	52	(7 or 12)	(1 or 0)	(1 or 0)
I/O	7X	12	0	0

(hex)   (decimal)

Figure 6.16   Typical microinstruction PLA table

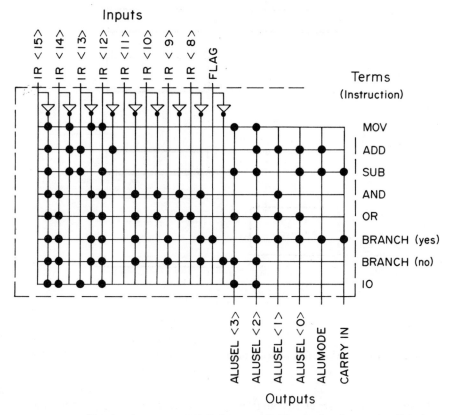

(Reprinted courtesy of IEEE Computer Society, Design Automation Group)
Figure 6.17   PLA layout for a programmable OP CODE generator

To satisfy these requirements economically, a convenient means of address retranslation is desirable. FPLA's are ideally suited for this application as shown in a typical system in Figure 6.18. The first FPLA translates the current op code from a 16-bit Instruction Register into one of forty-eight subroutine-start addresses in microcontrol store. Variable op code formats are handled by judicious programming of don't care states in the FPLA Input Table. The second FPLA is used to generate branch conditions based on the current microinstruction, as well as jump and status conditions in the machine. Note that the utilization of tri-state FPLA's (82S100) eliminates a multiplexer in the address path of the ROM Address Register.

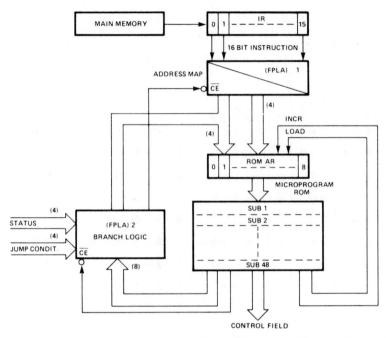

Figure 6.18   Subroutine address map and branch logic with tri-state FPLA's

Example 6.2:   Target Instruction Decoder for Microprogrammed Emulator.[2] One of the most difficult tasks of a general-purpose microprogrammed emulator shown in Figure 6.19 is the decoding of the target instruction. The circuit shown in Figure 6.20 provides a fairly general instruction decoder whose decoding can be changed to decode a variety of instruction sets by programming an FPLA. The equivalent circuit using PROM's would take over one hundred IC's.

The circuit has as input a sixteen bit instruction and two bits that tell whether address calculation has taken place. This is so that when the instruction is decoded and no memory reference is required, the decoder will generate the microinstruction address of the appropriate macroinstruction routine. If the instruction requires a memory reference, the address of the

---

[2] The material in this example has been adapted from publications of Signetics Corporation. Programs, figures, and tables are courtesy of and copyright by Signetics Corporation. All rights reserved.

BLOCK DIAGRAM OF MICROPROGRAMMED EMULATOR

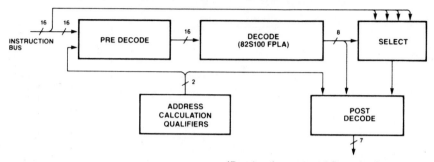

Figure 6.19   Block diagram of microprogrammed emulator

address calculation routine is generated. In this routine the address calculation bit is set. The microinstruction causes the decoder to be used again, but
the second time through, the presence of the address calculation bit causes
the decoder to generate the address of the appropriate microroutine, instead
of the address calculation routine.

The FPLA in the circuit has been programmed to decode the DEC PDP-11
series of instructions. These are tabulated in the FPLA Program Table of
Figure 6.21. Given a 16-bit opcode from a PDP-11, the circuit will return a
microcode starting address. In addition, if a memory reference is required,
the circuit will generate the address of the memory reference routine. The
microcode can then set a status bit so that, during the second pass through
the network, the memory reference routine is bypassed.

Example 6.3:   Timing Decoder and Sequence Controller for Data Acquisition System.[3] The functional diagram of Figure 6.22 shows a data acquisition
peripheral which samples four analog signals and sequentially supplies digitized data to a minicomputer. Computer commands vary sample timing.
Four digitized samples are sent to the computer via interrupts every one
millisecond.

The system operates with a basic repetition interval of 1Ms. Sample acquisition time begins at the start of each 1Msec interval, and samples are
held at various times after the beginning of the interval. Sample No. 1 is
always held at 200 μsec into the interval. Sample No. 2 follows No. 1 by 2.5
μsec. The timing of Samples 3 and 4 are varied before and after Sample 1 in

---

[3] The material in this example has been adapted from publications of Signetics Corporation.
Programs, figures, and tables are courtesy of and copyright by Signetics Corporation. All rights
reserved.

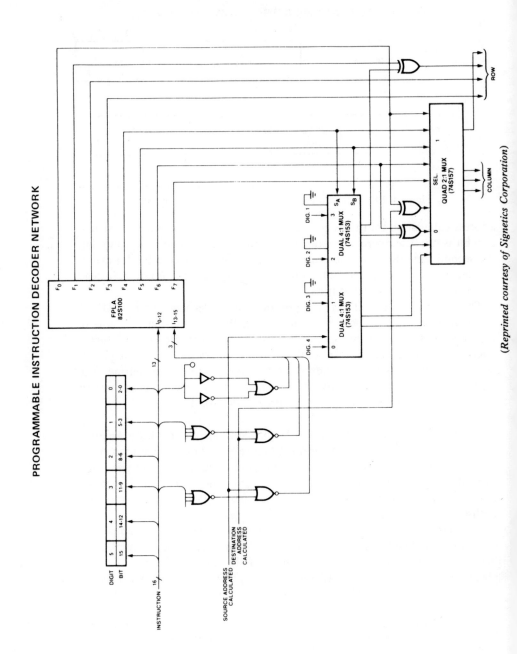

PROGRAMMABLE INSTRUCTION DECODER NETWORK

(Reprinted courtesy of Signetics Corporation)

NO.	15	14	13	12	11	10	9	8	7	6	5	4	3	2	1	0	O7	O6	O5	O4	O3	O2	O1	O0	COMMENTS
				PRODUCT TERM / INPUT VARIABLE													ACTIVE LEVEL / OUTPUT FUNCTION								
																	H	H	H	H	H	H	H	H	
0	-	L	H	-	-	-	-	-	-	-	-	-	-	H	-	-	•	•	•	A	•	A	A	•	CALCULATE SOURCE ADDRESS, WORD
1	-	-	L	H	-	-	-	-	-	-	-	-	-	H	-	-	•	•	•	A	•	A	A	•	
2	-	H	-	L	-	-	-	-	-	-	-	-	-	H	-	-	•	•	•	A	•	A	A	•	
3	H	L	H	-	-	-	-	L	-	-	-	-	-	H	-	-	•	•	•	A	•	A	A	A	
4	H	L	H	-	-	-	-	-	L	-	-	-	-	H	-	-	•	•	•	A	•	A	A	A	
5	H	H	L	-	-	-	-	L	-	-	-	-	-	H	-	-	•	•	•	A	•	A	A	A	CALCULATE SOURCE ADDRESS, BYTE
6	H	H	L	-	-	-	-	-	L	-	-	-	-	H	-	-	•	•	•	A	•	A	A	A	
7	H	-	L	H	-	-	-	L	-	-	-	-	-	H	-	-	•	•	•	A	•	A	A	A	
8	H	-	L	H	-	-	-	-	L	-	-	-	-	H	-	-	•	•	•	A	•	A	A	A	
9	-	L	H	-	-	-	-	-	-	-	-	-	-	L	H	-	•	•	A	•	•	A	•	A	
10	-	-	L	H	-	-	-	-	-	-	-	-	-	L	H	-	•	•	A	•	•	A	•	•	
11	-	H	-	L	-	-	-	-	-	-	-	-	-	L	H	-	•	•	A	•	•	A	•	•	CALCULATE DESTINATION ADDRESS, WORD
12	L	L	L	L	L	L	L	L	-	H	-	-	-	-	H	-	•	•	A	•	•	A	•	•	
13	-	L	L	L	H	-	-	-	-	-	-	-	-	-	H	-	•	•	A	•	•	A	•	•	
14	L	H	H	H	L	-	-	-	-	-	-	-	-	-	H	-	•	•	A	•	•	A	•	•	
15	L	H	H	H	H	L	L	-	-	-	-	-	-	-	H	-	•	•	A	•	•	A	•	•	
16	H	L	H	-	-	-	-	-	-	-	-	-	-	L	H	H	•	•	A	•	•	A	•	A	
17	H	H	L	-	-	-	-	-	-	-	-	-	-	L	H	H	•	•	A	•	•	A	•	A	CALCULATE DESTINATION ADDRESS, BYTE
18	H	-	L	H	-	-	-	-	-	-	-	-	-	L	H	H	•	•	A	•	•	A	•	A	
19	H	L	L	L	H	-	-	-	-	-	-	-	-	-	H	H	•	•	A	•	•	A	•	A	
20	L	L	L	L	L	L	L	L	L	L	L	L	L	L	L	-	A	•	•	•	A	A	A	A	INTERRUPT INSTR.
21	L	L	L	L	L	L	L	L	L	-	-	-	-	-	L	-	•	A	A	A	A	A	A	•	SPEC/JMP/RTS/SWAP
22	L	L	L	L	L	L	L	L	L	H	L	L	L	H	-	-	A	A	A	A	A	A	A	A	RESERVED
23	L	L	L	L	L	L	L	L	L	H	L	L	H	L	-	-	A	A	A	A	A	A	A	A	
24	L	L	L	L	L	L	L	L	L	H	L	L	H	H	-	-	A	A	•	•	A	A	A	A	SPL
25	L	L	L	L	L	L	L	L	L	H	L	H	L	-	-	-	A	•	•	•	A	•	•	•	COND. CODE CLR
26	L	L	L	L	L	L	L	L	L	-	L	H	H	-	-	-	A	•	•	•	A	A	A	•	COND. CODE SET
27	L	L	L	L	L	L	-	-	-	-	-	-	-	-	L	-	A	•	•	A	A	A	•	•	BRANCH, TRUE COND.
28	L	L	L	L	L	H	L	L	-	-	-	-	-	-	L	-	•	•	•	•	•	A	A	•	JSR
29	-	L	L	L	H	L	H	-	-	-	-	-	L	L	-	-	•	•	A	A	A	•	A	•	SINGLE OP., ≠1
30	-	L	L	L	H	H	L	-	-	-	-	-	L	L	-	-	•	•	A	A	A	•	•	•	SINGLE OP., ≠2
31	-	L	L	L	H	H	H	-	-	-	-	-	-	-	-	-	A	A	A	A	A	A	A	A	RESERVED
32	L	H	H	H	-	-	-	-	-	-	-	-	-	-	-	-	•	•	A	A	A	A	•	•	EIS
33	L	H	H	H	H	L	H	-	-	-	-	-	-	-	-	-	A	A	•	•	A	A	A	•	RESERVED
34	L	H	H	H	H	L	H	L	L	L	L	L	-	-	-	-	A	A	•	•	A	A	A	A	FLOATING POINT
35	L	H	H	H	H	H	L	-	-	-	-	-	-	-	-	-	A	•	A	A	A	A	A	A	RESERVED
36	L	H	H	H	H	H	H	-	-	-	-	-	-	-	-	-	A	A	A	A	A	A	A	•	SOB
37	H	L	L	L	L	-	-	-	-	-	-	-	-	-	-	-	A	A	A	A	A	A	A	•	BRANCH, FALSE COND.
38	H	L	L	L	H	L	L	L	-	-	-	-	-	-	-	-	A	•	•	•	•	A	A	•	EMT
39	H	L	L	L	H	L	H	-	-	-	-	-	-	-	-	-	A	•	•	•	A	A	A	•	TRP
40	H	L	L	L	H	H	L	H	L	L	-	-	L	L	-	-	•	A	A	A	A	•	•	•	MTPS
41	-	L	L	L	H	H	L	H	L	H	-	-	-	L	L	-	A	A	•	•	A	•	•	•	MT/F • I/D
42	-	L	L	L	H	H	L	H	H	L	-	-	-	L	L	-	A	A	•	A	•	•	•	•	
43	H	L	L	L	H	H	L	H	H	H	-	-	L	L	-	-	•	A	A	A	•	•	•	•	MKRS
44	H	H	H	L	-	-	-	-	-	-	-	-	-	L	L	-	•	A	•	•	•	•	A	•	SUBTRACT
45	H	H	H	H	-	-	-	-	-	-	-	-	-	-	-	-	A	A	•	A	A	A	A	A	EXT. FLOAT. PNT
46	L	L	H	L	H	H	L	H	L	L	-	-	-	-	-	-	A	A	•	A	A	A	A	•	MARK

(Reprinted courtesy of Signetics Corporation)

Figure 6.21   FPLA program table for PDP-11 decode

FUNCTIONAL DIAGRAM OF DATA ACQUISITION SYSTEM

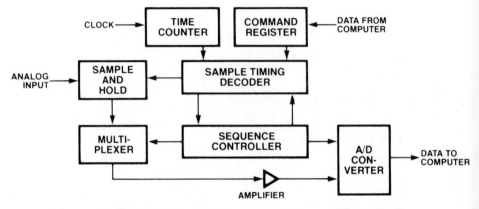

Figure 6.22   Functional diagram of data acquisition system

50 μsec steps by a 3-bit command from the computer. Sample 4 follows Sample 3 by 2.5 μsec. The timing commands and the resulting Sample 3 hold times (from start of 1Ms) are as shown below:

Command	0	1	2	3	4	5	6	
Sample 3 Time	50	100	150	200	250	300	350	... (μsec)

As shown in the circuit diagram of Figure 6.23, the counter outputs and the command bits are decoded in FPLA No. 1 to provide turn-off signals to the sample and hold gate flipflops. A 16-state sequential controller operates the multiplexers and A/D converter and interfaces with the computer interrupt system. The controller is implemented in FPLA No. 2 and is expanded into the remaining parts of FPLA No. 1 because more than eight outputs are required. Both FPLA Program Tables and I/O assignment are tabulated in Figures 6.24 and 6.25, respectively.

The Sequence Controller decodes counter outputs at the end of the 1 Msec interval and resets the counter synchronously. The sample gate flipflops are also turned on. The controller then waits until Sample 1 is held and starts the A/D Converter pulsing an output for one cycle. When the converter is no longer busy, the controller sets the interrupt output active until the computer recognizes it, and responds by reading the A/D output data. The multiplexer is advanced to Sample 2 and the process is repeated. The A/D conversion

CIRCUIT DIAGRAM OF DAS CONTROLLER

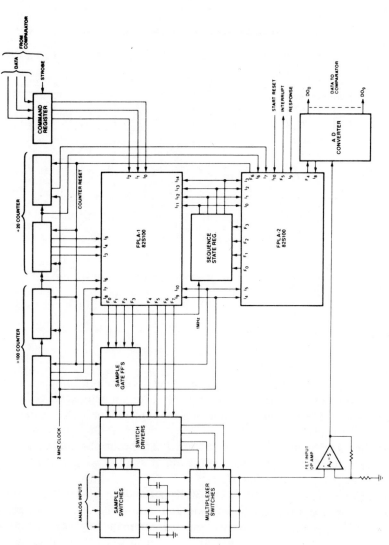

Figure 6.23 Circuit diagram of DAS controller

PROGRAM TABLE FOR FPLA 1

	PRODUCT TERM																ACTIVE LEVEL							
	INPUT VARIABLE																L	L	L	L	H	H	H	H
																	OUTPUT FUNCTION							
NO.	15	14	13	12	11	10	9	8	7	6	5	4	3	2	1	0	7	6	5	4	3	2	1	0
0	–	L	L	–	–	–	–	–	–	–	–	–	–	–	–	–	•	•	•	A	•	•	•	•
1	–	L	H	L	L	–	–	–	–	–	–	–	–	–	–	–	•	•	•	A	•	•	•	•
2	–	H	H	H	H	–	–	–	–	–	–	–	–	–	–	–	•	•	•	A	•	•	•	•
3	–	L	H	L	H	–	–	–	–	–	–	–	–	–	–	–	•	•	A	•	•	•	•	•
4	–	L	H	H	–	–	–	–	–	–	–	–	–	–	–	–	•	•	A	•	•	•	•	•
5	–	H	L	–	–	–	–	–	–	–	–	–	–	–	–	–	•	A	•	•	•	•	•	•
6	–	H	H	L	–	–	–	–	–	–	–	–	–	–	–	–	A	•	•	•	•	•	•	•
7	–	H	H	H	L	–	–	–	–	–	–	–	–	–	–	–	A	•	•	•	•	•	•	•
8	–	–	–	–	–	–	L	H	H	–	–	–	–	–	–	–	•	•	•	•	•	•	A	•
9	–	–	–	–	–	L	–	H	H	–	–	–	–	–	–	–	•	•	•	•	A	•	•	•
10	–	–	–	–	–	–	–	–	–	H	L	H	H	–	–	–	•	•	•	•	•	•	•	A
11	–	–	–	–	–	–	–	–	–	H	L	L	L	L	L	L	•	•	•	•	•	A	•	•
12	–	–	–	–	–	–	–	–	–	H	L	L	H	L	L	H	•	•	•	•	•	A	•	•
13	–	–	–	–	–	–	–	–	–	H	L	H	L	L	H	L	•	•	•	•	•	A	•	•
14	–	–	–	–	–	–	–	–	–	H	L	H	H	L	H	H	•	•	•	•	•	A	•	•
15	–	–	–	–	–	–	–	–	–	H	H	L	L	H	L	L	•	•	•	•	•	A	•	•
16	–	–	–	–	–	–	–	–	–	H	H	L	H	H	L	H	•	•	•	•	•	A	•	•
17	–	–	–	–	–	–	–	–	–	H	H	H	L	H	H	L	•	•	•	•	•	A	•	•

I/O ASSIGNMENT	Inputs	Outputs
	0-2: Command Register bits. 3-5: Count of 50 μsec intervals from ÷ 20 counter. 6: .5 μsec pulse every 50 μsec. 7: 2 μsec output from ÷ 100 counter. 8: .5 μsec output from ÷ 100 counter. This is also the signal used to clock the sequence state register. 9-10: Sample 1 and 3 gates. 11-14: Four sequence state bits.	0-3: Four sample Gate turn-off signals. 4-7: Four multiplexer control signals.

Figure 6.24 Program table for FPLA 1

takes longer than 2.5 μsec, so Sample 2 may finish before Sample 3 is held in the latest cases, and the sequencer may have to wait before converting. After the conversion and interrupt sequence is completed for all four samples, the sequencer waits for the end of the 1 Msec interval. One of the multiplexer switches is active at all times. A flow chart of the control sequence is shown in Figure 6.26. The system interface is through the following signals:

Clock: 2 MHz TTL square wave.

Analog Inputs: F_c = 100 KHz, 30 KHz Bandwidth Amplitude: ±1 volt.

Data from Computer: 3 bits of command data and a strobe. The strobe is pulsed to load the command register and after the computer has responded to all four interrupts in an interval.

Data to Computer: The A/D Converter provides 10 bits of parallel data in TTL compatible levels.

PROGRAM TABLE FOR FPLA-2

NO.	15	14	13	12	11	10	9	8	7	6	5	4	3	2	1	0	H 7	L 6	L 5	H 4	H 3	H 2	H 1	H 0
						INPUT VARIABLE														**OUTPUT FUNCTION**				
0	–	–	–	–	–	H	–	–	–	–	–	–	–	–	–	–	A	A	•	•	•	•	•	A
1	–	–	–	–	–	L	–	–	H	H	–	–	L	L	L	L	A	A	•	•	•	•	•	A
2	–	–	–	–	–	L	–	–	–	–	–	–	L	L	L	H	A	A	•	•	•	•	A	•
3	–	–	–	–	–	L	–	–	–	–	–	H	L	L	H	L	A	•	•	•	•	•	A	•
4	–	–	–	–	–	L	–	–	–	–	–	L	L	L	H	L	A	•	•	A	•	•	A	A
5	–	–	–	–	–	L	–	–	–	–	–	–	L	L	H	H	A	•	•	A	•	A	•	•
6	–	–	–	–	–	L	–	H	–	–	–	–	L	H	L	L	A	•	•	•	•	A	•	•
7	–	–	–	–	–	L	–	L	–	–	–	–	L	H	L	L	A	•	A	•	A	•	A
8	–	–	–	–	–	L	H	–	–	–	–	–	L	H	L	H	A	•	A	•	A	•	A
9	–	–	–	–	–	L	L	L	–	–	–	–	L	H	L	H	A	•	•	A	•	A	A	•
10	–	–	–	–	–	L	–	–	–	–	–	–	L	H	H	L	A	•	•	A	•	A	A	A
11	–	–	–	–	–	L	–	H	–	–	–	–	L	H	H	H	A	•	•	•	•	A	A	A
12	–	–	–	–	–	L	–	L	–	–	–	–	L	H	H	H	A	•	A	•	A	•	•	•
13	–	–	–	–	–	L	H	–	–	–	–	–	H	L	L	L	A	•	A	•	A	•	•	•
14	–	–	–	–	–	L	L	–	–	–	H	–	H	L	L	L	A	•	•	•	A	•	•	A
15	–	–	–	–	–	L	L	–	–	–	L	–	H	L	L	L	A	•	•	A	A	•	A	•
16	–	–	–	–	–	L	–	–	–	–	H	–	H	L	L	H	A	•	•	•	A	•	•	A
17	–	–	–	–	–	L	–	–	–	–	L	–	H	L	L	H	A	•	•	A	A	•	A	•
18	–	–	–	–	–	L	–	–	–	–	–	–	H	L	H	L	A	•	•	A	A	•	A	A
19	–	–	–	–	–	L	–	H	–	–	–	–	H	L	H	H	A	•	•	•	A	•	A	A
20	–	–	–	–	–	L	–	L	–	–	–	–	H	L	H	H	A	•	A	•	A	A	A	•
21	–	–	–	–	–	L	H	–	–	–	–	–	H	H	L	L	A	•	A	•	A	A	•	•
22	–	–	–	–	–	L	L	–	–	–	–	–	H	H	L	L	A	•	•	A	A	A	•	A
23	–	–	–	–	–	L	–	–	–	–	–	–	H	H	L	H	A	•	•	A	A	A	A	•
24	–	–	–	–	–	L	–	H	–	–	–	–	H	H	H	L	A	•	•	A	A	A	•	A
25	–	–	–	–	–	L	–	L	–	–	–	–	H	H	H	L	A	•	A	•	A	A	A	A
26	–	–	–	–	–	L	H	–	–	–	–	–	H	H	H	H	A	•	A	•	A	A	A	A

I/O ASSIGNMENT

0-3: Four sequence state bits.
4-5: Sample 1 and 3 gates.
6-7: ÷ 20 counter outputs to decode 1 Msec.
8: A/D Converter busy.
9: Computer interrupt response.
10: Start/Reset signal from computer.

0-3: Four sequence state bits for next step.
4: A/D Converter start pulse-high logic level for 1 μsec.
5: Interrupt to computer.
6: Reset signal to counter and Sample Gates

Figure 6.25   Program table for FPLA 2

Interrupt:	Low TTL level active while the controller has valid data for the computer to read.
Response to Interrupt:	A 2 μsec active-low pulse after the computer has read the A/D data.

Example 6.4:   We conclude our discussion with a microprogram control algorithm for a vertical miller under numerical control. In this example we will develop an LPA microprogram to operate a three-axis vertical miller

FLOWCHART OF A/D CONVERSION AND DATA INTERFACE SEQUENCE

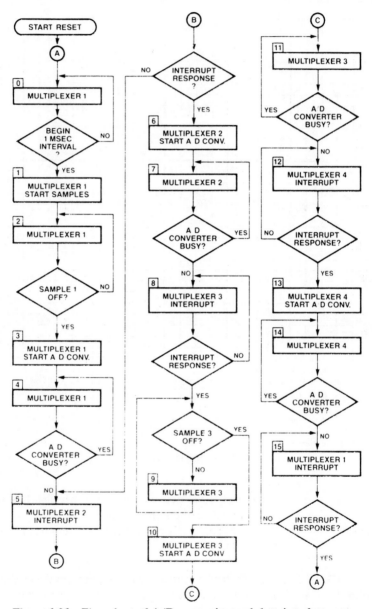

Figure 6.26   Flow chart of A/D conversion and data interface sequence

which is automatically controlled by some microprogrammable digital machine. At first we will explain the mechanisms of the miller, after which we will describe a typical ASM design for the control algorithm assuming an LPA monophase implementation.

Vertical Miller Characteristics—The vertical miller is a metal cutting machine which allows for general table movement in two dimensions and the cutting tool (endmill) movement in one dimension as shown in Figure 6.27. The table holds the workpiece to be machined by a cutter called an endmill. Horizontal motion is accomplished with drive motors on the table which are controlled by a firmware driven digital machine. Likewise, vertical motion of the endmill for depth of cutting into the workpiece is motor driven and controlled by the same microprogrammed digital machine. Three axes of motion are permitted: left/right or X direction, forward/reverse or Y direction, and up/down or Z direction.

We will devise an ASM chart as microprogram documentation to control the miller to cut rectangular grooves of any depth in a workpiece. This requires several passes through the groove, incrementally lowering the endmill with each pass until the final depth is reached. Several mechanical considerations arise in this application. The first consideration depends on the cornering requirements of the groove, and the second consideration depends on the type of endmill.

For a special cornering requirement we will assume that a separate microprogram is used. Therefore, if a radius specification cannot be met by a simple change of direction by 90°, the ASM algorithm branches to a radii microprogram, guides the cutting tool through the radial cut and returns to the current microprogram when the arc is completed. For our example, we will not be concerned with the special radii microprogram. Likewise, if our endmill does not permit us to cut into the workpiece in the vertical direction,[4] another special microprogram is utilized. Again, we will not concern ourselves with this microprogram other than to direct the endmill at the proper time by a jump to a special microprogram control sequence. Upon completion of this activity, a return to our current microprogram is made. A third consideration is the width of the groove and the diameter of the endmill. If a groove wider than the endmill diameter is required, we will again assume a special microprogram control sequence.

The above considerations and others are summarized in Table 6.3. Here we see that these considerations translate directly into input conditions for the decision blocks in the ASM chart.

---

[4] An endmill with bottom flutes or cutting edges will cut downward and sideways. An endmill without bottom flutes will only cut sideways.

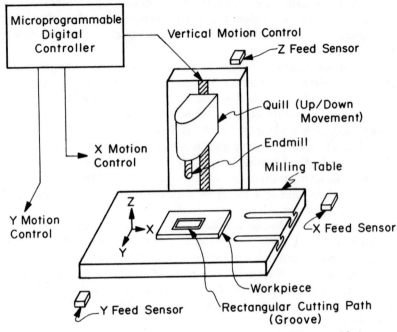

Figure 6.27   Microprogram controlled vertical milling machine

Table 6.3   Conditions For Vertical Miller Grooving Microprogram

Conditions	Mnemonic	Description
$YQBC_1$	YGED	True if groove width equals endmill diameter.
$YQBC_2$	YCAD	True if endmill capable of cutting in all directions.
$YQBC_3$	YCSR	True if groove corner requires a special routine.
$YQBC_4$	YPFC	True if current plane feed (X or Y) is complete.
$YQBC_5$	YCVC	True if current vertical feed (Z) is complete.
$YQBC_6$	YTDC	True if total depth is complete.

Let us now describe a stepwise procedure for cutting the rectangular groove. Refer to Figure 6.28. First, the workpiece is manually positioned directly under the endmill by the machine operator. Next, the microprogram controller is enabled and vertical endmill movement at the starting location of the groove begins. Our ASM documentation for head and table movement

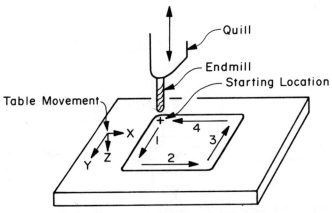

Figure 6.28   Endmill movement

in the machining sequence is shown in Figure 6.29. The operator then assumes control of the machine, retracts the endmill and removes the workpiece. The LPA microinstruction format is shown in Figure 6.30. The structure of the microprogram using the AND-TIE and OR-TIE is depicted in Figure 6.31.

Let us examine the actual algorithm design. We note that the cutter must essentially traverse four distinct paths (Y positive, X positive, Y negative and X negative). Also, the vertical movement must be initialized and checked after all four motions for a completed groove. Thus, we specify at least six states for the microprogram controller. From the ASM chart, the first state (0001) places the miller in an initialization mode. Here, the quill is set above the starting point. In the next state (0011), the quill is lowered. When complete, the controller enters state (0010) to cut the groove in the Y positive direction. The X positive direction state (0110) follows next and so on, until the quill has returned to the starting point. Now the total vertical distance traveled is checked. If the required depth is satisfied, we exit this microprogram. If not, we lower the quill further and repeat the process.

The mnemonics for the branch decisions (Table 6.3) are chosen to be descriptive. Likewise, each ASM block is "tagged" for clarity. For instance, state 0011 is tagged as Vertical Motion to indicate that the quill is moving. As mentioned earlier, special cornering paths and cutter widths require the controller to enter alternate microprograms. These microprograms initiate at states 1000 and 1100, respectively.

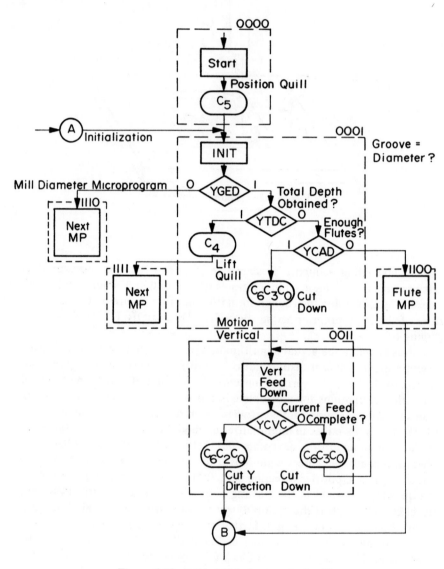

Figure 6.29   LPA ASM chart vertical miller

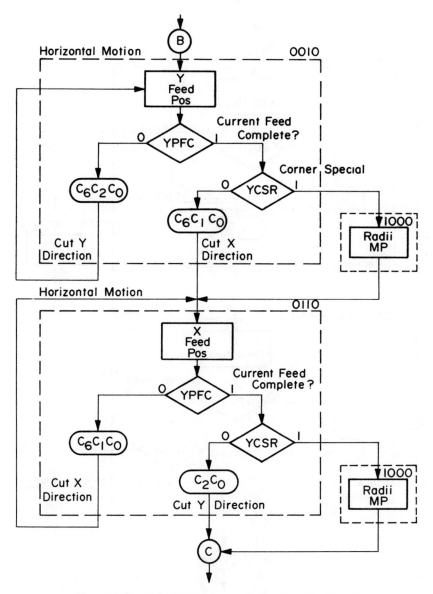

Figure 6.29   LPA ASM chart vertical miller (Continued)

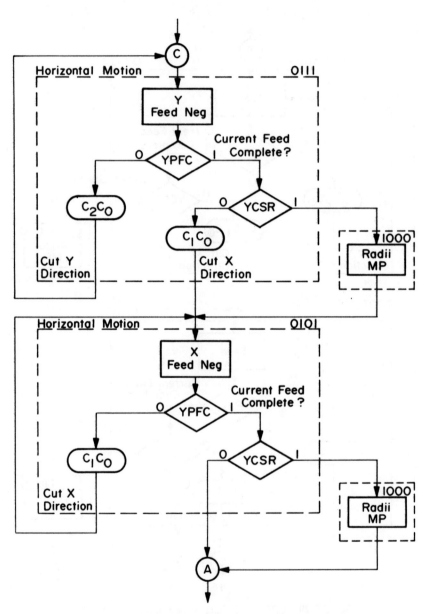

Figure 6.29 LPA ASM chart vertical miller (Continued)

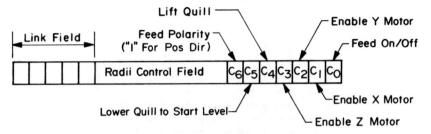

Figure 6.30   Link path addressable microinstruction format
rectangular milling cavity

6.6   STATE QUALIFIER PAIR ADDRESSABLE SEQUENCING

One obvious disadvantage of the LPA structure is the need to use two types of devices, an AND-TIE array and an OR-TIE array. A less obvious disadvantage becomes evident when the actual physical structure is chosen. Simply stated, for most PLA's, considerable peripheral logic is necessary (remember that a PLA may not even contain a simple latch). Hence, the number of devices increases.

When one type of device is desired, the State Qualifier Pair (SQP) control structure is typically used. One implementation is shown in Figure 6.32. In the SQP structure, the microinstruction format differs from the link path addressable structure in that an additional field must be utilized in the microinstruction. This field contains one or more possible "next addresses". In our implementation, TRUE BRANCH ADDRESS and FALSE BRANCH ADDRESS are shown in the field. Of course, we are not limited to two branches. More elaborate configurations of this basic control structure incorporate multi-way branch capability. However, for the case at hand, a simple ASM flowchart structure is possible. This simplicity in the algorithmic structure and the direct implementation with a ROM makes the SQP sequencing attractive.

The physical elements of the SQP structure include a ROM with expanded fields for next addresses and a BRANCH TEST field, branch control circuitry to select which conditions are to be tested (for branching), and finally a selector switch to choose between the TRUE BRANCH ADDRESS and the FALSE BRANCH ADDRESS. The selector switch is simply a demultiplexer. Note that our SQP scheme does not utilize much peripheral logic to the ROM in contrast to the link path addressable scheme. You should also observe that the branch control circuitry and BRANCH TEST field in each microinstruction are general enough to incorporate other alternative implementations.

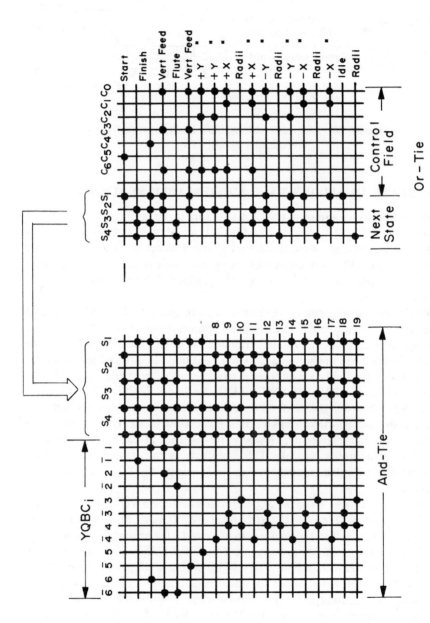

Figure 6.31 LPA AND-TIE, OR-TIE for vertical miller

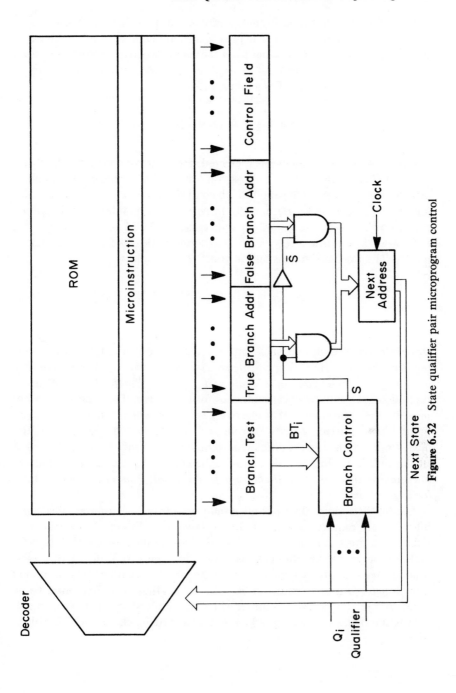

Figure 6.32   State qualifier pair microprogram control

Alternative structures for branch control circuitry lie between the single bit concept, BT, emanating from the microinstruction and the multiple bit concept, BT_0, BT_1, ..., emanating from the microinstruction. Both are shown in Figure 6.33. In the single bit method, all branch tests are enabled simultaneously. As a result, the Boolean expression:

$$S = BT \cdot (Q_0 + Q_1 + Q_2 + \cdots) \tag{6.1}$$

is applicable when a branch test is desired. Here, the single bit minimally increases ROM width. But this approach is less flexible for the eventual microprogrammer than the following branch control test method shown in the bottom half of Figure 6.33. Here, each branch test bit enables a single branch condition. Yet, even though we must increase the ROM width by one bit for each branch condition, Q_0, Q_1, ..., a more flexible control structure results. The Boolean expression for branching becomes:

$$S = BT_0 \cdot Q_0 + BT_1 \cdot Q_1 + BT_2 \cdot Q_2 + \cdots. \tag{6.2}$$

Regardless of the type of branch control circuitry, the SQP chart itself is straightforward. Only two rules apply when generating an SQP chart. *Rule 1 requires that each ASM block, which is equivalent to a state (and essentially a clock cycle), must contain a "state and a qualifier" pair.* This SQP structure allows for only two next addresses for each state. These next addresses must be the state names of respective next states which follow the two exit paths (there must only be two) from each ASM block as shown in Figure 6.34. Note also that no conditional outputs (microinstructions) are allowed as in the link path addressable control scheme. Thus, *Rule 2 states that all microinstructions must be direct outputs that result from enabling a particular ROM word.*

The SQP structure does permit a multi-way branch. However, this capability simply requires a wider ROM to include additional branch address fields. The chart must also be modified to include the multi-branch tests. A typical flow chart for this case is shown in Figure 6.35 for a three-way branch. Accordingly, Rule 1 must be modified to accomodate this additional branch field. One nice feature of SQP schemes is that the dotted boxes (state times) in the charts can be omitted since it is understood that every microinstruction (hence, a clock cycle) consists of a state block and qualifier block pair.

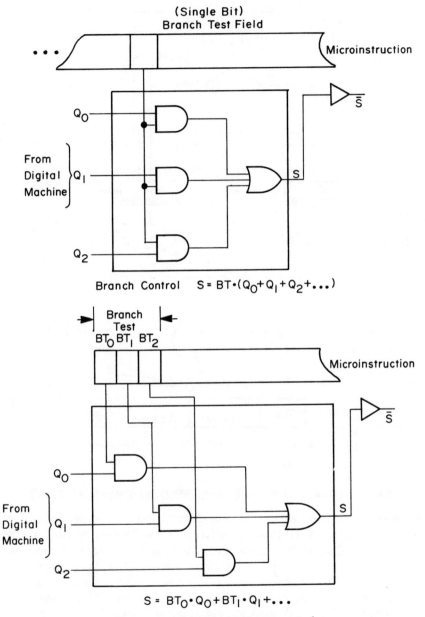

Figure 6.33   Typical branch test control

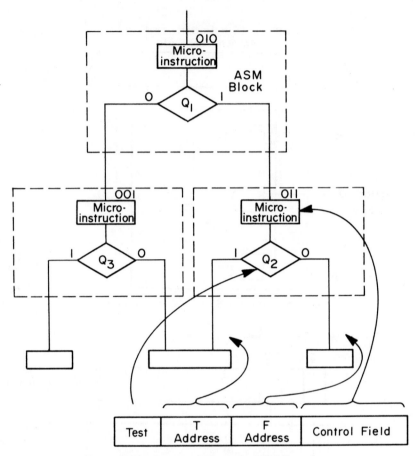

Figure 6.34 State qualifier pair ASM flow chart

6.7 STATE QUALIFIER PAIR ASSUMED ADDRESS FORMAT

Suppose now that we encounter some design constraint which simply does not permit a wide ROM. How do we change the SQP format to minimize the ROM width? Can we eliminate a branch address field of each microinstruction? If we do, what additional hardware is required in the microprogram control unit? The sequencing structure we next describe is purposely designed to reduce ROM width. The distinguishing feature of this new structure, called SQP with assumed address, is the utilization of peripheral hardware to generate an implicit next address. This implicit address is generated by incrementing the current address. The peripheral hardware now necessary

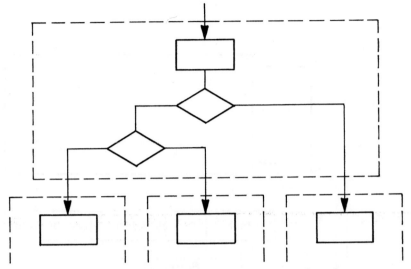

Figure 6.35   SQP structure with a three-way branch

is a counter or incrementer with associated switching circuitry similar to that shown in Figure 6.36.

The address of every conditional branch available from the incrementer will be called the "ASSUMED" address. In the ASM chart of Figure 6.37 for this variation of the SQP structure, we chose the incremented address when a true condition occurs. To be consistent, throughout the ASM chart we will follow this convention. So we see that it is possible to reduce ROM width at the expense of additional peripheral logic. Now the question is, how does this new format affect the ASM chart? The new format makes the chart simpler. Our only concern will be to assume that whenever a "true" condition appears, the incremented address will be the next state. This "rule" merely establishes a consistency within the physical implementation. In Figure 6.37, states 0010, 0011, 0100, 0101 are assigned to addresses for all "true" conditions.

The SQP chart is simpler than an LPA chart especially when we attempt to assign states to the actual tasks in a flow chart. The hardware implementation for an SQP dictates separate rules. Let us begin with the chart of Figure 6.38. The first rule concerns state assignments. If we wish to fully utilize the assumed address,

Rule 1:   *Assign incremental state values to the largest possible non-intersecting path or paths in the chart.* Such an assignment may be desirable

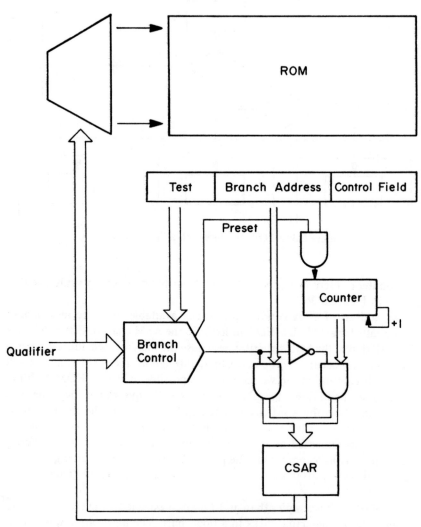

Figure 6.36   Microprogram control unit for state qualifier pair format
with assumed address

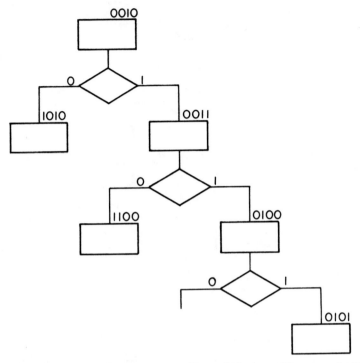

Figure 6.37 ASM chart for state qualifier pair format with assumed address

when electrical noise in the physical implementation creates fewer address errors in the incrementer than in the direct load of the branch address into the microinstruction memory address register (see Figure 6.36).

Rule 2: *Assign all conditional branch addresses consistently.* That is, either all non-incremental addresses should be selected as a result of a true test or all non-incremental addresses should be selected as a result of a false test. This subtle requirement dictates how we are to employ a special bit in the TEST field. This special bit performs the task of enabling a jam transfer of the False Branch address into the counter when a False Branch address is selected. In this manner the microprogram can physically continue through a new set of *sequential* addresses. If we consistently apply Rule 2, the microprogrammer can expect this bit to enable a jam transfer *only* when the False Branch address is employed. Naturally, we (the equipment designers) can reverse the interpretation of this special bit (enable it when a True Branch

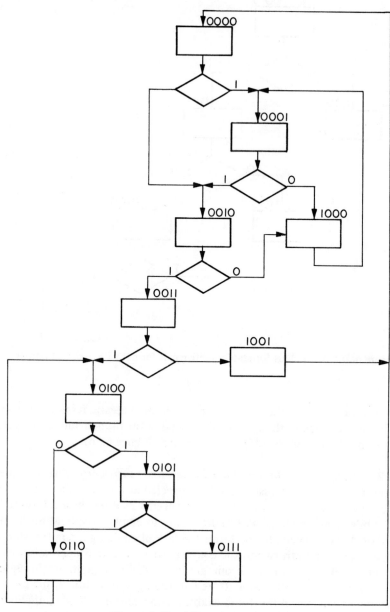

Figure 6.38   SQP assumed address

address is desired). But, we must now assign incremental addresses after all branch tests that are false.

6.8 PROPERTIES OF SQP STRUCTURES

The SQP structure has the following properties. It is implementable by a ROM structure with a microinstruction of four fields. These are a true address field, false address field, branch test field, and control field. Little additional circuitry is needed to select the branch address. Should a narrower ROM be desired, an address field can be deleted. This deleted address field is then replaced by an incrementer and an assumed address format for the ASM chart. Care must now be taken in the design of the branch control circuitry to insure that unconditional branches are possible.

Example 6.5: SQP Format for Vertical Miller Microprogram. In this example we return to the microprogram to cut rectangular grooves with the vertical miller. Now let us employ the SQP structure. Two ASM designs are developed. The first design utilizes the SQP scheme without an assumed address format. The ASM chart for this version is shown in Figure 6.39 and the microinstruction for this ASM design is depicted in Figure 6.40. The ROM microprogram is shown in Figure 6.41. If we compare these designs with the previous LPA microprogram, we see that the LPA scheme (Figure 6.31) uses nineteen horizontal lines in the OR-TIE while the SQP scheme (Figure 6.41) uses twelve machine states.[5] The SQP scheme is more compact. Although the LPA scheme employs more lines, it may still be faster since the LPA scheme uses programmable logic arrays which may be inherently faster than the SQP scheme which uses ROM's.

The second SQP version of the microprogram utilizes an assumed address format. The ASM chart (not shown) is identical to Figure 6.39. But the ROM is narrower by four bits since the deleted true address field is replaced by an incrementer. The microprogram for the assumed address format is also similar to the microprogram of Figure 6.41, except, of course, for the deletion of the true address field.

6.9 VARIABLE FORMAT SEQUENCING

Suppose that we now desire to reduce the ROM width even further than that possible by the SQP with assumed address (where the true branch field was

---

[5]This comparison is distorted because we are comparing two different devices: a programmable logic array and a ROM.

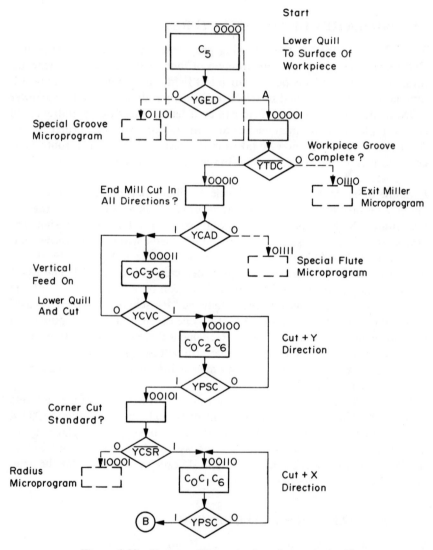

Figure 6.39   State qualifier pair chart for vertical miller

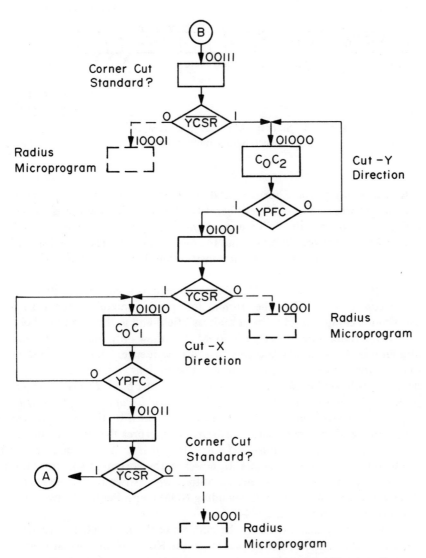

Figure 6.39   State qualifier pair chart for vertical miller (Continued)

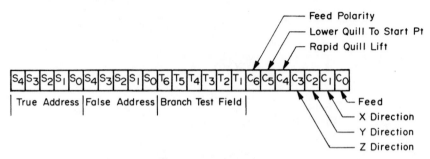

Figure 6.40   State qualifier pair microinstruction format for
rectangular milling cavity

deleted). What possible formats and sequencing structures are to be expected and what additional peripheral hardware in the microprogram control unit is now required? To answer the first question, a narrow ROM,
possibly the narrowest, assumes that the minimum width is dictated solely by
the number of control bits in a microinstruction. One possible microinstruction format, the variable format, is shown in Figure 6.42. In this case, a two
format structure is assumed. One format interprets a microinstruction as an
entire control field. The other format interprets a microinstruction as address fields comprised of a "next address" field and a "branch test" field.

In a microprogram stored in a ROM, we allow only these two formats,
although each could be arbitrarily placed in sequence. That is, several contiguous words may be pure control field instructions, followed by a next ad-
dress/branch test format, etc., as depicted in Figure 6.43. *The key to this implementation is the use of a Format Designator bit appended to each and
every microinstruction.* This bit, when programmed by the microprogrammer, commands the peripheral hardware to interpret the current word format. For example, if the Format Designator bit is a "1", the current word
can be interpreted as control bits. If, however, the Format Designator bit is a
"0", the current word is interpreted, differently, as two fields; the next address and branch test. The corresponding ROM controller for the two format
structure is shown in Figure 6.44.

For the two format structure, the address of the next microinstruction is
not always the next contiguous location in the ROM. If the Format Designator bit is "1", the next address is automatically the next contiguous address
in the ROM. However, if the Format Designator bit in the current word is
"0", the next address need not be the following ROM address. It depends on

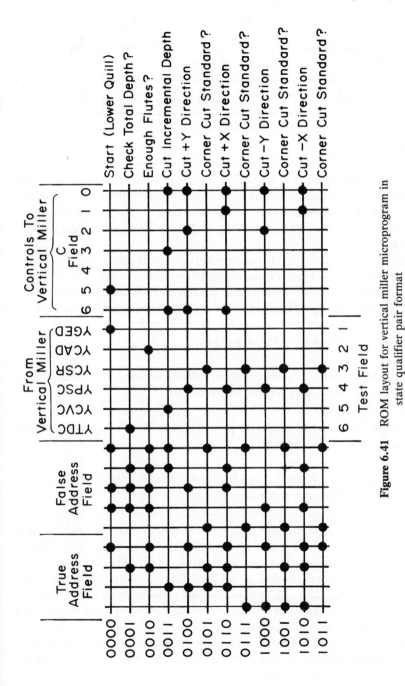

Figure 6.41 ROM layout for vertical miller microprogram in state qualifier pair format

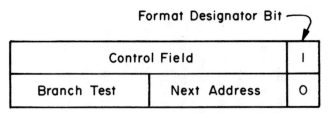

Figure 6.42 Variable format microinstruction

the branch control circuitry output. If the branch test lines energize qualifiers which test "false", then the next address is taken from the "next address" field of the current ROM word. If the branch test lines enable qualifiers which test "true", the next address is obtained from the current address incremented by "1".

A typical ASM chart for this two format structure is shown in Figure 6.45. This variable format example and ASM chart uses an "assumed address" specification similar to the SQP control scheme we have seen previously. This "assumed address" specification for the variable format scheme places some restrictions on the state assignments for the ASM design. The rules which we must follow (for the assumed address) are:

Rule 1: *All Format "1" instructions which follow Format "1" instructions must be assigned the next sequential state code.*

Rule 2: *All decision blocks must be preceded by a "blank" microinstruction (no control signals are possible).*

Rule 3: *Any state following a true branch test must be assigned the next sequential code of the state preceding the decision block.*

The preceding rules have been applied to the state assignments in Figure 6.45. For instance, states 0000, 0001, 0010, 0011, and 0100 have been assigned according to Rule 1. States 0100, 0101, 0110, 0111, 1000, and 1001 have been "introduced" according to Rule 2. Because of our two variable format, no control signals will appear at these state times since the current ROM word only contains test and address fields. The state assignments 1010 and 1101 have been made consistent with Rule 3.

We see that these ASM restrictions (at least for the assumed address format) introduce additional states that may not be required by the original

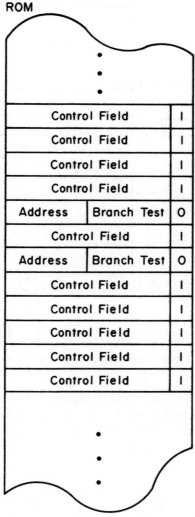

Figure 6.43   ROM microprogram with variable format

digital machine specifications. For instance, suppose the digital machine requires a simple ASM chart as in Figure 6.46a. Then, if we employ a dual format microcontrol structure, the chart must be altered as in Figure 6.46b to be consistent. Otherwise, the state assignments 1000, 0110, and 1001 violate Rule 1 for our dual format. Rule 1 then requires us to introduce an additional state, 0111, as in Figure 6.46b. Now the ASM chart complies with the

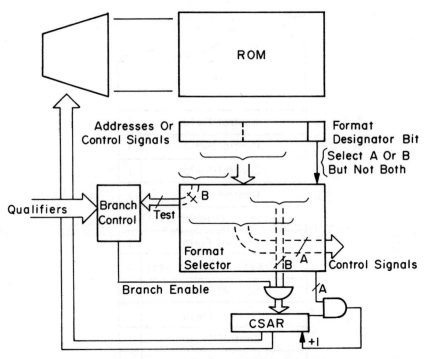

Figure 6.44 Variable format microprogrammable controller with assumed address

rules and with the hardware implementation at the cost of an additional state. The extra state in Figure 6.46b was required because we employed the assumed address for Format 1 (the next sequential ROM location). Even if we altered the Format 0 word from:

to:

Test	Branch Address	0

Test	True Branch	False Branch	0

Two Next Addresses

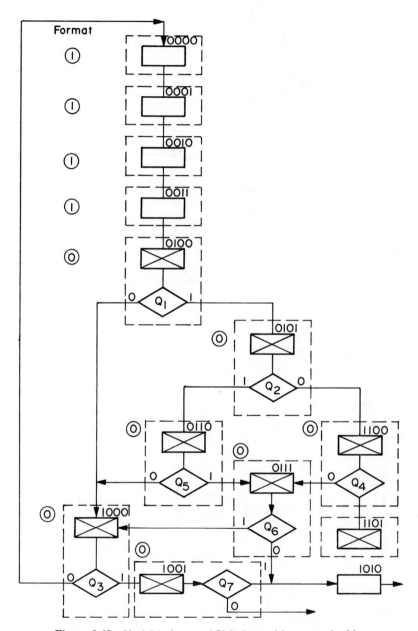

Figure 6.45 Variable format ASM chart with assumed address

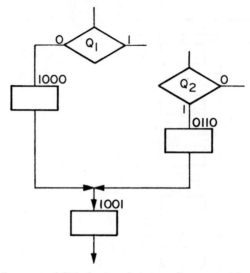

Figure 6.46a Improper ASM chart and state assignment with assumed address

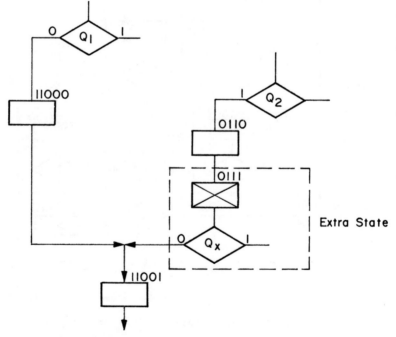

Figure 6.46b Corrected ASM chart and state assignment with assumed address

we still could not eliminate these extra states.[6] In order to eliminate extra states for the situation shown in Figure 6.46b, we would need another field in *both* Formats "1" and "0" microinstructions. This extra field must be an address field. Now the dual format distinguishes between microinstructions which always contain not only addresses but also sometimes contain control signals combined with an address field.

The dual format is only one method of numerous variable format control structures available. Its chief advantages are its simplicity and narrow ROM. As the number of formats increase, so does the complexity of state assignment in the ASM chart. This complexity in hardware may, however, be warranted if speed is more important than device specification. In this case, additional address fields would be imbedded in each ROM word, of course at the expense of a wider ROM.

6.10 FIRMWARE ENGINEERING DESIGN PROCEDURES VIA ASM

In general, the design of the control unit for a microprogrammable machine is an iterative process (see Figure 6.47). The stepwise procedure begins with a mapping process from sequential tasks to an ASM chart. Specifying the chart format (e.g., LPA, SQP, etc.) follows next. If no conflicts between task execution and chart format arise, the micro-operations and, in essence, the microinstructions can be identified. At this point, hardware considerations such as timing, device type, voltage levels, noise supression, etc. can be included. If, then, all design goals, including speed of execution, electrical power limits, and validity of task execution are met, the final steps of microprogram generation (ROM programming) and hardware build-up are initiated. Most importantly, the final step is to carefully yet completely document the design.

If at any point, conflicts between software development (microprogram specification) and hardware specification arise, the design process is repeated. A major asset of firmware engineering is to provide for a common form of documentation (via ASM charts). In so doing, the final documentation phase will be shortened considerably.

SUMMARY

In this chapter we developed a simple design procedure for microprogrammable machines. The procedures have focused on ASM design techniques

---

[6] Again, we are making the ROM wider than we originally had planned.

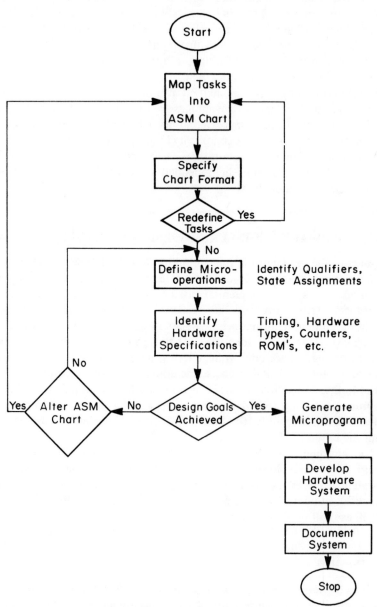

Figure 6.47   ASM design procedure

proposed by Clare for logic state machines. Three ASM techniques, link path addressable sequencing, state qualifier pair sequencing, and variable format, are described. All of these techniques focus upon the sequencing considerations of a typical microprogrammable controller with regard to the hardware. Except for the link path schemes, which may be implemented with programmable logic arrays, the sequencing schemes of this chapter assume that control of a state machine is stored in a ROM. The major point of this chapter is to demonstrate that by careful flow charting we can cleanly couple the hardware implementation rules to the microprogramming tasks. The approach is general. Hence, digital machines including computers can be designed in this manner.

Although each technique employs different flow chart principles, common among all of them are: (a) identification of machine clock cycles by state assignments, (b) employment of unambiguous sequencing rules compatible with specified physical hardware, and (c) common form of documentation understandable to the hardware as well as the software designer. This last property makes the ASM techniques effective in design environments where software and hardware must be developed simultaneously. Such is the nature of firmware engineering.

PROBLEMS

6.1   The LPA structure most nearly resembles which hardware control scheme proposed in Chapter 2. Why?

6.2   The SQP structure most nearly resembles which hardware control scheme of Chapter 2. Why?

6.3   If, in an LPA design, we find that conditional outputs are highly dependent on qualifiers, which LPA control structure appears more desirable, the monophase or the polyphase structure? Why?

6.4   In the LPA scheme, what relationship exists between the number of horizontal lines in Figure 6.9 and the ASM chart of Figure 6.7? Does this always hold true for LPA designs?

6.5   What flexibility is introduced in an LPA scheme when we use Field Programmable Logic Arrays? What is lost?

6.6   Which methods of this chapter are most applicable to sequential micro-programming (that is, few conditional branches)?

6.7   Which methods of this chapter support "subroutine" microprogramming (as well as conditional branches)?

6.8   T/F The penalty for a variable format ROM is that more state times are required to execute an algorithm than are required in a two address fixed format ROM.

6.9   T/F The n-bit address portion of a state qualifier ROM is a simple complete decode of the n-bits themselves.

6.10   T/F One disadvantage of the state qualifier pair ROM is that an AND-TIE and OR-TIE are always required.

6.11   In the vertical miller microprogram controller, suppose that we desire to mill out a rectangular cavity as shown below. Generate a control scheme and microinstruction format, including qualifiers for

a) LPA structure
b) SQP structure
c) SQP structure with assumed address

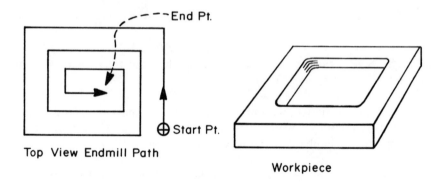

Top View Endmill Path

Workpiece

Assume that the endmill cannot cut the full depth in one pass. Do you need any additional control signals?

6.12   Design a branch control circuit for Figure 6.32. Assume three test bits and three qualifiers. How will you implement unconditional jumps?

6.13 What is the significant hardware difference between the SQP and SQP with assumed address?

6.14 What impact on microprogram software would you expect for the control schemes in Problem 13?

6.15 Assume that the vertical miller has feedrate feedback sensors that indicate when a "cut" is too heavy for that direction. What additional control bits and qualifiers would you use for

a) Example 6.6
b) Problem 11a
c) Problem 11b
d) Problem 11c

6.16 Assume that the vertical miller can move in three dimensions simultaneously. Assign a new microinstruction format and control bits to execute cutting paths in any direction.

6.17 Design an ASM scheme to cut circular arcs for the miller in Problem 16.

6.18 Make state qualifier pair (with assumed address) state assignments for

a) Problem 15a
b) Problem 15b

6.19 Revise the following ASM charts and state assignments to be consistent
with link path addressable sequencing.

a)

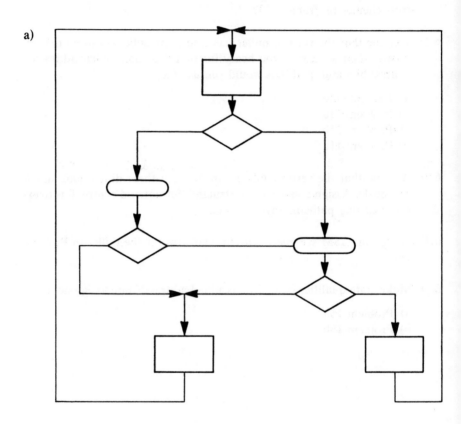

b)

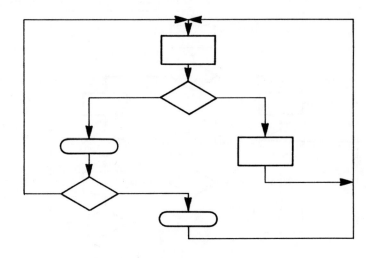

c)

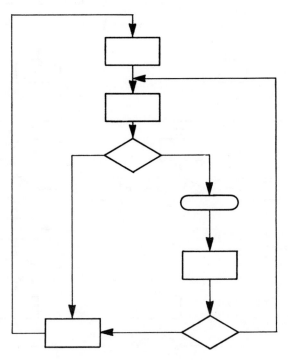

d)

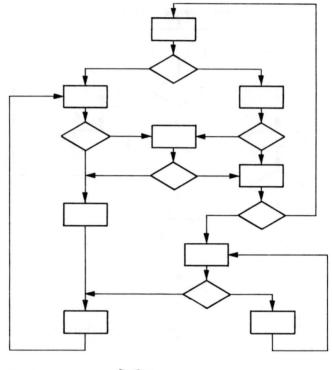

e)

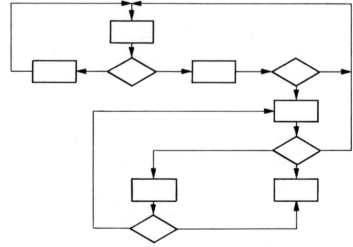

6.20 Revise the ASM charts and states of Problem 19 to be consistent with SQP sequencing without assumed address.

6.21 Revise the ASM charts and states of Problem 19 to be consistent with SQP assumed address sequencing.

6.22 Revise the ASM charts and states of Problem 19 to be consistent with two variable format sequencing of Section 6.9.

6.23 Given a microinstruction layout shown below, what ASM chart rules must be employed?

Control	Address		1
Test	Address	Address	0

6.24 Design a microcontrol structure with currently available LSI for Problem 23.

6.25 Suppose that two ROM's are utilized. One is for Format "1" words and the other is for Format "0" words.
   a) Design a hardware microcontroller for this method.
   b) Develop a set of consistent ASM rules for state implementation.
   c) What speed improvements over those methods in this chapter would you expect?

6.26 Implement the flow chart of Figure 6.29 with the Signetics 82S100.

6.27 The vertical miller examples in the text are typical of many motion controller algorithms. Design an ASM chart for a microprogrammable controller for an *X-Y* plotter. Assume that the pen has a simple lift/lower command (a binary command).
   a) Use an LPA structure
   b) Use an SQP structure
   c) Use a variable format structure

REFERENCES

The ASM structures presented in this chapter for microprogramming applications were originally introduced by Clare for the design of logic state machines in general.

In particular, see Chapter Six of Clare, Christopher R., *Designing Logic Systems Using State Machines.* McGraw Hill Book Company, New York, 1972.

The programmable logic array has become an interesting design tool for many digital machines which do not require the computational power of a computer (PLA's are notoriously inefficient for computation) but, nevertheless, need the flexibility of redesign, later on in the actual development of a digital machine. The following reference identifies several useful applications:

Signetics Field Programmable Logic Arrays, Signetics Corporation, Sunnyvale, California, 1977.

A thorough coverage on the status of firmware engineering is found in a set of papers delivered at the National Computer Conference NCC-81:

W. K. Giloi and R. Gueth, "Firmware Engineering: Methods and Tools for Firmware Specification and Design."
H. Berg, "Firmware Testing and Test Data Selection."
P. MA, "The Design of a Firmware Engineering Tool: The Microcode Compiler."
J. A. Fisher, D. Landskov, and B. D. Shriver, "Microcode Compaction: Looking Backward and Looking Forward."

Papers presented at MICRO-14 (Oct. 12-15, 1981, Mass., see IEEE Cat. #373) discuss novel firmware engineering techniques:

C. A. Papachristos, "Hardware Microcontrol Schemes Using PLA's."
S. Geyer and A. Lake, "Development Tools for User-Microprogramming."

Chapter Seven

MICROCONTROLLERS

7.1 INTRODUCTION

In the early 1970's, a number of sophisticated LSI devices appeared. Some of these devices are now regularly implemented in digital machines as microcontrollers for the sequencing and branching activity internal to the machine. Others have also been simultaneously employed both for internal and external control. LSI devices are common to process controller systems. Like many other digital machines, process controllers employ sophisticated LSI devices as microcontroller elements. *A microcontroller is an LSI device*[1] *or a set of LSI devices which provide for the control of a digital machine through a microprogrammable memory.* As we shall see, microcontrollers simplify the design of the *m*icroprogrammable control *u*nit, MCU.

Recall that the two paramount functions for control are:

a) declaration of control signals for each machine state, and
b) generation of the next machine state.

The microcontroller, depicted in Figure 7.1, performs all tasks necessary to sequence through the microprogram. In any MCU today, the microcontroller is more than a simple address decoder. In fact, most available microcontroller devices provide nearly all of the features of the sequential control architectures of Chapter 2 Thus, we now have ready access to a variety of devices, well suited to most demanding applications.

Microcontrollers perform successfully when they enhance the following programming tasks: *a) microroutine manipulation, b) indexing, and c) parameterization*. Microroutines are program segments employed by other programs to perform a particular task, hopefully several times. Microroutines are effective when the microprogram is called to do tasks repetitively. For example, the simple fetching of a microinstruction itself is a natural task for a microroutine. Executing a memory reference macroinstruction is another example. Indexing locates data efficiently and helps count the

---

[1] An LSI device, in the context of this chapter, is a physically small integrated circuit chip with few pins.

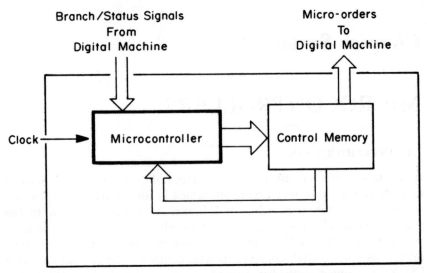

Figure 7.1 Microprogrammable control unit, MCU

number of accesses. A multiply microroutine could employ indexing to assist in the loop count. Scanning files is another indexing task. Parameterization makes use of information which characterizes the state of a digital machine. Parameters might describe the status of machine activity as a whole (e.g., fetch, execute, interrupt, etc.) or of primitive activity (e.g., ALU overflow, underflow, etc.).

7.2 MICROCONTROLLER CHARACTERISTICS

The basic elements of a microcontroller include an address register, incrementer, and stack, illustrated in Figure 7.2. The address register latches the microprogram memory address just prior to "accessing" the control memory. Any modification is accomplished before this register. Another important element is the incrementer. This element behaves much like the program counter. The incrementer generates the next sequential address. Finally, the microcontroller should facilitate microroutines. Hence, the stack implements necessary temporary storage for the return address and nesting of microroutine "calls".

Although not necessary for any microcontroller, the pipeline register, which stores the next address, is commonly found in many actual devices to overlap fetch and execute cycles of a microinstruction. This register, if utilized properly, can speed up microprogram execution. However, a faster

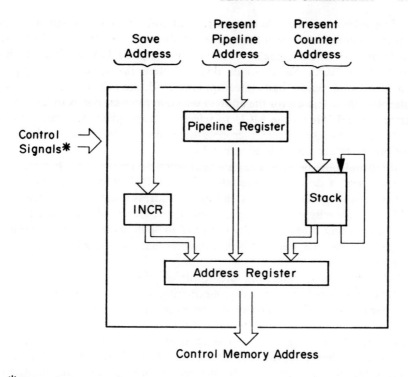

Figure 7.2 General microcontroller architecture

microprogram is not always guaranteed. The problem is that conditional branches may prematurely select the wrong "next" address. Hence, the pipeline register contents may need to be flushed out. This change of address impedes final address generation and, ultimately, execution speed of the microprogram.

Since microcontrollers do not generate micro-orders (these originate in the control memory), control of the microcontroller is accomplished via "instruction" inputs. These signals constitute the implicit linkage from digital machine to MCU. Such signals might declare the status of the digital machine (wait, ready, halt, interrupt, overload, etc.). The microcontroller interprets these signals for the address selection process. For example, an interrupt would inform the MCU to select the appropriate interrupt microroutine and save the current microprogram address in the stack. Typical control functions are shown in Figure 7.2.

Microcontroller designs today are very much device-oriented. Fortunately, several types of devices are available. A main distinction among microcontroller devices is their ease of extending the address space. Some increase the address space only through paging techniques. Others already have a sufficient addressing range, typically from 512 to 4096 control words. To utilize existing devices, we need to forecast the eventual total length of the control memory.

Other important features of microcontroller devices relate to their ability to handle previously mentioned programming tasks, microroutines, indexes and parameterization. A variety of supportable mechanisms internal as well as external to the devices are found. Of course, the fastest methods tend to favor internal mechanisms since less data/address movement across buses is involved. Furthermore, internal mechanisms typically require less hardware outside the actual microcontroller device. In some designs, the number of devices or the "chip count" is an important design constraint. Less wiring is possible. Minimization of attendant discrete devices such as transistors is oftentimes desirable.

7.3 PROGRAMMING THE MICROCONTROLLER

All of the programming tasks in Section 7.1 are common to assembly language programming. Hence, a good assembly language programmer tends to become a good microprogrammer. There is, however, a big difference between programming at the machine level and microprogramming a microcontroller. This is evident when we look at one application for a microcontroller, namely process control.

Several distinguishing features separate process controllers from digital computers. Like digital computers, process controllers perform mathematical operations on data, although very infrequently. However, process controllers generally do far more. They also facilitate rapid movement of data, provide for elaborate interfacing mechanisms primarily through hardware, and manage events through a real-time clock. In fact, process controllers commonly consider data as signals to and from external devices. Such signals may be as simple as a single wire on-off control (e.g., to a relay) and as complex as an n-bit parallel signal (e.g., to a digital-to-analog converter).

To program a microcontroller for a process controller, we must know the external sequence of events. (Many commercial process controllers are called event controllers.) Interfacing between the microcontroller and the external devices also becomes important. Typically, the interface is a strange mixture of serial asynchronous data transfer (e.g., a teletype), banks of relays and/or photo-optical couplers, and parallel input/output ports (e.g., in analog-to-digital and digital-to-analog conversion). In fact, many signals are incompatible for direct input to the microcontroller without substantial signal conditioning.

For example, in the case depicted in Figure 7.3, pressure and temperature are primary signals to be monitored. Signal conditioning would perform a transduction on each to generate a voltage or current variable. This voltage or current would then be "digitized". Finally, direct coupling to the microcontroller is made.

Notice that the microcontroller performs many tasks uncommon to digital computers. One of them is to control the action of the analog-to-digital converter. It must initiate a conversion request by issuing a "start-of-conversion" signal. Later, it must receive the "end-of-conversion" signal. Some "signal conditioners" or transducers also require control (e.g., input signal level as gain control, nonlinear compensation, etc.) which the microcontroller can provide.

Process controllers which employ microcontrol generally need to perform four tasks: *a) monitor signals at input points rapidly, b) set or reset latches or registers connected to control points in the machine, c) facilitate connections between many input and output points, and d) move data between sources and destinations.*

An example of a microcontroller application can be found in computerized numerical control machines. The Allen Bradley 7320, depicted in Figure 7.4, uses a microprogrammed processor to implement sequences of tasks for milling machines and machining centers. In fact, the ASM tasks in Chapter 6 are rudimentary examples of such microcode employed by the 7320. Another

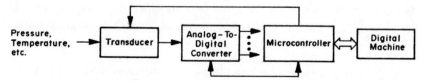

Figure 7.3 A typical microcontroller configuration

microcontroller implementation is the HP 3582A Spectrum Analyzer (see Figure 7.5). Here, significant data processing as well as signal conditioning is required of the digital machine. A further example of microcontrol is illustrated by the Horizon Technology Corporation energy management system, the Sentrol 110 (see Figure 7.6). All of these machines employ some forms of microcontrol. This diversity of applications attests to the widespread usage of microprogrammed processors which are primarily implemented in LSI devices.

Example 7.1: Distributed Controller.[2] In industrial or commercial processes it is often necessary to provide many contact closure type control points and/or contact sense points. A simple control system of this type can be implemented using the circuit of Figure 7.7, and any serial compatible send/receive terminal such as a Teletype or CRT controller.

The circuit has the following features:

A. Up to 56 jumper selectable addressed units may be connected in series to a single control circuit. Addresses are in octal, excluding 00, 11, 22, 33, 44, 55, 66, 77.
B. Up to 16 contact closure output points (TTL level) for each unit. Points A through P functions ("S"et and "R"eset).
C. Up to 16 contact closure input points (TTL level) for each unit. Points A through P function (Read).

The serial IN(S1) and serial OUT(S0) drivers are not defined in this circuit. A typical output communications sequence is (#34AS), where:

"#" = Attention character that resets the address function in
        all units on the serial communications circuit.
"3" = The 1st address character.
"4" = The 2nd address character.
"S" = The control function.

When sensing a contact point, replace the "R" or "S" function with a "?" function to read the sense point. The unit responds (in ASCII) with a "1" for a closed contact and a "0" for an open contact point.

Several different modifications of this basic circuit are possible to send BCD or ASCII data using the same or a modified decoding scheme. The decoding function for this circuit is shown in the FPLA program table of Figure 7.8.

---

[2]The material in this section has been adapted from publications of Signetics Corporation. Programs, figures, and tables are courtesy of and copyright by Signetics Corporation. All rights reserved.

Figure 7.4 Allen Bradley 7320
computerized numerical
control system

Figure 7.6 Horizon Technology
Corporation Sentrol 110

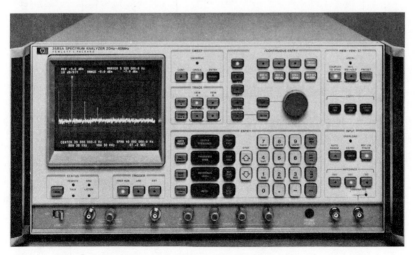

Figure 7.5 Hewlett Packard Model 3582A spectrum analyzer

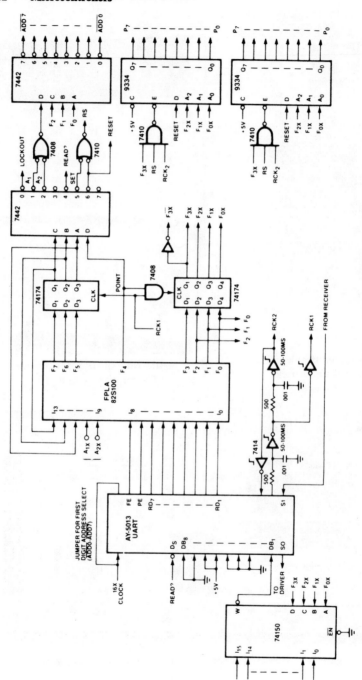

Figure 7.7 Distributed process controller

(Reprinted courtesy of Signetics Corporation)

COMMENT	NO.	15	14	13	12	11	10	9	8	7	6	5	4	3	2	1	0	7 (L)	6 (L)	5 (L)	4 (H)	3 (H)	2 (H)	1 (H)	0 (H)
=	0	−	−	−	−	−	−	−	L	L	L	H	L	L	L	H	H	A	A	•	•	•	•	•	•
TRANS. ERR.	1	−	−	−	−	−	−	−	H	H	−	−	−	−	−	−	−	A	A	A	•	•	•	•	•
A1 ERR.	2	−	−	L	L	H	−	L	−	−	−	−	−	−	−	−	−	A	A	A	•	•	•	•	•
A2 ERR.	3	−	−	L	H	L	L	−	−	−	−	−	−	−	−	−	−	A	A	A	•	•	•	•	•
"S" ET	4	−	−	H	−	−	H	H	L	L	L	H	H	L	L	H	H	•	A	•	•	•	•	•	•
"R" ESET	5	−	−	H	−	−	H	H	L	L	L	H	H	L	L	H	L	•	•	A	•	•	•	•	•
READ "?"	6	−	−	H	−	−	H	H	L	L	H	H	H	H	H	H	H	•	A	A	•	•	•	•	•
A	7	−	−	H	−	−	H	H	L	L	L	L	L	L	L	L	H	•	•	•	A	•	•	•	A
B	8	−	−	H	−	−	H	H	L	L	L	L	L	L	L	H	L	•	•	•	A	•	•	A	•
C	9	−	−	H	−	−	H	H	L	L	L	L	L	L	L	H	H	•	•	•	A	•	•	A	A
D	10	−	−	H	−	−	H	H	L	L	L	L	L	L	H	L	L	•	•	•	A	•	A	•	•
E	11	−	−	H	−	−	H	H	L	L	L	L	L	L	H	L	H	•	•	•	A	•	A	•	A
F	12	−	−	H	−	−	H	H	L	L	L	L	L	L	H	H	L	•	•	•	A	•	A	A	•
G	13	−	−	H	−	−	H	H	L	L	L	L	L	L	H	H	H	•	•	•	A	•	A	A	A
H	14	−	−	H	−	−	H	H	L	L	L	L	L	H	L	L	L	•	•	•	A	A	•	•	•
I	15	−	−	H	−	−	H	H	L	L	L	L	L	H	L	L	H	•	•	•	A	A	•	•	A
J	16	−	−	H	−	−	H	H	L	L	L	L	L	H	L	H	L	•	•	•	A	A	•	A	•
K	17	−	−	H	−	−	H	H	L	L	L	L	L	H	L	H	H	•	•	•	A	A	•	A	A
L	18	−	−	H	−	−	H	H	L	L	L	L	L	H	H	L	L	•	•	•	A	A	A	•	•
M	19	−	−	H	−	−	H	H	L	L	L	L	L	H	H	L	H	•	•	•	A	A	A	•	A
N	20	−	−	H	−	−	H	H	L	L	L	L	L	H	H	H	L	•	•	•	A	A	A	A	•
O	21	−	−	H	−	−	H	H	L	L	L	L	L	H	H	H	H	•	•	•	A	A	A	A	A
P	22	−	−	H	−	−	H	H	L	L	L	H	H	L	L	L	L	•	•	•	A	•	•	•	•
I CHARACTER ADDRESS DECODE	23	−	−	L	L	H	−	H	L	L	L	H	H	L	L	L	L	•	•	•	•	•	•	•	•
	24	−	−	L	L	H	−	H	L	L	L	H	H	L	L	L	H	A	•	A	•	•	•	•	A
	25	−	−	L	L	H	−	H	L	L	L	H	H	L	L	H	L	A	•	A	•	•	•	A	•
	26	−	−	L	L	H	−	H	L	L	L	H	H	L	L	H	H	A	•	A	•	•	•	A	A
	27	−	−	L	L	H	−	H	L	L	L	H	H	L	H	L	L	A	•	A	•	•	A	•	•
	28	−	−	L	L	H	−	H	L	L	L	H	H	L	H	L	H	A	•	A	•	•	A	•	A
	29	−	−	L	L	H	−	H	L	L	L	H	H	L	H	H	L	A	•	A	•	•	A	A	•
	30	−	−	L	L	H	−	H	L	L	L	H	H	L	H	H	H	A	•	A	•	•	A	A	A
II CHARACTER ADDRESS DECODE	31	−	−	L	H	L	H	−	L	L	L	H	H	L	L	L	L	•	A	A	•	•	•	•	•
	32	−	−	L	H	L	H	−	L	L	L	H	H	L	L	L	L	•	A	A	•	•	•	•	•
	33	−	−	L	H	L	H	−	L	L	L	H	H	L	L	H	L	•	A	A	•	•	•	A	•
	34	−	−	L	H	L	H	−	L	L	L	H	H	L	L	H	H	•	A	A	•	•	•	A	A
	35	−	−	L	H	L	H	−	L	L	L	H	H	L	H	L	L	•	A	A	•	•	A	•	•
	36	−	−	L	H	L	H	−	L	L	L	H	H	L	H	L	H	•	A	A	•	•	A	•	A
	37	−	−	L	H	L	H	−	L	L	L	H	H	L	H	H	L	•	A	A	•	•	A	A	•
	38	−	−	L	H	L	H	−	L	L	L	H	H	L	H	H	H	•	A	A	•	•	A	A	A
ILLEGAL CODES	39	−	−	−	−	−	−	−	−	L	L	L	−	−	−	−	−	A	A	A	•	•	•	•	•
	40	−	−	−	−	−	−	−	−	L	L	H	−	−	−	−	−	A	A	A	•	•	•	•	•
	41	−	−	−	−	−	−	−	−	L	H	L	−	−	−	−	−	A	A	A	•	•	•	•	•
	42	−	−	−	−	−	−	−	−	H	H	L	−	−	−	−	−	A	A	A	•	•	•	•	•
	43	−	−	−	−	−	−	−	−	H	H	H	−	−	−	−	−	A	A	A	•	•	•	•	•

(Reprinted courtesy of Signetics Corporation)

Figure 7.8   FPLA program table

7.4   CHOOSING A MICROCONTROLLER

Selection of an LSI microcontroller is highly dependent upon the application. However, we can identify some general guidelines. Since the primary function of the device is to control, such activity should not consume an inordinate amount of the total processing time, and microprogramming should be relatively straightforward. With regard to the latter task, the microcontroller should be flexible enough to generate any address sequences (sequential, conditional, unconditional, and repetitive) that will be required of the particular application. In addition, the address space should be large enough or at least easily expandable. Either cascading devices or extending pages are satisfactory; that is, if the "controlling" speed is not degraded beyond the requirements of the system to be controlled.

Oftentimes the microcontroller device contains considerable internal logic. Determining the suitability of the device then becomes a difficult task. Consequently, we need to have some procedure to measure the power of the microcontroller and compare its performance to others. One useful procedure is to isolate the combinational circuits from the memory circuits. At first, focus on each capability separately. The combinational circuits dictate how address selection is decided. Determine how many branch addresses are possible and how many branch condition signals are permitted. The memory circuits indicate how deeply microroutines can be nested. After separate analysis, then combine the two capabilities and repeat the analysis. Now, determine how much peripheral logic is required. Is the device actually stand-alone? Remember that each additional logic circuit external to the microcontroller increases the address generation time (besides increasing the physical wiring, cooling, and power requirements).

In the next sections we will examine available microcontroller devices. Although the selection is not complete, it is representative and sufficient for most applications. As you analyze each device, consider its potential microprogramming power as previously described.

7.5   CONTROL STORE SEQUENCER, 8X02—3

The Signetics Control Store Sequencer[3] is a low-power Schottky LSI device, designed for use in high-performance microprogrammed systems. The basic function of this device is to set up the microprogram address from which the microinstruction is fetched. All microinstructions are assumed to reside in

---

[3]The material in this section has been adapted from publications of Signetics Corporation. The author assumes full responsibility for the material so published herein. Programs, figures, and tables are courtesy and copyright © 1976 by Signetics Corporation. All rights reserved.

the Control Store (ROM's, PROM's, or RAM's, in the case of Writable Control Store).

The fundamental design philosophy of the sequencer is to provide an LSI device that can handle most of the essential sequencing functions normally required for efficient microprogramming and be easy to use. Direct addressing to 1024 words is possible. Additional address requirements are provided by external page registers, which can be either entirely or partially controlled via the microprogram.

The Control Sequencer architecture is shown in Figure 7.9. The address register is a 10-bit D-type FF which holds the current address. The register changes state when the CLOCK is in a Low-to-High transition (edge triggered). The address register can be loaded with different address sources under control of the three Address Control (AC_{2-0}) lines and one Test input line. These sources are:

All 0's for reset
Current address +1 for simple increment
Current address +2 for skip
10-bit branch address from outside
Stack register field output

There is a four-level Stack Register File and a 2-bit Stack Pointer, both of which respond automatically to operations requiring a PUSH (write to Stack Register File) or POP (read Stack Register File). The file is organized as a

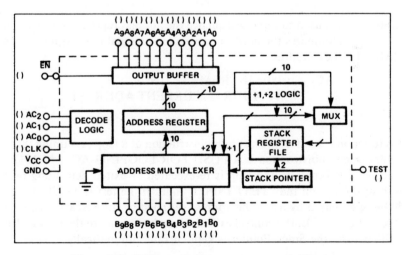

Figure 7.9 8X02 control store sequencer architecture

4-word-by-10-bit matrix and operates as a LIFO. The Stack Pointer operates as an UP/DOWN counter.

The activities that take place within various logic elements are shown in Table 7.1. The AC_{2-0} and the TEST INPUT are input variables for this chart. Following is a detailed description of all the possible functions performed by the Control Store Sequencer. Let us begin with the TEST and SKIP function.

This function is used to facilitate transfer of control based on the result of a test on the "Test Input" line.

AC_{2-0} = 000: TEST & SKIP (TSK)
       PERFORM TEST ON "TEST INPUT" LINE

       IF TEST IS
           FALSE: NEXT ADDR = CURRENT
                   ADDR +1, STACK POINTER
                   UNCHANGED.

       IF TEST IS
           TRUE: NEXT ADDR = CURRENT
                   ADDR +2, i.e., SKIP NEXT
                   MICROINSTRUCTIONS:
                   STACK POINTER UNCHANGED.

This function is used to serially sequence the address register by 1. This simple function eliminates the need to provide ten external address lines to do a BRANCH to next address.

AC_{2-0} = 001: INCREMENT (INC)
       NEXT ADDR = CURRENT ADDR +1

This function is used as the last microinstruction of a loop (assuming that the beginning microinstruction is a PUSH FOR LOOPING AC_{2-0} = 101). By means of this function, the loop is re-executed or exited depending on the result of the test on the "TEST INPUT" line. If the test is TRUE, the loop will be re-executed by using the address supplied by the Stack Register File. If the test is FALSE, the control exits the loop by moving to the next address. In either case, the Stack Pointer is kept current automatically.

MNEMONIC	DESCRIPTION	FUNCTION AC$_2$ 1 0	TEST	NEXT ADDRESS	STACK	STACK POINTER
TSK	TEST & SKIP	0 0 0	FALSE TRUE	CURRENT +1 CURRENT +2	N.C. N.C.	N.C. N.C.
INC	INCREMENT	0 0 1	X	CURRENT +1	N.C.	N.C.
BLT	BRANCH TO LOOP IF TEST INPUT TRUE	0 1 0	FALSE TRUE	CURRENT +1 STACK REG FILE	X POP (READ)	DECR DECR
POP	POP STACK	0 1 1	X	STACK REG FILE	POP (READ)	DECR
BSR	BRANCH TO SUBROUTINE IF TEST INPUT TRUE	1 0 0	FALSE TRUE	CURRENT +1 BRANCH ADDR.	N.C. PUSH (CURR +1)	N.C. INCR
PLP	PUSH FOR LOOPING	1 0 1	X	CURRENT +1	PUSH (CURR. ADDR)	INCR
BRT	BRANCH IF TEST INPUT TRUE	1 1 0	FALSE TRUE	CURRENT +1 BRANCH ADDR.	N.C. N.C.	N.C. N.C.
RST	SET MICRO-PROGRAM ADDR. OUTPUT TO ZERO	1 1 1	X	ALL O's	N.C.	N.C.

X = DON'T CARE
N.C. = NO CHANGE

TABLE 7.1   8X02 next address control function

AC$_{2-0}$ = 010: BRANCH TO LOOP IF TEST CON-
DITION TRUE (BLT) PERFORM TEST ON
"TEST INPUT" LINE

IF TEST IS
TRUE: NEXT ADDR = ADDR FROM
REG FILE (POP), STACK
POINTER DECR BY 1.

IF TEST IS
FALSE: NEXT ADDR = CURRENT
ADDR +1, STACK POINTER
DECR BY 1.

This function is used to POP or read the Stack Register File unconditionally. It is usually used as the last microinstruction of a microroutine where the control will be returned to the main microprogram.

AC$_{2-0}$ = 011: POP STACK (POP)
NEXT ADDR = STACK REG FILE
STACK POINTER DECREMENTED BY 1

This function facilitates the transfer of control based on the result of the test on "TEST INPUT" line. If the test is FALSE, no branch will take place and the next instruction will be executed. If the test is TRUE, the address register is loaded with the B$_{9-0}$ (Branch Address) lines and, in the meantime, the (current address +1) is written or pushed into the Stack Register File. The latter condition allows branching to a microroutine whose beginning address is supplied by B$_{9-0}$. Simultaneously, the return address is saved in the Stack Register File.

AC$_{2-0}$ = 100: BRANCH TO SUBROUTINE IF
TEST INPUT TRUE (BSR)

IF TEST IS
FALSE: NEXT ADDR = CURRENT
ADDR +1, NO PUSH ON
STACK, STACK POINTER
UNCHANGED.

IF TEST IS
  TRUE: NEXT ADDRESS = BRANCH
         ADDRESS ($B_{9\text{-}0}$), PUSH CUR-
         RENT ADDR $+1 \rightarrow$ STACK
         REG FILE, STACK POINTER
         INCREMENTED BY 1.

This function is generally used as the first microinstruction of a program loop. The current address is saved in the Stack Register File. This function works hand in hand with the BLT function.

$AC_{2\text{-}0}$ = 101: PUSH FOR LOOPING (PLP)
         NEXT ADDR = CURRENT ADDR $+1$
         STACK POINTER INCR BY 1
         PUSH (CURRENT ADDR) $\rightarrow$ STACK REG
         FILE

This function is used to facilitate transfer of control based on the result of the test on the TEST INPUT line. If the test is TRUE, the next address is supplied by the $B_{9\text{-}0}$ lines; if the test is FALSE, the control proceeds to the next address.

$AC_{2\text{-}0}$ = 110: BRANCH IF TEST CONDITION
         TRUE (BRT)

IF TEST IS
  FALSE: NEXT ADDR = CURRENT
         ADDRESS $+1$.

IF TEST IS
  TRUE: NEXT ADDR = BRANCH
         ADDRESS ($B_{9\text{-}0}$).

This function is used to reset the address to all 0's. The state of the $B_{9\text{-}0}$ lines has no bearing on the next address setup.

$AC_{2\text{-}0}$ = 111: RESET TO 0 (RST)
         NEXT ADDR = 0, FOR RESET

The 8X02 is totally compatible with all bipolar TTL logic elements. A typical hardware setup is shown in Figure 7.10. This figure generally represents the control loop of a 16-bit CPU. To control the 8X02 as it is configured in Figure 7.10, the firmware basically has to provide fields for:

AC_{2-0}: 3 bits for address control

ACK INH: 1 bit for clock inhibit

S_{2-0}: 3 bits for multiplexer select. In a simpler design, a 1-bit field connected directly to the "TEST" input pin of the 8X02 may satisfy the design requirement.

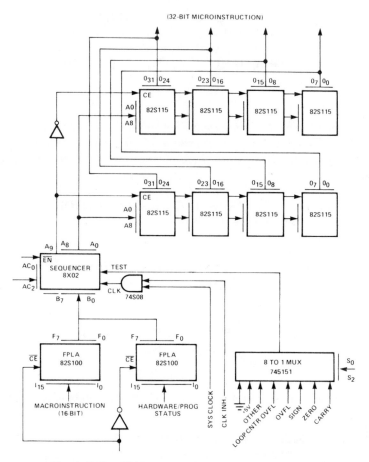

Figure 7.10 8X02 as part of control loop configuration

7.6   AM 2900 MICROPROGRAM CONTROL

Microprogramming sequencing is accomplished with the AM 2909 sequencer[4] depicted in Figure 7.11. This is essentially a 4-bit sequential address controller. It has two control line inputs, S_0 and S_1, with the capability to select one of four next addresses. The four sources include: a) a set of direct external inputs (D_0 through D_3), b) the top of a four word PUSH-POP stack, c) a program counter register (incrementer), and d) inputs from an external address register via the OR inputs (OR_0 through OR_3) which are enabled by the $\overline{RE}$ line. The 2909 also contains the 4×4 file for nested subprogram calls, a stack pointer, and a microprogram address register.

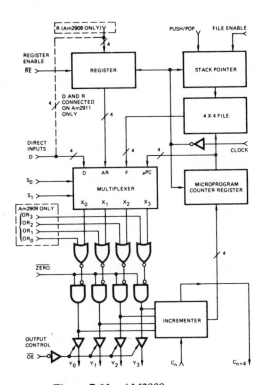

Figure 7.11   AM2909 sequencer

---

[4]The material in this section has been adapted from publications of Advanced Micro Devices Corporation. The author assumes full responsibility for the material so published. Programs, figures, and tables are courtesy and copyright © 1976 by Advanced Micro Devices Corporation. All rights reserved.

Appropriate decode logic inside the chip dictates which multiplexer output is enabled. Note also that the incrementer has a C_n input carry line and a C_{n+4} output carry line to allow for cascading 2909 chips. This allows us to extend the address space. Conditional branches are enabled via the OR_0 through OR_3 input lines to the sequencer chip. When three cascaded sequencers are used, addressing is extendable to 4096 unique microprogram locations. A modified version of the 2909, 2911, is also available. It is identical to the 2909 except that the "OR" inputs (OR_0, OR_1, OR_2, OR_3) in Figure 7.11 are omitted.

The AM microprogramming sequencer is supported by the AM29811. The AM29811 is a device designed specifically for next address control of the AM2911 Microprogram Sequencer. The device generates outputs required of a computer control unit or a structured state machine using microprogramming techniques.

Sixteen instructions are available by using a 4-bit instruction field I_{0-3}. In addition, a test input is available such that conditional instructions can be performed based on a condition code test input. The full instruction set consists of such functions as conditional jumps, conditional jump-to-subroutine, conditional return-from-subroutine, conditional repeat loops, and conditional branch to starting address.

One AM29811 can be used to control any number of AM2911 Microprogram Sequencers. The AM2911 is a 4-bit slice itself. Thus, one AM29811 Next Address Control Unit and three AM2911 Microprogram Sequencers can be used to build a microprogram sequencer capable of controlling 4K words of microprogram memory. A typical computer configuration for the AM29811 is illustrated in Figure 7.12.

There are four main modes of sequencing with the AM architectures. These modes are: a) Starting Addresses, b) Jumps, c) Sequencing, and d) Microroutining. The four cases are shown below with the significant control paths.

APPLICATION

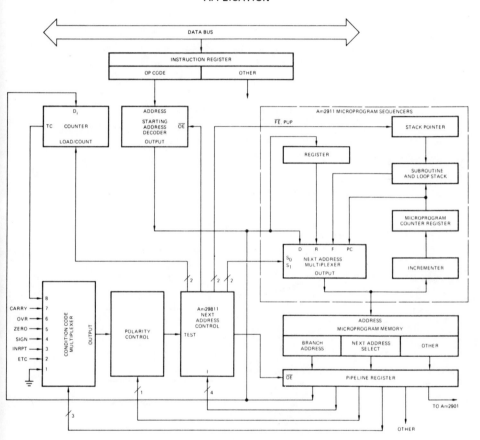

Figure 7.12   AM2911, 29811

Mode 1—STARTING ADDRESSES

This is typically used to enter a microroutine, e.g., "MULT" or "DIV". A mapping PROM is used to decode the op code field of the instruction register in the main section of the computer. The next step generates the address for the next address MUX followed by the eventual transfer to the microinstruction address register.

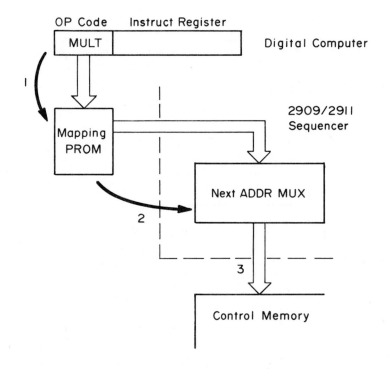

Mode 2—JUMPS

In the Jump mode, the AM29811 enables the Jump field of the pipeline register via signal, $\overline{OE}$. Later, S_0 and S_1 are generated by the AM29811 to latch this JUMP address into the next address MUX of the AM2911. A JUMP now occurs.

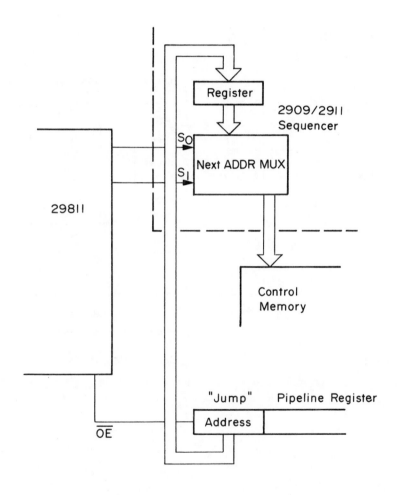

Mode 3—SEQUENCING

In this mode, the microprogram counter in the AM2909/2911 is automatically incremented and chosen as the next address for the microprogram memory. S_0 and S_1 are appropriately generated by the AM29811.

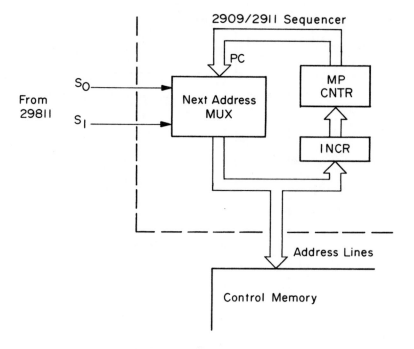

Mode 4—MICROROUTINE ENTRY

In this mode, the stack pointer in the AM2909/2911 is enabled by $\overline{FE}$ and PUP signals from the AM29811. A microroutine starting address is retrieved from the 4 × 4 stack and the current address is preserved in the stack.

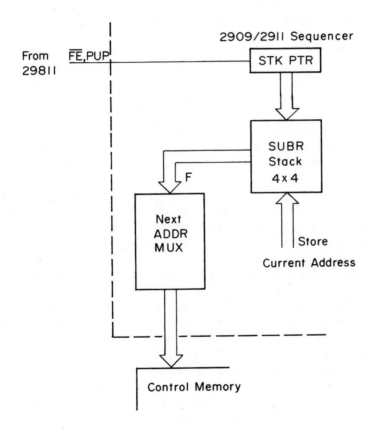

7.7 INTEL 3001 MICROCONTROLLER

The Intel 3001 MCU chip[5] is the microprogram control sequencer for the 3000 series. We see from Figure 7.13 that no address incrementer is available. Thus, all sequencing is either conditional or unconditional jumps. The MCU chip contains a microprogram address register which serves as an internal latch for the next address, two output buffer latches, MA 8 through MA 4 for row address, and MA 3 through MA 0 for column address. These outputs are the microprogram memory address lines. The MCU also contains flags and flag latches to facilitate conditional jumps via interpretation of carry or shift signals. The input to the 3001 consists of a 7-bit jump function bus which also is combined with a primary and secondary function bus, PX and SX. The jump function bus and primary and secondary buses are combined to form the next address in the microprogram. The 3001 can be combined with other Intel hardware to form a computer (depicted in Figure 7.14).

The two noteworthy features of the Microprogram Control Unit are: a) next-address sequencing is a branch (either conditional or unconditional), and b) the independent MCU resident logic for branch tests on the CPE carry/shift signals. Next-address sequencing is accomplished without the need for a hardware or software program counter. In fact, every address is a jump address. The MCU uses a versatile two-dimensional addressing scheme, one field for a row address and another field for the column address. Such a scheme is quite useful when one or more microinstructions are found in several microroutines. Less time-space penalty occurs than usually found in other branching schemes.

The next address is formed from a specified JUMP set for the current microinstruction. Within the 9-bit microinstruction next-address field, from two to five bits select the JUMP set while the remaining bits supply part of the destination address. Each microinstruction is identified with a row-column address in the 32 row $\times$ 16 column two-dimensional address matrix. Rows are determined with a 5-bit code while columns are determined with a 4-bit code generating a 512 cell memory map. The JUMP set is determined by: a) the current location in the matrix and b) the MCU jump function. A typical JUMP set for JZR (Jumpt to Zero Row) is shown in Figure 7.15. The eleven jump functions are listed in Table 7.2 and the JUMP sets for each function are shown in Figure 7.16.

---

[5] The material in this section has been adapted from publications of Intel Corporation. The author assumes full responsibility for the material so published herein. Programs, figures, and tables are courtesy and copyright © 1975 by Intel Corporation. All rights reserved.

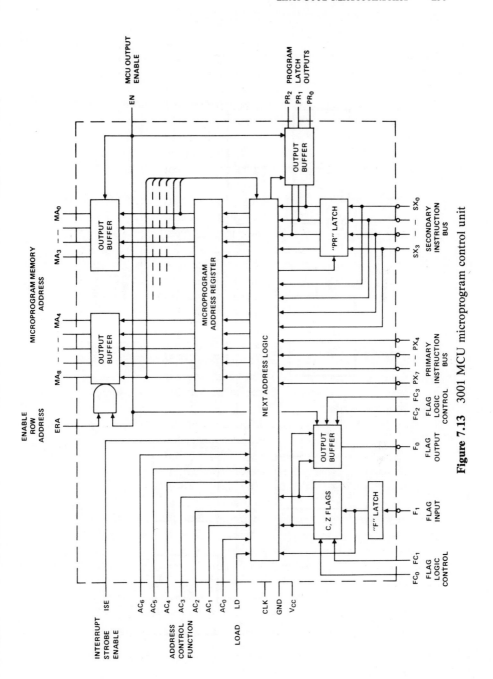

Figure 7.13 3001 MCU microprogram control unit

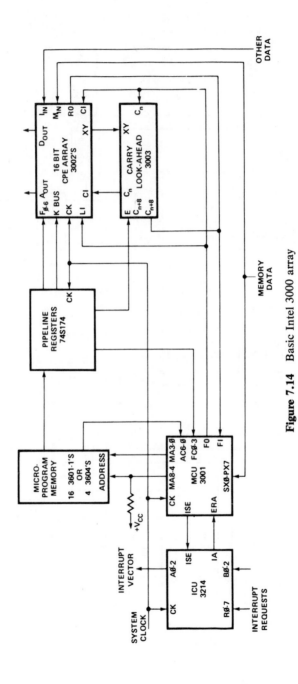

Figure 7.14 Basic Intel 3000 array

The jump functions utilize tests on the independent flags we mentioned earlier. These flags monitor carry/shift signals from the central processing element or CPE, configured somewhat like Figure 7.17. Note that the MCU supplies carry/shift inputs to the CPE array and handles carry/shift output from the CPE. In typical configurations, the MCU's Flag Output, FO, is connected to the Carry Input, CI, and the Left Input, LI, of the CPE array. Thus, the Flag Output furnishes carry/shift data to the CPE. Under control of the Flag Output Function Bus, the MCU can force the Flag Output to zero, one, the current state of the C-Flag, or the current state of a Z-Flag. The MCU's Flag Input, FI, is connected to the Carry Output, CO, and the Right Output, RO, of the CPE. The Flag Input receives the carry/shift output of the CPE and is automatically stored in the MCU's F-latch. From control in the Flag Input Function Bus, the MCU can save the state of the Flag Input in the C-Flag, Z-Flag, both flags, or neither flag. The FO field in a

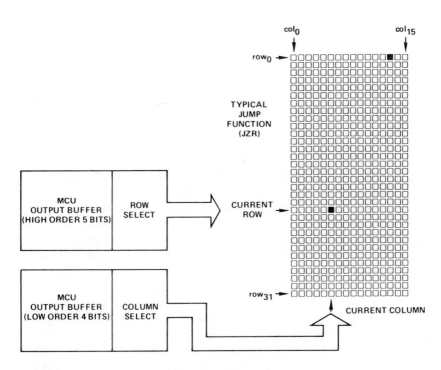

Figure 7.15   JZR jump set

Table 7.2   3001 jump instructions

MNEMONIC	DESCRIPTION	FUNCTION							NEXT ROW					NEXT COL			
		AC_6	5	4	3	2	1	0	MA_8	7	6	5	4	MA_3	2	1	0
JCC	Jump in current column	0	0	d_4	d_3	d_2	d_1	d_0	d_4	d_3	d_2	d_1	d_0	m_3	m_2	m_1	m_0
JZR	Jump to zero row	0	1	0	d_3	d_2	d_1	d_0	0	0	0	0	0	d_3	d_2	d_1	d_0
JCR	Jump in current row	0	1	1	d_3	d_2	d_1	d_0	m_8	m_7	m_6	m_5	m_4	d_3	d_2	d_1	d_0
JCE	Jump in column/enable	1	1	1	0	d_2	d_1	d_0	m_8	m_7	d_2	d_1	d_0	m_3	m_2	m_1	m_0
JFL	Jump/test F-latch	1	0	0	d_3	d_2	d_1	d_0	m_8	d_3	d_2	d_1	d_0	m_3	0	1	f
JCF	Jump/test C-flag	1	0	1	0	d_2	d_1	d_0	m_8	m_7	d_2	d_1	d_0	m_3	0	1	c
JZF	Jump/test Z-flag	1	0	1	1	d_2	d_1	d_0	m_8	m_7	d_2	d_1	d_0	m_3	0	1	z
JPR	Jump/test PR-latches	1	1	0	0	d_2	d_1	d_0	m_8	m_7	d_2	d_1	d_0	p_3	p_2	p_1	p_0
JLL	Jump/test left PR bits	1	1	0	1	d_2	d_1	d_0	m_8	m_7	d_2	d_1	d_0	0	1	p_3	p_2
JRL	Jump/test right PR bits	1	1	1	1	1	d_1	d_0	m_8	m_7	1	d_1	d_0	1	1	p_1	p_0
JPX	Jump/test PX-bus	1	1	1	1	0	d_1	d_0	m_8	m_7	m_6	d_1	d_0	x_7	x_6	x_5	x_4

SYMBOL	MEANING
d_n	Data on address control line n
m_n	Data in microprogram address register bit n
p_n	Data in PR-latch bit n
x_n	Data on PX-bus line n (active LOW)
f, c, z	Contents of F-latch, C-flag, or Z-flag, respectively

microinstruction determines the carry/shift input to the CPE while the FI field handles the carry/shift output from the CPE. Flag operations are summarized in Table 7.3.

The jump functions also provide the important feature for handling interrupts. In the MCU, the JZR micro-order activates the Interrupt Strobe Enable, ISE, output from the MCU. If an interrupt is pending, an alternate row address is forced onto the microprogram memory row address lines. As a result, the next microinstruction is accessed, not from row 0 of column 15 (as required by JZR), but typically from row 31 of column 15. Address row 31, column 15 should be the starting location of the interrupt service routine.

Example 7.2: Macroinstruction Decoding with the Intel 3000 Architecture. There are eight input lines, PX4-7 and SX0-3, in the MCU which are especially designed with jump instructions to enhance macroinstruction decoding. In a computer structure, these lines would be tied to the memory data bus of the system and also to the M-input pins of the 3002 CPE array much like Figure 7.18. Suppose that a 16-bit macroinstruction format is chosen as in Figure 7.19. Then the upper four bits of the address mode field would be tied to PX4-7 while the next four bits, the "operation mode" field, would be tied to SX0-3. The last eight bits are used as a displacement.

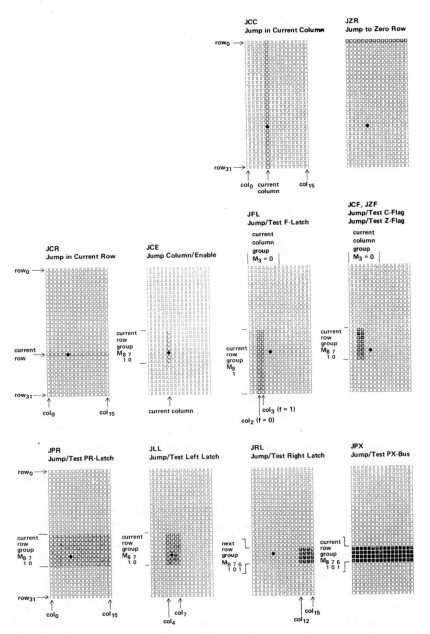

(Reprinted courtesy of Intel Corporation)

Figure 7.16 3001 jump sets

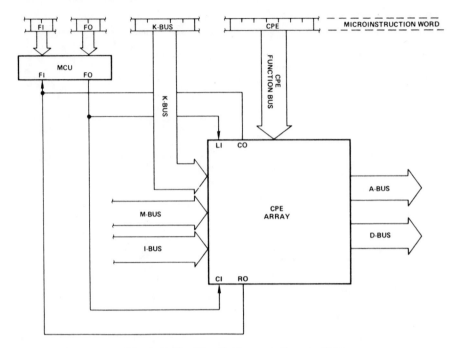

Figure 7.17   Flag field connections to CPE

During the JPX micro-order, the displacement would be stored in the CPE array while a 16-way branch is enabled by the four bits on the PX lines. The four bits on SX are automatically stored in the PR latch for later use. The four bits on the PX lines would be used for initial address processing of the macroinstruction. In the case of the CPU design example, the initial processing involves address calculations and/or operand fetching. Table 7.4 lists the initial processing modes for the design example. Using the instruction format shown in Figure 7.19, the high order four bits (bits 12 to 15) will be used to select one of the modes listed in Table 7.4. Thus, by executing a JPX operation, a 16-way branch on the PX0-PX3 bus can be performed to determine the address mode specified. At the same time, the SX bus bits (the Operation Code field) will be stored in the PR latches for later use. A possible assignment of the first four bits (bits 12 through 15) might be as shown in Table 7.5. In addition to the initial address mode processing, input/output, register to register, and other special function operations can be specified in the first four bits, as shown in Table 7.5.

Table 7.3 Flag micro-orders

TYPE	MNEMONIC	DESCRIPTION	FC₁	0
	SCZ	Set C-flag and Z-flag to f	0	0
Flag	STZ	Set Z-flag to f	0	1
Input	STC	Set C-flag to f	1	0
	HCZ	Hold C-flag and Z-flag	1	1

TYPE	MNEMONIC	DESCRIPTION	FC₃	2
	FF0	Force FO to 0	0	0
Flag	FFC	Force FO to C-flag	0	1
Output	FFZ	Force FO to Z-flag	1	0
	FF1	Force FO to 1	1	1

LOAD FUNCTION	NEXT ROW					NEXT COL			
LD	MA₈	7	6	5	4	MA₃	2	1	0
0	see Appendix A					see Appendix A			
1	0	x_3	x_2	x_1	x_0	x_7	x_6	x_5	x_4

SYMBOL	MEANING
f	Contents of the F-latch
x_n	Data on PX- or SX-bus line n (active LOW)

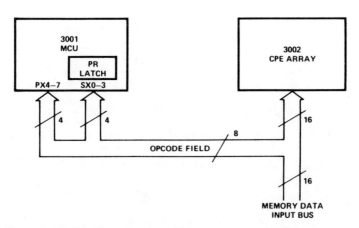

Figure 7.18 Macroinstruction decode connections for 3001 and 3002

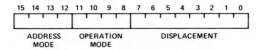

Figure 7.19 Macroinstruction format

Table 7.4   Mode bit assignments

In the description below, the letters A, X, B, S, P, W, and E represent the contents of the respective registers. D represents the 8-bit displacement treated as a positive number ranging from 0 to 255. D' represents D−128. ( ) are used to designate contents of memory. For example, (B+D) means the contents of the memory location whose address is equal to the sum of the contents of B and the displacement D. It is assumed that, when the instruction is fetched, P is incremented prior to instruction execution.

MEMORY REFERENCE MODES

1.   Direct: Address = B+D

2.   Indirect: Address = (B+D)

3.   Indirect relative: Address = (B+D)+B

4.   Indirect indexed: Address = (B+D)+X

5.   Indirect indexed relative: Address = (B+D)+B+X

IMMEDIATE MODES

6.   If D≠0, Data = D−128

     If D=0, Date = (P), P=P+1

JUMP MODES

7.   Jump relative: P=P+D−128

8.   Jump indirect: P=(E+D)+E

9.   Call relative: P=(E+D)+E

10.   Call indirect: P=E'+(E') where E'=E+(E+D)

REGISTER MODE

11.   Fetch source register

Table 7.5   Memory modes

ADDRESS MODE BITS	MODE	INITIAL PROCESS	SUBSEQUENT PROCESSING
0000	No operation		
0001	Jump relative	P+D'	Condition testing
0010	Jumps (index, etc.)	(E+D)+E	
0011	Immediate	D' or (P)	LAI, AAI, etc.
0100	Direct memory reference	B+D	
0101	Indirect memory reference	(B+D)	
0110	Indirect index	(B+D)+X	LAA, LDA, etc.
0111	Indirect index relative	(B+D)+X+B	
1000	I/O input	D → MAR	
1001	I/O input	X → MAR	
1010	I/O output	D → MAR	
1011	I/O output	X → MAR	
1100	Move group		
1101	Special function group		Shift A
1110	Indirect relative memory reference	(B+D)+B	
1111	No operation		

LOAD FUNCTION	NEXT ROW					NEXT COL			
LD	MA_8	7	6	5	4	MA_3	2	1	0
0	see Appendix A					see Appendix A			
1	0	x_3	x_2	x_1	x_0	x_7	x_6	x_5	x_4

SYMBOL	MEANING
f	Contents of the F-latch
x_n	Data on PX- or SX-bus line n (active LOW)

7.8   MC10801 MICROPROGRAM CONTROL FUNCTION

The Motorola MC10801 Microprogram Control Function[6] is an LSI building block for digital processor systems. This circuit controls machine operations by generating the addresses and sequencing pattern for microprogram control storage. The MC10801 is compatible with a wide range of control memory sizes and organizations. Each part is four bits wide and can be connected in parallel for larger memory addresses. Maximum system flexibility is maintained with five separate data ports.

---

[6]The material in this section has been adapted from publications of Motorola Corporation. The author assumes full responsibility for the material as published herein. Programs, figures, and tables are courtesy and copyright © 1976 by Motorola Corporation. All rights reserved.

The Microprogram Control Function as shown in the block diagram (Figure 7.20) contains a control memory address register CR0, multi-purpose registers CR1–CR3, an incrementer, a subroutine LIFO, and the associated next address, status, and bus control logic in a single MECL Bipolar LSI circuit. Nine select (CS) lines and four instruction inputs (IC) control all operations within the part.

Architectural Description. The MC10801 Microprogram Control Function is composed of eight master slave registers, CR0 through CR7, as shown in Figure 7.21. Additional gates, multiplexers, and a next address logic block transfer information to and from these registers. Five 4-bit data ports (CR0, CR3, NA, 1 Bus, and $\emptyset$ Bus) are available to enter and output address information. In addition, three single line terminals (B, $\overline{XB}$, and D_{in}) provide status inputs for decisions within the part. Each of the eight registers fills an important function in the storage and generation of control memory addresses. The individual registers and data transfer paths in Figure 7.21 are described below.

CR0—Control Memory Address Register. Register CR0 holds the present microprogram control memory address and its outputs are gated to package pins CR00 through CR03. In a system these outputs address the control memory storage block. The next address logic block in Figure 7.21 generates next address information to the CR0 register inputs.

Next Address Logic. The next address logic block performs one of sixteen sequence instructions as selected by the instruction control lines IC0 through IC3 inputs. These sixteen control instructions (see Table 7.6) determine the source of control memory address information within each MC10801. Possible sources are CR1, CR2, CR4, NA inputs, 1 Bus, $\emptyset$ Bus, and the incrementer. During each microcycle the next address block generates a new control memory address in parallel with other processor functions, such as the ALU.

CR1—Repeat Register. Register CR1 is primarily designed to be an index counter for repeating single microinstructions or repeating subroutines. A second function performed by CR1 is a control memory address save register. In this mode the present control memory address in CR0 is transferred to CR1 on a JLA-Jump and Load Address instruction (Table 7.6). At a later time it is possible to return to the stored address by transferring CR1 back to CR0 on a RPI-Repeat Instruction command.

CR2—Instruction Register. Register CR2 is used primarily as an instruction or op code storage register. After fetching a machine instruction, the control memory starting address can be stored in CR2. As with register CR1, the operation of CR2 is controlled by the instruction inputs IC0–IC3 and the next address logic. The 1 Bus is the source for CR2.

Microprogram Control Function BLOCK DIAGRAM—MC10801

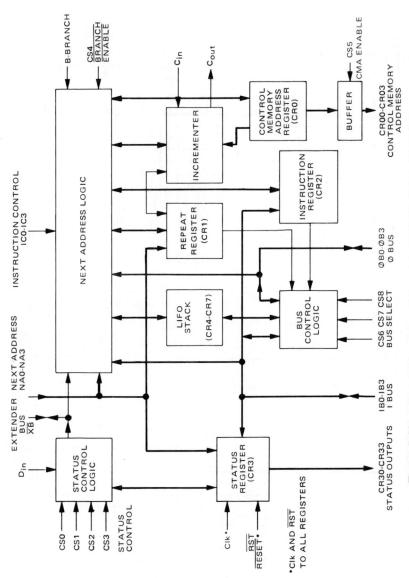

Figure 7.20 Microprogram control function block diagram—MC10801

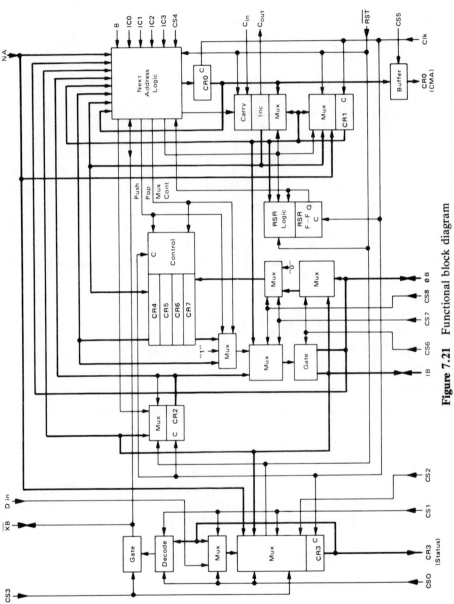

Figure 7.21 Functional block diagram

Table 7.6   MC10801 control instructions

INC—Increment
JMP—Jump to N.A. Inputs
J1B—Jump to 1 Bus
J1N—Jump to 1 Bus and Load CR2
JP1—Jump to Primary Instruction (CR2)
JEP—Jump to External Port (∅ Bus)
JL2—Jump to N.A. Inputs and Load CR2
JLA—Jump to N.A. Inputs and Load Address into CR1
JSR—Jump to Subroutine
RTN—Return from Subroutine
RSR—Repeat Subroutine (Load CR1 from N.A. Inputs)
RPI—Repeat Instruction
BRC—Branch to N.A. Inputs on Condition; otherwise Increment
BSR—Branch to Subroutine on Condition; otherwise Increment
ROC—Return from Subroutine on Condition; otherwise Jump to N.A. Inputs
BRM—Branch and Modify Address with Branch Inputs (Multi-way Branch)

CR3—Status Register. Register CR3 is normally used as a status register for storing flag conditions. This 4-bit register can be parallel loaded from either the NA or 1 Bus inputs. The CR3 status information may be used in conjunction with other external information for generating branch conditions.

Another use for CR3 is to extend the control memory address. This is accomplished by organizing the control memory in a word-page format. The word address is contained in CR0 and the page address in CR3. With two MC10801's each page can be 256 words (eight CR0 bits) and sixteen pages may be addressed with four CR3 bits or 256 possible pages using all eight CR3 bits.

CR4–CR7 LIFO Stack. Registers CR4 through CR7 are connected as a last-in-first-out (LIFO) stack for nesting subroutines within microprograms. When jumping to a subroutine, the return destination is automatically pushed onto the top of the LIFO (CR4). When returning from subroutine, CR4 is loaded into the control memory address register CR0. Push and pop stack operations are controlled by the IC0–IC3 inputs and the next address logic.

Incrementer. The 4-bit incrementer is used in several of the Table 7.6 microprogram control instructions. One is the INC-Increment command which linearly steps through a microprogram. A second function is to increment CR1 when it is used as an index counter for repeating microinstructions or subroutines as described in the earlier CR1 section. Increment is also used with the JSR-Jump to Subroutine, BSR-Branch to Subroutine, and JLA-Jump and Load Address commands to generate the proper return address. Operation of the incrementer is controlled by the IC0–IC3 code and the C_{in} input.

The incrementer is expanded with the carry in (C_{in}) and carry out (C_{out}) terminals when MC10801 circuits are operated in parallel.

RSR Logic and RSR Flipflop. The repeat subroutine (RSR) logic and flipflop blocks in Figure 7.19 provide a means for setting the MC10801 in an instruction repeat sequence as described in the previous CR1 section. The RSR flipflop is automatically set when a repeat constant is loaded into CR1 with a RSR-Repeat Subroutine instruction. It is cleared when CR1 reaches the final repeat count.

Functional Description. The MC10801 generates the microprogram address sequencing from sixteen control instructions which are encoded on the IC0–IC3 inputs. Each control instruction determines the data source for the next microprogram control memory address. This next address information is then stored in register CR0 on a positive going clock signal.

The sixteen sequence control instructions are each described in Table 7.7 which also shows the associated mnemonics, binary select codes, and register transfers. Several instructions require making decisions on the status of the branch (B), extender bus ($\overline{XB}$), RSR flipflop output (RSQ), or select line (CS4). Both decision alternatives are given for these instructions.

7.9   9408 MICROPROGRAM SEQUENCER

The Fairchild 9408 Microprogram Sequencer[7] controls the order in which microinstructions are fetched from the control memory. It contains a 10-bit program counter, a four-level last-in-first-out stack, and associated control logic. Thus, it can control up to a maximum of 1024 words of memory. For larger word capacities external paging can be used. The 9408 is controlled by a 4-bit instruction input. The instruction repertoire includes Fetch, Conditional and Unconditional Branches, Branch to Subroutine and Return from Subroutine.

There are seven test inputs, four of which participate in conditional branches and three in multi-way branches. The conditional test lines are flipflop buffered. These flipflops can be tested individually by appropriate branch instructions. The remaining three "multi-way" test inputs are used to

[7] The material in this section has been adapted from publications of Fairchild Camera and Instrument Corporation. The author assumes full responsibility for the material as published herein. Programs, figures, and tables are courtesy and copyright © 1976 by Fairchild Camera and Instrument Corporation. All rights reserved.

Table 7.7 MC10801 sequence control instructions

FUNCTIONAL DESCRIPTION

Four instruction control inputs, IC0 — IC3, and nine select lines, CS0 – CS8, control the flow of data within the MC10801 Microprogram Control Function. The following information describes programming these inputs to perform the various circuit functions. All truth tables are expressed in negative logic with V_{OL} being a logic 1 and V_{OH} a logic 0.

TABLE 2[5]

MNEM	IC3	IC2	IC1	IC0	DESCRIPTION	RESET CONDITION $\overline{RST}$	BRANCH OR REPEAT CONDITION[2]	CR0[7]	CR1	CR2	LIFO STACK CR4 – CR7[6]	RSQ[3]
X	X	X	X	X	RESET CONDITION	0	X	0	0	0	"PUSH" CR0 TO STACK	0
INC	1	1	0	0	INCREMENT	1	X	CR0 plus C_{in}	–	–	–	–
JMP	0	0	0	0	JUMP TO NEXT ADDRESS	1	X	NA	–	–	–	–
JIB	1	0	0	0	JUMP TO I BUS	1	X	IB·NA	–	–	–	–
JIN	1	0	0	1	JUMP TO I BUS & LOAD CR2	1	X	IB·NA	–	IB	–	–
JPI	1	0	1	0	JUMP TO PRIMARY INST.	1	X	CR2·NA	–	–	–	–
JEP	1	1	1	0	JUMP TO EXTERNAL PORT	1	X	ØB·NA	–	IB	–	–
JL2	0	0	0	1	JUMP & LOAD CR2	1	X	NA	–	–	–	–
JLA	0	0	1	0	JUMP & LOAD ADDRESS	1	X	NA	CR0 plus C_{in}	–	–	–
JSR	0	0	0	1	JUMP TO SUBROUTINE	1	RSQ+RIN·$\overline{XB}$=0 RSQ+RIN·$\overline{XB}$=1	NA NA	–	–	"PUSH" CR0 TO STACK "PUSH" CR0 plus C_{in}	–
RTN	1	1	1	1	RETURN FROM SUBROUTINE	1	RSQ+RIN·$\overline{XB}$=0 RSQ+RIN·$\overline{XB}$=1	CR4 CR4	–	–	"POP" STACK TO CR0 "POP" STACK TO CR0	0
RSR	1	0	1	1	REPEAT SUBROUTINE	1	X	CR0 plus C_{in}	NA	–	–	1
RPI	1	0	1	1	REPEAT INSTRUCTION	1	RSQ+RIN·$\overline{XB}$=0 RSQ+RIN·$\overline{XB}$=1	CR1·NA CR1·NA	CR1 plus C_{in}	–	–	0
BRC	0	1	0	1	BRANCH ON CONDITION	1	XB·(CS4+$\overline{B}$)=0 XB·(CS4+$\overline{B}$)=1	NA CR0 plus C_{in}	–	–	–	–
BSR	0	1	0	0	BRANCH TO SUBROUTINE	1	$\overline{XB}$·(CS4+$\overline{B}$)=0 $\overline{XB}$·(CS4+$\overline{B}$)=1	NA CR0 plus C_{in}	–	–	"PUSH" CR0 plus C_{in}	–
ROC	0	1	1	1	RETURN ON CONDITION	1	XB·(CS4+$\overline{B}$)=0 XB·(CS4+$\overline{B}$)=1	CR4 NA	–	–	"POP" STACK TO CR0	–
BRM	0	1	1	0	BRANCH & MODIFY	1	CS4=1 CS4=0	NA CR00=NA0·B CR01=NA1·XB CR02=NA2 CR03=NA3	–	–	–	–

REGISTER AND FLIP FLOP OUTPUTS [4][5] $V_{OL}\smile V_{OH}$

NOTES:
1. X = DON'T CARE STATE
   – = NO CHANGE
2. EQUATIONS APPLY AS SHOWN, WHERE:
   RIN = (CR13·CR12·CR11·CR10)
   $\overline{XB}$ = EXTERNAL EXTENDER BUS NODE (see Table 3)
   $\overline{B}$ = COMPLEMENT OF BRANCH INPUT
3. RSQ = OUTPUT OF RSR FLIP FLOP
4. ALL REGISTERS AND RSR FLIP FLOP CHANGE STATE ON V_{OL} TO V_{OH} (POSITIVE GOING) CLOCK TRANSITION
5. NEGATIVE LOGIC USED THROUGHOUT
6. TABLE 8 SHOWS LIFO STACK TRUTH TABLE
7. CR0 CHIP OUTPUTS ENABLED WHEN CS5=1

form the least significant three bits of the branch address for a multi-way branch. Thus, branching will occur to one of eight unique locations depending on the bit pattern present on these three inputs.

The 9408 is designed to operate in pipeline or non-pipeline mode as specified by the user. The device operates synchronously with the clock input and can be initialized using the Master Reset input. A typical microcontroller configuration is depicted in Figure 7.22.

Functional Description. As can be seen from the block diagram, Figure 7.23, the 9408 consists of a 10-bit program counter, 4-word-by-10-bit last-in-first-out stack with associated control, input multiplexer, pipeline multiplexer, instruction decode network, and a 4-bit test register using four edge triggered D flipflops.

The two-port pipeline multiplexer receives the program counter (PC) output as one input port (non-pipeline mode). The second input is provided by the input multiplexer output (pipeline mode). The port selection is controlled by the Pipeline Select (PLS) and Master Reset (MR) inputs, a LOW level on either input forces non-pipeline mode of operation. A LOW level on the MR input also clears the PC. Thus, when the 9408 is initialized by the MR input, the A_0–A_1 outputs will be LOW irrespective of the PLS input. A LOW on the PLS specifies non-pipeline mode and a HIGH specifies pipeline mode of operation.

The PC is a 10-bit edge triggered register. The input to the PC is always the address of the next microinstruction. Because of the edge triggered nature of the PC register, its output remains static for a full clock cycle. Thus, in the non-pipeline mode, the PC output can be used to address a control memory output in an external microinstruction register. However, in the case of the pipeline mode, the 9408 provides the next address information as soon as available, so that execution of a microinstruction can be overlapped with the fetching of the next microinstruction. In order that the microinstruction is stable for the full clock cycle, the output of the control memory should be buffered with an external microinstruction register.

There are four possible sources of data into the input multiplexer. One of the ports is the output of the last-in-first-out (LIFO) stack and the second port is the output of a 10-bit incrementer. The incrementer always adds one to the content of the PC. The third and fourth are the branch and the multi-way ports. The branch port is the 10-bit Branch Address input (BA_0–BA_9). The multi-way branch port is made up of the seven most significant Branch Address inputs (BA_3–BA_9) and three Multi-way inputs (MW_0–MW_2).

The 4-word-by-10-bit LIFO stack receives the incrementer output as its data input. The Stack Control Logic generates the appropriate control signals.

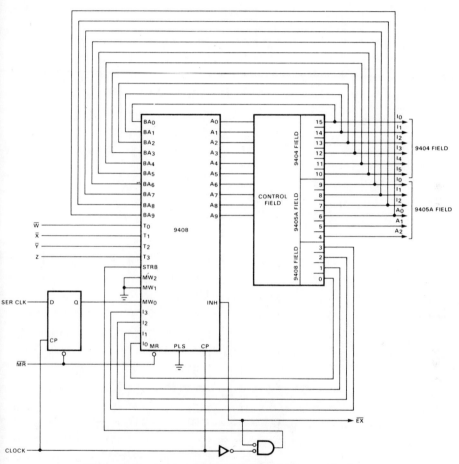

Figure 7.22 A microprogrammed controller employing a
Fairchild 9408 microcontroller

BLOCK DIAGRAM

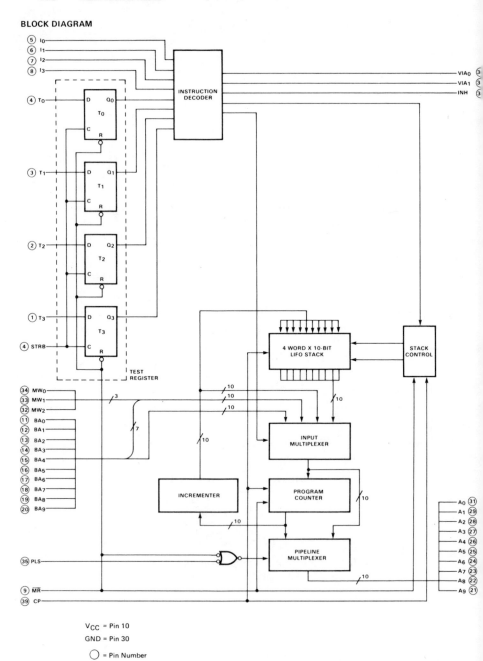

V_{CC} = Pin 10

GND = Pin 30

◯ = Pin Number

Figure 7.23   9408 block diagram

The 4-bit test register consists of four type D flipflops. The four Test inputs (T_0–T_3) are the data inputs and are loaded on LOW to HIGH transition of the Strobe (STRB) input. The LOW level on the MR input resets the test flipflops.

The Instruction decode network receives the 4-bit Instruction input (I_0–I_3) and the test register output. The VIA outputs (VIA_0 and VIA_1) and the Inhibit (INH) outputs of the 9408 are generated by the instruction decode logic. In addition, this logic also generates appropriate logic signals for the Stack Control logic and Input Multiplexer. The 9408 has a four-level subroutine nesting capability.

The 9408 has a repertoire of sixteen instructions; the desired instruction is specified by appropriate logic levels on the I_0–I_3 inputs (see Table 7.8). These instructions can be divided into three groups: unconditional branches, conditional branches, and miscellaneous. Table 7.8 is a list of the 9408 instructions.

SUMMARY

Microcontrollers are LSI devices that implement many control functions required in a microprogrammable control unit. With the widespread availability of such devices, only a particularly complex application would require a totally new device. This chapter describes five such devices, providing us with general features of each architecture.

Because microcontrollers are general-purpose control elements, the devices can be found in many applications beyond digital computers. This versatility also distinguishes microcontrollers from microprocessors. Of course, microprocessors can perform most of the functions of the microcontrollers. However, microprocessors already possess a predefined macroinstruction set. Microcontrollers sometimes do not. In fact, new macroinstructions can be utilized with a microcontroller. This is true because no constraints are placed on the contents of the control memory.

It is noteworthy that many microcontroller devices come with processor elements. The Intel 3001 MCU couples directly to the Intel 3002 CPE. Likewise, the AMD 2909 efficiently controls the 2901 CPU. Therefore, when significant computational power is required in an application, compatible processors can be found. More importantly, the two processing elements just mentioned belong to the class of bit-slice architectures. Processing elements that perform computational tasks on two or four binary bits are commonly called bit-slice devices. Processor slices are cascaded to provide the desired bit length. Such architectures offer interesting solutions to many digital machine applications.

Table 7.8   9408 instruction set

	MNEMONIC	DEFINITION	$I_3I_2I_1I_0$	$T_3T_2T_1T_0$	$O_9O_8O_7\cdots O_2O_1O_0$	VIA_1VIA_0	INH	DESCRIPTION OF OPERATION
	BRV_0	Branch VIA_0	L H L L	X X X X	$BA_9 BA_8\text{-}\text{-}BA_1 BA_0$	L L	H	$BA_0 \cdot BA_9 \to PC$
Unconditional	BRV_1	Branch VIA_1	L H L H	X X X X	$BA_9 BA_8\text{-}\text{-}BA_1 BA_0$	L H	H	$BA_0 \cdot BA_9 \to PC$
Branch	BRV_2	Branch VIA_2	L H H L	X X X X	$BA_9 BA_8\text{-}\text{-}BA_1 BA_0$	H L	H	$BA_0 \cdot BA_9 \to PC$
	BRV_3	Branch VIA_3	L H H H	X X X X	$BA_9 BA_8\text{-}\text{-}BA_1 BA_0$	H H	H	$BA_0 \cdot BA_9 \to PC$
Instructions	BMW	Branch Multiway	L L H H	X X X X	$BA_9 BA_3\text{-}\text{-}MW_2 MW_0$	L L	H	$MW_0 \cdot MW_2$, $BA_3 \cdot BA_9 \to PC$
	BSR	Branch to Subroutine	L L L H	X X X X	$BA_9 BA_8\text{-}\text{-}BA_1 BA_0$	L L	H	$BA_0 \cdot BA_9 \to PC$ & Push the Stack
	BTH_0	Branch on T_0 HIGH	H H L L	X X X H / X X X L	$BA_9 BA_8\text{-}\text{-}BA_1 BA_0$ / PC+1	L L	H	If Test Register 0 is HIGH: $BA_0 \cdot BA_9 \to PC$ If Test Register 0 is LOW: $PC+1 \to PC$
	BTH_1	Branch on T_1 HIGH	H H L H	X X H X / X X L X	$BA_9 BA_8\text{-}\text{-}BA_1 BA_0$ / PC+1	L L	H	If Test Register 1 is HIGH: $BA_0 \cdot BA_9 \to PC$ If Test Register 1 is LOW: $PC+1 \to PC$
	BTH_2	Branch on T_2 HIGH	H H H L	X H X X / X L X X	$BA_9 BA_8\text{-}\text{-}BA_1 BA_0$ / PC+1	L L	H	If Test Register 2 is HIGH: $BA_0 \cdot BA_9 \to PC$ If Test Register 2 is LOW: $PC+1 \to PC$
	BTH_3	Branch on T_3 HIGH	H H H H	H X X X / L X X X	$BA_9 BA_8\text{-}\text{-}BA_1 BA_0$ / PC+1	L L	H	If Test Register 3 is HIGH: $BA_0 \cdot BA_9 \to PC$ If Test Register 3 is LOW: $PC+1 \to PC$
Conditional	BTL_0	Branch on T_0 LOW	H L L L	X X X L / X X X H	$BA_9 BA_8\text{-}\text{-}BA_1 BA_0$ / PC+1	L L	H	If Test Register 0 is LOW: $BA_0 \cdot BA_9 \to PC$ If Test Register 0 is HIGH: $PC+1 \to PC$
Branch	BTL_1	Branch on T_1 LOW	H L L H	X X L X / X X H X	$BA_9 BA_8\text{-}\text{-}BA_1 BA_0$ / PC+1	L L	H	If Test Register 1 is LOW: $BA_0 \cdot BA_9 \to PC$ If Test Register 1 is HIGH: $PC+1 \to PC$
Instructions	BTL_2	Branch on T_2 LOW	H L H L	X L X X / X H X X	$BA_9 BA_8\text{-}\text{-}BA_1 BA_0$ / PC+1	L L	H	If Test Register 2 is LOW: $BA_0 \cdot BA_9 \to PC$ If Test Register 2 is HIGH: $PC+1 \to PC$
	BTL_3	Branch on T_3 LOW	H L H H	L X X X / H X X X	$BA_9 BA_8\text{-}\text{-}BA_1 BA_0$ / PC+1	L L	H	If Test Register 3 is LOW: $BA_0 \cdot BA_9 \to PC$ If Test Register 3 is HIGH: $PC+1 \to PC$
Miscellaneous	RTS	Return from Subroutine	L L L L	X X X X	Contents of the Stack Addressed by Read Pointer	L L	L	Pop the Stack
Instructions	FTCH	FETCH	L L H L	X X X X	PC+1	L L	L	$PC+1 \to PC$

L - LOW Level
H - HIGH Level
X - Don't Care

For instance, some machines required to handle variable word-length data. Others employ input/output ports that must change from single bit to parallel 4 or 8-bit ports. Controlling banks of relays is one example. Of course, a bit-slice design involves critical hardware decisions and creation of a new instruction set. However, such versatility is invaluable to the designer (even parts from different manufacturers can be mixed into one design). Hence, critical hardware decisions far outweigh the constraints imposed upon a designer employing microprocessor-based architecture. A microprocessor-based system may employ a microprocessor with a predefined instruction set, but be designed/configured in a variety of ways according to the *end users* specifications.

PROBLEMS

7.1   Nearly all microcontrollers have incrementers. Suppose a microcontroller similar to the one in Figure 7.24 below was available. What useful functions could this microcontroller perform?

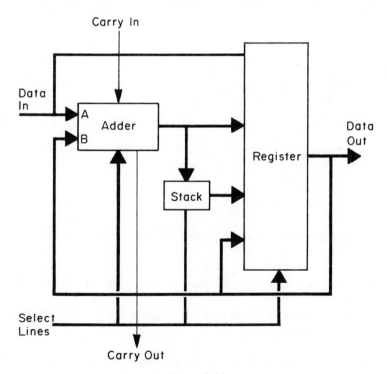

Figure 7.24

7.2   For each microcontroller below, devise a circuit to implement relative addressing at the microprogram level, if possible.

    a. Signetics 8X02
    b. AMD 2911 and 29811
    c. Fairchild 9408
    d. Motorola MC10801
    e. Intel 3001

7.3   For those microcontrollers in the text which do not have a "repeat" register (to execute microinstructions repetitively), design peripheral circuits to accomplish this control task.

7.4   The Intel 3000 address space consists of 32 rows and 16 columns. Since every address is a branch address and two-dimensional addressing is available, what benefits can be derived from such an arrangement?

7.5   Make a table of significant features for several microcontrollers. Tabulate

    a. Access speed
    b. Memory space range
    c. Number of conditional branches
    d. Memory extension method
    e. Microroutine nest levels
    f. Pipeline method

7.6   For the following microcontrollers, how would you implement a circuit to control a variable format microinstruction?

    a. MC10801
    b. AMD 2909/11 with a 29811.

7.7   Devise a circuit to perform a single level microroutine nest for the Intel 3001.

7.8   How does the 8X02 count the number of loops in a microroutine?

7.9   In the 9408, is there any provision for loading one flag without disturbing any other flag?

7.10   Which microcontrollers provide the capability to internally store status information in the microcontroller device itself?

REFERENCES

A brief discussion of the procedures necessary to design microcontrollers is available in two application notes from Scientific Micro Systems, Inc.: "Design of a General-Purpose Microcontroller," July 1973, and "Design of Microprogrammable Systems," December, 1970.

A two-part article summarizes and compares several bit-slice architectures and their respective microcontroller devices: "How Bit-Slice Families Compare: Part I, Evaluating Processor Elements," *Electronics,* August 3, 1978, and "How Bit-Slice Families Compare: Part II, Sizing Up the Microcontrollers," *Electronics*, August 17, 1978.

Considerable documentation is available for all of the devices in this chapter as well as others not discussed. For Signetics information, see "How to Design with the Control Store Sequencer, 8X02," Signetics Corporation, Sunnyvale, California, 1976. For AMD 2900 data, see "Advanced Micro Devices Data Book" and "Microprogramming Handbook," Advanced Micro Devices Corporation, Sunnyvale, California, 1976. For Intel 3000 series architecture, see "Intel Series 3000 Microprogramming Manual," Intel Corporation, Santa Clara, California, 1975. For the Motorola MC10801 data, see "M10800, High Performance MECL LSI Processor Family," Motorola Corporation, Phoenix, Arizona, 1976. For Fairchild data, see "Macrologic Bipolar Microprocessor Databook," Fairchild Camera and Instrument Corporation, Mountain View, California, 1976.

Discussion of signal conditioning and control signal definitions for many digital machine applications can be found in Robert J. Bibbero, *Microprocessors in Instruments and Control,* John Wiley, New York, 1977.

APPENDIX A: Program A.1

```
00100 PROGRAM MCC (INPUT,OUTPUT)
00110*
00120*   WRITTEN BY  WILLIAM O. WHITE        3/10/79
00130*
00140 COMMON CONMAT(20,20), NOCON(300,20)
00150 INTEGER CONMAT(20,20), NOCON(300,20), CONFLIC(20,20)
00160 INTEGER TABLE1(20,20), TABLE2(20,20), IT(20)
00170*
00180 CALL INITIAL
00190*
00200 CALL HEADING
00210*
00220* READ THE INPUT MICRORDERS INTO MATRIX 'CONFLIC'
00230*
00240 DO 10 I = 1,20
00250    READ 110,(CONFLIC(I,J),J = 1,20)
00260    IF (CONFLIC(I,1).EQ.09) GOTO 12
00270 10 CONTINUE
00280 110 FORMAT (20I1)
00290*
00300* TRANSFER MICRORDERS INTO MATRIX 'CONMAT' USING THE CORRECT CI
00310*
00320 12  I = 0
00330 15  I = I + 1
00340 20  DO 25 J = 1,20
00350 25  IF (CONFLIC(I,J).EQ.1) GO TO 30
00360     IF (I.NE.20) GO TO 15
00370     GO TO 40
00380 30  DO 33 K = 1,20
00390 33  IF (CONFLIC(I,K).NE.0) CONMAT(K,J) = CONFLIC(I,K)
00400     IF (I.NE.0) GO TO 15
00410 40  DO 45 I = 1,20
00420        DO 44 J = 1,20
00430           IF (CONMAT(J,I).NE.0) CONMAT(J,J) = 1
00440 44     CONTINUE
00450 45 CONTINUE
00460*
00470* FIND CI'S THAT DON'T CONFLICT
00480*
00490     KFLAG = 9
00500     JFLAG = 9
00510     IFLAG = 0
00520     M = 1
00530     N = 1
00540 50  IF (M+N.EQ.20) GO TO 60
00550     DO 55 I = 1,20
00560        IF ((CONMAT(I,M).EQ.1).AND.(CONMAT(I,M+N).EQ.1)) IFLAG = 9
00570        IF (CONMAT(I,M).EQ.1) JFLAG = 0
00580 55     IF (CONMAT(I,M+N).EQ.1) KFLAG = 0
00590     IF((IFLAG.EQ.0).AND.(JFLAG.EQ.0).AND.(KFLAG.EQ.0))CALL COMBINE(M,M+N)
00600     IFLAG = 0
00610     JFLAG = 9
00620     KFLAG = 9
00630     N = N + 1
00640     GO TO 50
```

```
00650 60   IF (M.EQ.19) GO TO 80
00660      M = M + 1
00670      N = 1
00680      GO TO 50
00690*
00700* LOOK FOR MCC'S THAT ARE SUBSETS TO OTHER MCC'S
00710*
00720 80   IFLAG = 0
00730      JFLAG = 0
00740      DO 90 I = 1,300
00750 90   IF (NOCON(I,1).EQ.0) GO TO 91
00760 91   N = I - 2
00770 92   DO 95 J = 1,N
00780         DO 94 K = 1,20
00790            DO 93 L = 1,20
00800 93            IF (NOCON(N+1,K).EQ.NOCON(J,L)) IFLAG = 9
00810         IF (IFLAG.EQ.0) JFLAG = 9
00820         IFLAG = 0
00830 94      CONTINUE
00840      IF (JFLAG.EQ.0) GO TO 150
00850      JFLAG = 0
00860 95   CONTINUE
00870 96   N = N - 1
00880      IF (N.EQ.1) GO TO 97
00890      GO TO 92
00900 97   CONTINUE
00919 GO TO 115
00920 150 DO 155 M = 1,20
00921 155 NOCON(N+1,M) = 0
00922      GO TO 96
00930*
00940* COMPACT MCC ARRAY
00950*
00960 115 IM = 1
00970      DO 117 J = 1,20
00980         DO 116 K = 1,20
00990 116 IF (NOCON(J,1).NE.0) CONMAT(IM,K) = NOCON(J,K)
01000      IF (NOCON(J,1).NE.0) IM = IM + 1
01010 117 CONTINUE
01020      DO 120 J = IM,20
01030         DO 121 K = 1,20
01040 121    CONMAT(J,K) = 0
01050 120  CONTINUE
01060      PRINT 129
01070 129  FORMAT ("MCC #",4X,"MICRORDERS")
01080      DO 118 J = 1,20
01090 118  PRINT 132,J,(CONMAT(J,K),K = 1,20)
01100 132  FORMAT (2X,I2,3X,20I3.0)
01110      DO 170 J = 1,20
01120         DO 169 K = 1,20
01130            IF (CONMAT(J,K).EQ.0) GO TO 169
01140               DO 168 L = 1,20
01150 168            IF (TABLE1(L,CONMAT(J,K)).EQ.0) GO TO 180
01160 169      CONTINUE
01170 170  CONTINUE
01180      GO TO 190
01190 180  TABLE1 (L,CONMAT(J,K)) = J
01200      GO TO 169
```

```
01210 190   PRINT 191
01220 191   FORMAT (5X,"COVER TABLE")
01230       PRINT 192,(JJ,JJ = 1,20)
01240 192   FORMAT (20I3)
01250       PRINT 193
01260 193   FORMAT (" ")
01270       DO 200 J = 1,20
01275 194   FORMAT (20I3.0)
01280 200   PRINT 194,(TABLE1(J,K),K = 1,20)
01290*
01300* MAKE REDUCED COVER TALBE
01310*
01320       DO 201 I = 1,20
01330         DO 202 J = 1,20
01340 202    IF (CONMAT(J,I).NE.0) IFLAG = 9
01350         IF (IFLAG.EQ.0) GO TO 203
01360 201   IFLAG = 0
01370 203   IM = 1
01380 204   DO 205 J = 1,20
01390         IF ((TABLE1(1,J).NE.0).AND.(TABLE1(2,J).EQ.0)) GO TO 210
01400 205   CONTINUE
01410       GO TO 220
01420 210   TABLE2(IM) = TABLE1(1,J)
01430       DO 215 K = 1,I
01440         IF (CONMAT(TABLE1(1,J),K).EQ.0) GOTO 215
01450           DO 214 L = 1,I
01460 214       TABLE1(L,CONMAT(TABLE1(1,J))) = 0
01470 215   CONTINUE
01480       IM = IM + 1
01490       GO TO 205
01500 220   PRINT 221
01510 221   FORMAT (5X,"REDUCED COVER TABLE")
01520       PRINT 192,(JJ,JJ=1,20)
01530       PRINT 193
01540       DO 225 J = 1,20
01550 225   PRINT 194,(TABLE1(J,K),K = 1,20)
01560*
01570* FIND A MINIMAL SOLUTION
01580*
01590       IBIG = 0
01600 240 DO 250 J = 1,I
01610         DO 245 K = 1,20
01620           DO 243 L = 1,20
01630 243      IF (TABLE1(J,K).EQ.L) IT(L) = IT(L) + 1
01640 245     CONTINUE
01650 250 CONTINUE
01660       DO 260 J = 1,20
01670 260 IF (IT(J).GT.IBIG) IBIG = J
01680       TABLE2 (IM) = IBIG
01690       DO 270 J = 1,I
01700         IF (CONMAT(IBIG,J).EQ.0) GOTO 270
01710           DO 265 K = 1,I
01720             TABLE1(K,CONMAT(IBIG,J)) = 0
01730 265     CONTINUE
01740 270 CONTINUE
01750       DO 280 J = 1,I
01760         DO 275 K = 1,20
01770 275    IF (TABLE1(J,K).NE.0) IFLAG = 9
```

```
01780 280 CONTINUE
01790     IF (IFLAG.EQ.0) GO TO 300
01800     DO 290 JJ = 1,20
01810 290 IT(JJ) = 0
01820     IFLAG = 0
01830     IBIG = 0
01840     IM = IM + 1
01850     GO TO 240
01860 300 PRINT 410
01870 410 FORMAT ("A SOLUTION")
01880     PRINT 425,(TABLE2(I),I = 1,20)
01890 425 FORMAT(20I3.0)
01900 STOP
01910 END
01920 SUBROUTINE INITIAL
01930 COMMON CONMAT(20,20), NOCON(300,20), CONFLIC(20,20)
01940 INTEGER CONMAT(20,20), NOCON(300,20), CONFLIC(20,20)
01950    DO 10 I = 1,20
01960       DO 9 J = 1,20
01970          CONFLIC(I,J) = 0
01980          CONMAT(I,J) = 0
01990 9   CONTINUE
02000 10 CONTINUE
02010    DO 20 I = 1,300
02020       DO 19 J = 1,20
02030 19   NOCON(I,J) = 0
02040 20 CONTINUE
02050 RETURN
02060 END
02070 SUBROUTINE HEADING
02080 PRINT 100
02090 PRINT 101
02100 PRINT 102
02110 PRINT 103
02120 PRINT 104
02130 PRINT 105
02140 PRINT 102
02150 PRINT 106
02160 PRINT 107
02170 PRINT 108
02180 PRINT 102
02190 PRINT 104
02200 100 FORMAT("INSTRUCTIONS: YOU CAN INPUT MICROCODE UP TO TWENTY LINES")
02210 101 FORMAT("AND NO MORE THAN TWENTY COLUMNS, IN THE FOLLOWING FORMAT:")
02220 102 FORMAT(" ")
02230 103 FORMAT("EX.",6X,"COLUMNS")
02240 104 FORMAT(2X,"1          THRU      20")
02250 105 FORMAT(2X,"10000101010111100101")
02260 106 FORMAT("PLEASE INPUT YOUR MICROCODE WITH NO SPACES BETWEEN ONE'S")
02270 107 FORMAT("AND ZERO'S. A INPUT OF 797 WILL TERMINATE INPUT SEQUENCE OR")
02280 108 FORMAT("WHEN A LIMIT OF TWENTY LINES IS REACHED.")
02290 RETURN
02300 END
02310 SUBROUTINE COMBINE(I,J)
02320 COMMON CONMAT(20,20), NOCON(300,20)
```

```
02330 INTEGER CONMAT(20,20), NOCON(300,20), FLAG, ATTACH
02340     FLAG = 0
02350     ATTACH = 0
02360     IF (NOCON(1,1).NE.0) GO TO 10
02370     NOCON(1,1) = I
02380     NOCON(1,2) = J
02390     RETURN
02400 10  DO 15 K = 1,300
02410 15  IF (NOCON(K,1).EQ.I) GO TO 30
02420     DO 17 K = 1,300
02430 17  IF (NOCON(K,1).EQ.0) GO TO 20
02440     RETURN
02450 20  NOCON(K,1) = I
02460     NOCON(K,2) = J
02470     RETURN
02480 30  DO 40 L = 2,20
02490        IF (NOCON(K,L).NE.0) GO TO 60
02500        IF (NOCON(K,L).EQ.0) GO TO 42
02510 40  CONTINUE
02520 42  IF (FLAG.EQ.0) GO TO 70
02530 43  FLAG = 0
02540     IF (NOCON(K+1,1).NE.NOCON(K,1)) GO TO 80
02550     K = K + 1
02560     GO TO 30
02570 60  DO 65 M = 1,20
02580 65  IF ((CONMAT(M,NOCON(K,L)).EQ.1).AND.(CONMAT(M,J).EQ.1)) FLAG = 9
02590     GO TO 40
02600 70  NOCON(K,L) = J
02610     ATTACH = 9
02620     GO TO 43
02630 80  IF (ATTACH.EQ.9) RETURN
02640     NOCON(K+1,1) = I
02650     NOCON(K+1,2) = J
02660     RETURN
02670 END
READY.
```

APPENDIX A: Program A.2

```
PROGRAM CONFLICTDIA (INPUT, OUTPUT) ;

   (*******************************************************************
    *                                                                 *
    *  THIS PROGRAM CONSTRUCTS A CONFLICT DIAGRAM OF A MICROPROGRAM.   *
    *  IT THEN TAKES THIS DIAGRAM AND PUTS IT INTO COMPATIBILITY       *
    *  CLASSES. THESE CLASSES ARE THEN PUT INTO DECODERS, MAXIMUM OF   *
    *  THREE TO EIGHT DECODER)  AS EACH OF THESE DECODERS ARE BUILT,   *
    *  THEY ARE ENCODED.  THE WORDS FROM THE MICROPROGRAM ARE THEN     *
    *  RECORDED INTO MICROINSTRUCTIONS USING THE ENCODING FROM THE     *
    *  DECODERS.                                                       *
    *                                                                 *
    *      PROGRAMMED BY KAELEEN NORRIS                                *
    *                                                                 *
    *                                                                 *
    *                                                                 *
       *********************************************************)

   TYPE TOTALSET = SET OF 1..20 ;
        CONFLICTREC = RECORD MORDER : INTEGER ;
                            COUNT  : INTEGER ;
                            AVAIL  : BOOLEAN
                     END ;
        CONFLICTDIAGRAM = ARRAY [1..20] OF TOTALSET ;
        MICROPROGRAM = ARRAY [1..20, 1..20] OF INTEGER ;
        ARRAYDECODER = ARRAY [1..20, 1..8] OF INTEGER ;
        CHARARRAY    = ARRAY [1..3] OF CHAR ;
        ARRAYMI      = ARRAY [1..8, 1..3] OF CHAR ;
        ARRAYCONFLIC = ARRAY [1..20] OF CONFLICTREC ;

   VAR MPROGRAM : MICROPROGRAM ;
       DIAGRAM : CONFLICTDIAGRAM ;
       DECODER    : ARRAYDECODER ;
       CONFLICTCNT : ARRAYCONFLIC ;
       NUMWORDS, NUMMORDERS, DECODERCNT, MICOUNT : INTEGER ;
       INDEX1, INDEX2 : INTEGER ;


   PROCEDURE COMPATIBILITIES (CONFLICTCNT : ARRAYCONFLIC ; VAR DECODER :
                             ARRAYDECODER ; NUMMORDERS : INTEGER ;
                             VAR DECODERCNT : INTEGER ; DIAGRAM :
                             CONFLICTDIAGRAM) ;

      (* THIS PROCEDURE FINDS THE MICRO-ORDERS THAT ARE COMPATIBLE   *
       * AND PUTS THEM IN THE DECODER ARRAY.                         *)

     VAR INDEX, INDEX1, COUNT, CHECKER : INTEGER ;
         INDEX2 : INTEGER ;
         MOREDATA : BOOLEAN ;
```

```
BEGIN (* PROCEDURE COMPATIBILITIES *)
  FOR INDEX := 2 TO NUMMORDERS DO
    CONFLICTCNT[INDEX].AVAIL := TRUE ;
  INDEX := 1 ;
  DECODERCNT := 1 ;
  CHECKER := CONFLICTCNT[INDEX].MORDER ;
  INDEX1 := INDEX + 1 ;
  MOREDATA := TRUE ;
  WHILE MOREDATA AND (NOT (INDEX1 > NUMMORDERS)) DO
    BEGIN (* ACTUAL PROCESSING *)
      COUNT := 2 ;
      DECODER[DECODERCNT, 1] := CHECKER ;
      REPEAT
        IF NOT (CONFLICTCNT[INDEX1].MORDER IN DIAGRAM[CHECKER]) THEN
          IF CONFLICTCNT[INDEX1].AVAIL THEN
            BEGIN (* SET UP DECODER *)
              CONFLICTCNT[INDEX1].AVAIL := FALSE ;
              FOR INDEX2 := 1 TO NUMMORDERS DO
                IF INDEX2 IN DIAGRAM[CONFLICTCNT[INDEX1].MORDER] THEN
                  IF NOT (INDEX2 IN DIAGRAM [CHECKER]) THEN
                    DIAGRAM[CHECKER] := DIAGRAM[CHECKER] + [INDEX2] ;
                DECODER[DECODERCNT, COUNT] := CONFLICTCNT[INDEX1].MORDER ;
                COUNT := COUNT + 1
            END ; (* SET UP DECODER *)
          INDEX1 := INDEX1 + 1 ;
      UNTIL (COUNT = 8) OR (INDEX1 > NUMMORDERS) ;
      MOREDATA := FALSE ;
      FOR INDEX1 := INDEX TO NUMMORDERS DO
        IF CONFLICTCNT[INDEX1].AVAIL THEN
          MOREDATA := TRUE ;
      INDEX := INDEX + 1 ;
      WHILE NOT CONFLICTCNT[INDEX].AVAIL AND NOT(INDEX > NUMMORDERS) DO
        INDEX := INDEX + 1 ;
      IF NOT (INDEX > NUMMORDERS) THEN
      BEGIN
        CHECKER := CONFLICTCNT[INDEX].MORDER ;
        DECODERCNT := DECODERCNT + 1 ;
        INDEX1 := INDEX + 1
      END
    END (* ACTUAL PROCESSING *)
END ; (* PROCEDURE COMPATIBILITIES *)

PROCEDURE WRITEOUT (NUMWORDS, NUMMORDERS : INTEGER ; MPROGRAM : MICROPROGRAM ;
                    DECODERCNT : INTEGER ; DECODER : ARRAYDECODER) ;

  (* THIS PROCEDURE WRITES OUT ALL OF THE TABLES *)

  TYPE LINEARRAY = ARRAY [1..20, 1..40] OF CHAR ;

  VAR COLUMNCOUNT, INDEX, INDEX1 : INTEGER ;
      LINE      : LINEARRAY ;
      LINECOUNT : INTEGER ;
```

```
PROCEDURE CONVERTBIN (NUMCHARS : INTEGER ; VAR MINSTRUCT : ARRAYMI ;
                      CODE, MICOUNT : INTEGER) ;

    (* THIS PROCEDURE PUTS THE ENCODED VALUES INTO CHARACTER VALUES *)

  VAR INDEX : INTEGER ;

  BEGIN (* PROCEDURE CONVERTBIN *)
    FOR INDEX := NUMCHARS DOWNTO 1 DO
      BEGIN (* CONVERSION *)
        MINSTRUCT [MICOUNT, INDEX] %= CHR(ORD(#O#) + (CODE MOD 2)) ;
        CODE := CODE DIV 2
      END (* CONVERSION *)
  END ; (* PROCEDURE CONVERTBIN *)

PROCEDURE ENCODING (COUNT, INDEX : INTEGER ; DECODER : ARRAYDECODER ;
                    VAR LINE : LINEARRAY ;
                    NUMWORDS, COLUMNCOUNT : INTEGER) ;

    (* THIS PROCEDURE DOES THE ENCODING AND WRITING SEQUENCE *)

  VAR INDEX1, LINECOUNT, MICOUNT : INTEGER ;
      INDEX2 : INTEGER ;
    MINSTRUCT : ARRAYMI ;

  BEGIN (* PROCEDURE ENCODING *)
    MICOUNT := 1 ;
    WRITELN (OUTPUT, #O DECODER #, INDEX : 2) ;
    IF COUNT = 3 THEN
    WRITELN (OUTPUT, # OOO    NOP#)
    ELSE WRITELN (OUTPUT, # OO    NOP#) ;
    WHILE DECODER[INDEX, MICOUNT] <> O DO
      BEGIN (* MAJOR PROCESSING *)
        CONVERTBIN (COUNT, MINSTRUCT, MICOUNT, MICOUNT) ;
        WRITE (OUTPUT, # #) ;
        FOR INDEX1 := 1 TO COUNT DO
          WRITE (OUTPUT, MINSTRUCT[MICOUNT, INDEX1]) ;
        WRITELN (OUTPUT, #    #, DECODER[INDEX, MICOUNT] : 2) ;
        FOR LINECOUNT := 1 TO NUMWORDS DO
          IF MPROGRAM[LINECOUNT, DECODER[INDEX, MICOUNT]]= 1 THEN
                (* SETTING UP MICROINSTRUCTION *)
              FOR INDEX1 := O TO (COUNT - 1) DO
                LINE[LINECOUNT, COLUMNCOUNT + INDEX1] :=
                      MINSTRUCT[MICOUNT, INDEX1 + 1] ;
        MICOUNT := MICOUNT + 1
      END ; (* MAJOR RPOCESSING *)
    FOR INDEX1 := 1 TO NUMWORDS DO
      IF LINE[INDEX1, COLUMNCOUNT] = # # THEN
            (* PUT NOP"S IN THE REST OF THE PLACES *)
          FOR INDEX2 := O TO (COUNT - 1) DO
            LINE[INDEX1, COLUMNCOUNT + INDEX2] := #O#
  END ; (* PROCEDURE ENCODING *)
```

```
BEGIN (* PROCEDURE WRITEOUT *)
  COLUMNCOUNT := 1 ;
  FOR INDEX := 1 TO 20 DO
    FOR INDEX1 := 1 TO 20 DO
      LINE [INDEX, INDEX1] := # # ;
  WRITELN (OUTPUT, #O ROM#) ;
  FOR INDEX := 1 TO NUMWORDS DO
    BEGIN (* WRITE OUT ORIGINAL MICROPROGRAM *)
      WRITE (OUTPUT, # #, INDEX : 2, # #) ;
      FOR INDEX1 := 1 TO NUMMORDERS DO
        WRITE (OUTPUT, MPROGRAM[INDEX, INDEX1] : 2) ;
      WRITELN (OUTPUT)
    END ; (* WRITE OUT  ORIGINAL MOCROPROGRAM *)
  FOR INDEX := 1 TO DECODERCNT DO
    BEGIN (* DO ENCODING AND WRITING OF DECODERS *)
      IF DECODER[INDEX, 2] = O THEN
        BEGIN (* DECODER HAS ONLY ONE ELEMENT *)
          WRITELN (OUTPUT, #O DECODER #, INDEX: 2) ;
          WRITELN (OUTPUT, # 1   #, DECODER[INDEX, 1] : 2) ;
          FOR LINECOUNT := 1 TO NUMWORDS DO
            BEGIN   SET UP MICROINSTRUCTIONS *)
              IF MPROGRAM[LINECOUNT, DECODER[INDEX, 1]] = 1
                THEN LINE[LINECOUNT, COLUMNCOUNT] := #1#
                ELSE LINE[LINECOUNT, COLUMNCOUNT] := #O# ;
              LINE[LINECOUNT, COLUMNCOUNT + 1] := # # ;
              LINE[LINECOUNT, COLUMNCOUNT + 2] := # # ;
            END ; (* SET UP MICROINSTRUCTIONS *)
          COLUMNCOUNT := COLUMNCOUNT + 3
        END (* DECODER HAS ONLY ONE ELEMENT *)
      ELSE IF DECODER[INDEX, 4] = O THEN
        BEGIN (* 2 TO 4 DECODER NEEDED *)
          ENCODING (2, INDEX, DECODER, LINE, NUMWORDS,
                      COLUMNCOUNT) ;
          COLUMNCOUNT := COLUMNCOUNT + 4
        END   (* 2 TO 4 DECODER NEEDED *)
      ELSE
        BEGIN (* 3 TO 8 DECODER NEEDED *)
          ENCODING (3, INDEX, DECODER, LINE, NUMWORDS,
                      COLUMNCOUNT) ;
          COLUMNCOUNT := COLUMNCOUNT + 5
        END (* 3 TO 8 DECODER NEEDED *)
    END ; (* DO ENCODING AND WRITING OF DECODERS *)
  WRITELN (OUTPUT, #O ENCODED ROM#) ;
  FOR INDEX := 1 TO NUMWORDS DO
    BEGIN
      WRITE (OUTPUT, # #) ;
      FOR INDEX2:= 1 TO (COLUMNCOUNT - 1) DO
        WRITE (OUTPUT, LINE[INDEX, INDEX2]) ;
      WRITELN (OUTPUT) ;
    END
END ; (* PROCEDURE WRITEOUT *)
```

```
BEGIN (* PROGRAM CONFLICTDIA *)
  REPEAT
    FOR INDEX1 := 1 TO 20 DO
      FOR INDEX2 := 1 TO 8 DO
        DECODER [INDEX1, INDEX2] := 0 ;
    READ (INPUT, NUMWORDS, NUMMORDERS) ;
    FOR INDEX1 := 1 TO NUMWORDS DO
     BEGIN
      FOR INDEX2 := 1 TO NUMMORDERS DO
        READ (INPUT, MPROGRAM[INDEX1, INDEX2]) ;
      READLN (INPUT)
     END ;
    FINDCONFLICTS (MPROGRAM, DIAGRAM, NUMWORDS, NUMMORDERS, CONFLICTCNT) ;
    COMPATIBILITIES (CONFLICTCNT, DECODER, NUMMORDERS, DECODERCNT,
                     DIAGRAM) ;
    WRITEOUT (NUMWORDS, NUMMORDERS, MPROGRAM, DECODERCNT, DECODER) ;
  UNTIL EOF(INPUT)
 END. (* PROGRAM CONFLICTDIA *)
4 7  0 0 1 0 1 0 0
0 0 1 1 1 0 0
0 1 1 0 1 0 0
0 1 1 1 1 0 0
9 7 0 0 1 0 1 0 0
0 0 1 1 1 0 0
0 1 0 0 1 1 0
0 1 0 0 1 1 1
0 1 1 0 1 0 0
0 1 1 1 1 0 0
1 1 0 0 1 1 0
1 1 0 0 1 1 1
1 1 1 1 1 1 1
12 6 0 0 0 1 1 0
0 0 1 0 0 1
0 0 1 1 0 1
0 1 0 0 1 0
0 1 0 0 1 1
0 1 1 0 0 1
0 1 1 0 1 1
0 1 1 1 0 1
1 0 1 0 0 1
1 0 1 1 0 1
1 1 1 0 0 1
1 1 1 1 0 1
READY.
```

APPENDIX B: Program B.1

```
PROGRAM MAXCOMPCLASS (INPUT,OUTPUT);
(**********************************************************************)
(*           LYNN SHIMANUKI                                          *)
(*           MAXIMAL COMPATIBILITY CLASSES                           *)
(* INPUT DATA:  FIRST CARD - NUMBER MICROINSTRUCTIONS, NUMBER MICRO-ORDERS *)
(*              ONE CARD PER MI - NUMBER MOS, EACH MO                *)
(**********************************************************************)
CONST SP5 = #    #;
      MAXMO = 20;   (*MAXIMUM NUMBER OF MICRO-ORDERS*)
      MAXMI = 20;   (*MAXIMUM NUMBER OF MICROINSTRUCTIONS*)
TYPE AROINT = ARRAY [1..MAXMO] OF INTEGER;
     SOINT = SET OF O..MAXMO;
     AROS = ARRAY [1..MAXMO] OF SOINT;
     MIREC = RECORD NUMMO :. INTEGER;
                    MO : AROINT;
             END;
     MIARR = ARRAY [1..MAXMI] OF MIREC;
     CTREC = RECORD NUMCT : INTEGER;
                    CT : AROINT;
                    CTSET : SOINT;
             END;
     CTARR = ARRAY [1..MAXMO] OF CTREC;
VAR MI : MIARR;
    COVTAB : CTARR;
    MCC,CSSLIST : AROS;
    TOTMI,TOTMO,TOTMCC,TOTCSS: INTEGER;
    TOTSET,COVERED,SOLSET,REDSET : SOINT;

(*==================================================================*)
PROCEDURE PRINTLINE(VAR PUTOUT:TEXT; TOTMO:INTEGER; SYMBOL:CHAR);
    (*** PRINTS A LINE OF SYMBOL. ***)
 VAR I:INTEGER;
   BEGIN  (* PRINTLINE *)
   IF SYMBOL=#_#
     THEN WRITE(PUTOUT,#+#)
     ELSE WRITE(PUTOUT,# #);
   FOR I:=1 TO (TOTMO*5) DO  WRITE(PUTOUT,SYMBOL);
   WRITELN(PUTOUT);
   IF SYMBOL=#=# THEN WRITELN(PUTOUT,#O#);
   END;   (* PRINTLINE *)

(*==================================================================*)
PROCEDURE READMI(VAR PUTIN,PUTOUT:TEXT; VAR MI:MIARR; VAR TOTMI,TOTMO:INTEGER;
                                             VAR TOTSET:SOINT);
    (*** READS AND PRINTS MICROINSTRUCTIONS. ***)
 VAR I,J:INTEGER;
   BEGIN  (* READIN *)
   READLN(PUTIN,TOTMI,TOTMO);
   WRITELN(PUTOUT,#1     MI     MICRO-ORDERS#);
   PRINTLINE(PUTOUT,TOTMO,# #);
   FOR I:=1 TO TOTMI DO  WITH MI[I] DO
      BEGIN (*MICROINSTRUCTIONS*)
      READ(PUTIN,NUMMO);
      WRITE(PUTOUT,SP5,I:2,SP5,#(#);
      FOR J:=1 TO NUMMO DO
         BEGIN (*READ IN MICRO-ORDERS*)
         READ(PUTIN,MO[J]);
         WRITE(PUTOUT,MO[J]:3);
         END;  (*MOS*)
      READLN(PUTIN);
      WRITELN(PUTOUT,#  )#);
      END;   (*MIS*)
   PRINTLINE(PUTOUT,TOTMO,#=#);
   TOTSET:=[];
   FOR I:=1 TO TOTMO DO  TOTSET:=TOTSET+[I];
   END;   (* READMI *)
```

332

```
(*========================================================================*)
PROCEDURE GETMCCS(VAR MCC:AROS; VAR NUMMCC:INTEGER; MI:MIARR; TOTSET:SOINT;
                                              TOTMI,TOTMONTEGER);
     (*** FINDS MAXIMUM COMPATIBLE CLASSES. ***)
 VAR NOCON:AROS;
     EMPTYSET:SOINT;
     I,J,KNTEGER;

PROCEDURE TESTCLASS(CLASS:SOINT);
     (*** TESTS IF CLASS ALREADY IN LIST, ADDS IF NOT. ***)
 VAR TEST:BOOLEAN;
     I:INTEGER;
     (*GLOBAL:  NUMMCC,MCC *)
  BEGIN  (*TESTCLASS *)
  TEST:=TRUE;
  FOR I:=1 TO NUMMCC DO
     IF CLASS=MCC[I] THEN TEST:=FALSE;
  IF TEST
   THEN BEGIN (*ADD TO LIST*)
        NUMMCC:=NUMMCC+1;
        MCC[NUMMCC]:=CLASS;
        END;  (*ADD*)
  END;   (* TESTCLASS *)

PROCEDURE GENERATEMCC(CLASS,COMSET:SOINT; NOCON:AROS; TOTMO:INTEGER);
     (*** RECURSIVE PROCEDURE THAT GENERATES MCCS. ***)
 VAR NEWCLASS,NEWCOM:SOINT;
     I:INTEGER;
  BEGIN  (* GENERATEMCC *)
  FOR I:=1 TO TOTMO DO
     IF (I IN COMSET) AND NOT(I IN CLASS)
       THEN BEGIN
            NEWCLASS:=CLASS+[I];
            NEWCOM:=COMSET*NOCON[I];
            IF NEWCLASS=NEWCOM
             THEN TESTCLASS(NEWCLASS)
             ELSE GENERATEMCC(NEWCLASS,NEWCOM,NOCON,TOTMO);
            END;
  END;   (* GENERATEMCC *)


  BEGIN  (* GETMCCS *)
  FOR I:=1 TO TOTMO DO  NOCON[I]:=TOTSET;
  FOR I:=1 TO TOTMI DO  WITH MI[I] DO
     FOR J:=1 TO NUMMO DO
        BEGIN (*FIND NO-CONFLICT SET FOR EACH MICRO-ORDER*)
        FOR K:=1 TO NUMMO DO  NOCON[MO[J]]:=NOCON[MO[J]]-[MO[K]];
        NOCON[MO[J]]:=NOCON[MO[J]]+[MO[J]];
        END;  (*NO-CONFLICTS*)
  NUMMCC:=O;
  EMPTYSET:=[];
  FOR I:=1 TO TOTMO DO
     GENERATEMCC(EMPTYSET,NOCON[I],NOCON,TOTMO);
  END;   (* GETMCCS *)
```

```
(*----------------------------------------------------------------------------*)

PROCEDURE PRINTMCCS(VAR PUTOUT:TEXT; MCC:AROS; TOTMO,TOTMCC:INTEGER);
    (*** PRINTS MAXIMUM COMPATIBLE CLASSES. ***)
 VAR I,J:INTEGER;
   BEGIN  (* PRINTMCCS *)
   WRITELN(PUTOUT,#O        MAXIMAL COMPATIBILITY CLASSES#);
   PRINTLINE(PUTOUT,TOTMO,#_#);
   FOR I:=1 TO TOTMCC DO
      BEGIN (*PRINT MCCS*)
      WRITE(PUTOUT,# C#,I:2,#  =  (#);
      FOR J:=1 TO TOTMO DO
         IF J IN MCC[I] THEN  WRITE(PUTOUT,J:3);
      WRITELN(PUTOUT,#  )#);
      END;  (*PRINT MCC*)
   PRINTLINE(PUTOUT,TOTMO,#=#);
   END;   (* PRINTMCCS *)

(*===========================================================================*)

PROCEDURE PRINTTABLE(VAR PUTOUT:TEXT; CURSET:SOINT; COVTAB:CTARR;
                                         TOTMO:INTEGER);
    (*** PRINTS COVER TABLE. ***)
 VAR DONE:BOOLEAN;
    I,LINE:INTEGER;
   BEGIN  (* PRINTCT *)
   PRINTLINE(PUTOUT,TOTMO,#_#);
   FOR I:=1 TO TOTMO DO
      IF I IN CURSET THEN  WRITE(PUTOUT,I:5);
   WRITELN(PUTOUT);
   PRINTLINE(PUTOUT,TOTMO,#_#);
   LINE:=O;
   REPEAT
      LINE:=LINE+1;
      DONE:=TRUE;
      FOR I:=1 TO TOTMO DO  WITH COVTAB[I] DO
         IF I IN CURSET
         THEN IF NUMCT>=LINE
           THEN BEGIN (*PRINT MCC OF MO*)
                WRITE(PUTOUT,#  C#,CT[LINE]:2);
                DONE:=FALSE;
                END   (*PRINT MCC*)
           ELSE WRITE(PUTOUT,SP5);
      WRITELN(PUTOUT);
   UNTIL DONE;
   PRINTLINE(PUTOUT,TOTMO,#=#);
   END;   (* PRINTCT *)
```

```
(*--------------------------------------------------------------------------*)

PROCEDURE COVERTABLE(VAR COVTAB:CTARR; VAR REDSET,COVERED,SOLSET:SOINT;
        VAR PUTOUT:TEXT; TOTSET:SOINT; MCC:AROS; TOTMO,TOTMCC:INTEGER);
    (*** CREATES COVER TABLE AND REDUCED COVER TABLE. ***)
 VAR I,J:INTEGER;
   BEGIN (* COVERTABLE *)
   COVERED:=[];   SOLSET:=[];
   FOR I:=1 TO TOTMO DO  WITH COVTAB[I] DO
     BEGIN (*EACH MO*)
     CTSET:=[];  NUMCT:=0;
     FOR J:=1 TO TOTMCC DO
         IF I IN MCC[J]
         THEN BEGIN (*FIND ALL MCCS THAT CONTAIN MO*)
                 NUMCT:=NUMCT+1;
                 CT[NUMCT]:=J;
                 CTSET:=CTSET+[J];
                 END;  (*FIND MCCS*)
     IF (NUMCT=1) AND NOT(CT[1] IN SOLSET)
       THEN BEGIN (*NOTE MOS COVERED BY SINGLE MCC*)
             COVERED:=COVERED+MCC[CT[1]];
             SOLSET:=SOLSET+[CT[1]];
             END;  (*NOTE MOS*)
     END;  (*EACH MO*)
   REDSET:=TOTSET-COVERED;
   WRITELN PUTOUT,#O     COVER TABLE#);
   PRINTTABLE(PUTOUT,TOTSET,COVTAB,TOTMO);
   WRITELN(PUTOUT,#O     REDUCED COVER TABLE#);
   PRINTTABLE(PUTOUT,REDSET,COVTAB,TOTMO);
   END;  (* COVERTABLE*)

(*========================================================================*)

PROCEDURE GETRCTCOMBOS(VAR RSSLIST:AROS; VAR NUMRSS:INTEGER; COVTAB:CTARR;
                       ..CC:AROS; REDSET,TOTSET,COVERED,SOLSET:SOINT);
    (*** FINDS ALL COMPLETE SOLUTION SETS. ***)
 VAR COUNT:AROINT;
     AVAIL,RSS,NOCOV:SOINT;
     I,J,START:INTEGER;


PROCEDURE CHECK(NEWRSS:SOINT);
    (*** IF NEWRSS IS NOT ALREADY IN SOLUTION SET, ADDS TO LIST. ***)
 VAR ALREADYIN:BOOLEAN;
     I:INTEGER;
     (*GLOBALS:  RSSLIST,NUMRSS *)
   BEGIN  (* CHECK *)
   ALREADYIN:=FALSE;
   FOR I:=1 TO NUMRSS DO
     IF NEWRSS=RSSLIST[I] THEN  ALREADYIN:=TRUE;
   IF NOT(ALREADYIN)
     THEN BEGIN (*ADD TO LIST*)
         NUMRSS:=NUMRSS+1;
         RSSLIST[NUMRSS]:=NEWRSS;
         END;  (*ADD*)
   END;  (* CHECK *)
```

```
FUNCTION FINDMCC(I:INTEGER; CURAVAIL:SOINT):INTEGER;
    (*** GETS NEXT MCC OF MICRO-ORDER I. ***)
    (* GLOBAL:  COVTAB,COUNT *)
  BEGIN  (* FINDMCC *)
  WITH COVTAB[I] DO
    BEGIN (*GET NEXT MCC THAT CONTAINS MO*)
    REPEAT
       COUNT[I]:=COUNT[I]+1;
    UNTIL (CT[COUNT[I]] IN CURAVAIL) OR (COUNT[I]>NUMCT);
    IF COUNT[I]>NUMCT
     THEN FINDMCC:=O
     ELSE FINDMCC:=CT[COUNT[I]];
    END; (*GET NEXT MCC*)
  END;   (* FINDMCC *)


PROCEDURE GETRSS(I:INTEGER; CURRSS,CURNOCOV,CURAVAIL:SOINT);
    (*** RECURSIVE PROCEDURE THAT FINDS PARTIAL SOLUTIONS. ***)
 VAR NEWRSS,NEWNOCOV,NEWAVAIL:SOINT;
     NEWMCC:INTEGER;
     (*GLOBAL:  REDSET,COVTAB,COUNT *)
  BEGIN  (* GETRSS *)
  IF CURNOCOV<>[]
   THEN BEGIN (*FIND COMBO*)
        I:=I+1;
        WHILE NOT((I IN REDSET) AND (I IN CURNOCOV)) DO  I:=I+1;
        REPEAT (*AT EACH LEVEL*)
           NEWMCC:=FINDMCC(I,CURAVAIL);
           IF NEWMCC<>O
            THEN BEGIN (*TAKE ONE PATH*)
                 NEWNOCOV:=CURNOCOV-MCC[NEWMCC];
                 NEWRSS:=CURRSS+[NEWMCC];
                 NEWAVAIL:=CURAVAIL-COVTAB[I].CTSET;
                 IF NEWNOCOV=[]
                  THEN CHECK(NEWRSS)
                  ELSE GETRSS(I,NEWRSS,NEWNOCOV,NEWAVAIL);
                 END; (*PATH*)
        UNTIL NEWMCC=O;
        COUNT[I]:=O;
        END;  (*COMBO*)
     END;   (* GETRSS *)


  BEGIN  (* GETRCTCOMBOS *)
  AVAIL:=[];
  FOR I:=1 TO TOTMO DO
     IF I IN REDSET  THEN WITH COVTAB[I] DO
     BEGIN (*INITIALIZE*)
     COUNT[I]:=O;
     FOR J:=1 TO NUMCT DO
        IF NOT(CT[J] IN AVAIL)
        THEN AVAIL:=AVAIL+[CT[J]];
     END; (*INITIALIZE*)
  NUMRSS:=O;  START:=O;
  RSS:=[];
  NOCOV:=TOTSET-COVERED;
  GETRSS(START,RSS,NOCOV,AVAIL);
  IF NUMRSS=O  THEN NUMRSS:=1;
  FOR I:=1 TO NUMRSS DO
     RSSLIST[I]:=RSSLIST[I]+SOLSET;
  END;   (* GETRCTCOMBOS *)
```

```
(*==============================================================================*)

PROCEDURE PRINTLIST(VAR PUTOUT:TEXT; CSSLIST:AROS; TOTMCC,TOTCSS:INTEGER);
    (*** PRINTS LIST OF COMPLETE SOLUTION SETS. ***)
 VAR I,J:INTEGER;
   BEGIN  (* PRINTLIST *)
   WRITELN(PUTOUT,#O      COMPLETE SOLUTIONS#);
   PRINTLINE(PUTOUT,TOTMO,#_#);
   FOR I:=1 TO TOTCSS DO
       BEGIN (*PRINT COMPLETE SOLUTIONS*)
       WRITE(PUTOUT,# SOLUTION#,I:2,#:#);
       FOR J:=1 TO TOTMCC DO
           IF J IN CSSLIST[I]  THEN WRITE(PUTOUT,#  C#,J:2);
       WRITELN(PUTOUT);
       END;  (*PRINT COMPLETE SOLUTIONS*)
   PRINTLINE(PUTOUT,TOTMO,#=#);
   END;  (* PRINTLIST *)

(*----------------------------------------------------------------------------*)

PROCEDURE PRINTSOLTAB(VAR PUTOUT:TEXT; COVTAB:CTARR; MCC,CSSLIST:AROS;
                                                     TOTCSS,TOTMO:INTEGER);
     (*** PRINTS TABLES OF SOLUTIONS. ***)
 VAR DONE:BOOLEAN;
     CTSS:AROS;
     I,J,SOL:INTEGER;
   BEGIN  (*PRINTSOLTAB *)
   FOR SOL:=1 TO TOTCSS DO
   BEGIN (*PRINT ALL SOLUTIONS*)
   WRITELN(PUTOUT,#O      TABLE FOR SOLUTION#,SOL:2);
   PRINTLINE(PUTOUT,TOTMO,#_#);
   FOR I:=1 TO TOTMO DO  WITH COVTAB[I] DO
       BEGIN (*PRINT HEADING*)
       WRITE(PUTOUT,I:5);
       CTSS[I]:=CTSET*CSSLIST[SOL];
       END;
   WRITELN(PUTOUT);
   PRINTLINE(PUTOUT,TOTMO,#_#);
   REPEAT
       DONE:=TRUE;
       FOR I:=1 TO TOTMO DO  WITH COVTAB[I] DO
           IF CTSS[I]=[]
             THEN WRITE(PUTOUT,SP5)
             ELSE BEGIN (*FIND MCC*)
                  J:=1;
                  WHILE NOT(J IN CTSS[I]) DO  J:=J+1;
                  WRITE(PUTOUT,#  C#,J:2);
                  CTSS[I]:=CTSS[I]-[J];
                  DONE:=FALSE;
                  END;  (*MCC*)
       WRITELN(PUTOUT);
   UNTIL DONE;
   WRITELN(PUTOUT);
   END;
   PRINTLINE(PUTOUT,TOTMO,#*#);
   END;  (* PRINTSOLTAB *)
```

338 **Appendix B**

```
(*==========================================================================*)

BEGIN  (* PROGRAM MAXCOMPCLASS *)
WHILE NOT EOF(INPUT) DO
   BEGIN  (*DO PROBLEM*)
   READMI(INPUT,OUTPUT,MI,TOTMI,TOTMO,TOTSET);
   GETMCCS(MCC,TOTMCC,MI,TOTSET,TOTMI,TOTMO);
   PRINTMCCS(OUTPUT,MCC,TOTMO,TOTMCC);
   COVERTABLE(COVTAB,REDSET,COVERED,SOLSET,OUTPUT,TOTSET,MCC,TOTMO,TOTMCC);
   GETRCTCOMBOS(CSSLIST,TOTCSS,COVTAB,MCC,REDSET,TOTSET,COVERED,SOLSET);
   PRINTLIST(OUTPUT,CSSLIST,TOTMCC,TOTCSS);
   PRINTSOLTAB(OUTPUT,COVTAB,MCC,CSSLIST,TOTCSS,TOTMO);
   END;  (*PROBLEM*)
END.  (* PROGRAM MAXCOMPCLASS *)

    5    11
   6    1   2   3   4   5   6
   4    3   7   8   9
   5    1   2   8   9   10
   3    4   8   11
   2    6   8
READY.
```

APPENDIX B: Program B.2

```
00100 PROGRAM CONFLIK (INPUT,OUTPUT)
00110*
00120* WRITTEN BY WILLIAM O. WHITE    3/10/79
00130*
00140* PURPOSE: THIS PROGRAM IS DESIGNED TO REDUCE THE WIDTH OF A
00150*          MICROPROGRAMMED ROM. IT DOES THIS BY BUILDING A
00160*          CONFLICT MATRIX AND THEN PUTTING COMPATIBLE MICRO-
00170*          ORDERS INTO SETS. THESE "SETS" WILL HAVE TO BE EN-
00180*          CODED. A DECODER WILL HAVE TO BE USED TO INTERPRET
00190*          THE ENCODED FIELDS AND TO ACTIVATE THE CORRECT CONTROL
00200*          POINTS.
00210*
00220* INPUT:   THE REQUIRMENTS ARE THAT THE WIDTH OF THE ROM NOT
00230*          EXCEED TWENTY COLUMNS NOT THAT THE LENGTH NOT EXCEED
00240*          TWENTY ROWS. YOU ALSO HAVE THE OPTION OF WHAT TYPE OF
00250*          DECODER TO USE. (I.E. "2 TO 4" "3 TO 8" "4 TO 16")
00260*
00270* OUTPUT:  THE "SETS" OR "FIELDS" OF NON-CONFLICTING MICRORDERS.
00280*          THESE "SETS" WILL BE IN THE CONSTRAINTS OF THE TYPE OF
00290*          DECODER YOU WISH TO USE. IN EACH "SET" THE NUMBER OF
00300*          MICRORDERS WILL BE ONE LESS THAN THE MAXIMUN OUTPUT.
00310*          THIS IS TO ALLOW FOR A "NO-OP".
00320*
00330* SUBROUTINES:
00340*          INITIAL: THIS WILL INITIAL ALL ARRAY'S TO ZERO.
00350*          COMBINE: COMBINES MICRORDERS THAT DO NOT CONFLICT.
00360*                   IF MICRORDERS HAVE ALREADY BEEN COMBINED, THIS
00370*                   SUBROUTINE WILL CHECK THE INCOMING MICRORDER IS
00380*                   COMPATIBLE WITH THE PREVIOUSLY COMBINED MICRORDERS.
00390*
00400* ARRAY'S: CONFLIC: USED TO STORE THE ROM WORDS.
00410*          CONMAT:  IS THE CONFLICT MATRIX.
00420*          NOCON:   IS USED TO STORE THE "SETS".
00430*
00440* VARIBLES:TYPE: USED TO HOLD THE TYPE OF DECODER TO BE USED.
00450*          I,J,K,L,M,N: INDEXES.
00460*          JFLAG: A FLAG TO CHECK THAT A COLUMN IS NOT ALL ZERO'S.
00470*          KFLAG: A FLAG TO CHECK THAT A COLUMN IS NOT ALL ZERO'S.
00480*          IFLAG: A FLAG THAT SHOWS IF THE COMPATIBLITIY OF TWO
00490*                 MICRORDERS IS GOOD.
00500*          ICT: A COUNTER.
00510*
00520*
00530 COMMON CONFLIC(20,20), CONMAT(20,20), NOCON(20,20)
00540 COMMON/T/ TYPE
00550 INTEGER CONFLIC(20,20), CONMAT(20,20), NOCON(20,20)
00560 INTEGER TYPE
00570 CALL INITIAL
00580 PRINT 100
00590 PRINT 101
00600 PRINT 102
00610 PRINT 103
00620 PRINT 104
00630 PRINT 105
```

```
00640 PRINT 102
00650 PRINT 106
00660 PRINT 107
00670 PRINT 108
00680 PRINT 102
00690 PRINT 104
00700 100 FORMAT ("INSTRUCTIONS: YOU CAN INPUT MICROCODE UP TO TWENTY LINES")
00710 101 FORMAT ("AND NO MORE THAN TWENTY COLUMNS,IN THE FOLLOWING FORMAT:")
00720 102 FORMAT (" ")
00730 103 FORMAT ("EX.",6X,"COLUMNS")
00740 104 FORMAT (2X,"1        THRU        20")
00750 105 FORMAT (2X,"01101011011000010000")
00760 106 FORMAT("PLEASE INPUT YOUT MICROCODE WITH NO SPACES BETWEEN ONE'S AN")
00770 107 FORMAT("ZERO'S. A INPUT OF '9' WILL TERMINATE INPUT SEQUENCE OR WHEN")
00780 108 FORMAT ("A LIMIT OF TWENTY LINES IS REACHED.")
00790 109 FORMAT ("PLEASE INPUT THE TYPE OF DECODER YOU WISH TO USE.")
00800 111 FORMAT ("EX. '2 TO 4' '3 TO 8' '4 TO 16'")
00810*
00820* READ THE INPUT MICRORDERS INTO MATRIX CONFLIC
00830*
00840 DO 10 I = 1,20
00850    READ 110,(CONFLIC(I,J),J=1,20)
00860 10 IF (CONFLIC(I,1).EQ.9) GOTO 12
00870 110 FORMAT (20I1)
00880 12 PRINT 102
00890 PRINT 109
00900 PRINT 111
00910 PRINT 102
00920 READ 110, TYPE
00930 IF (TYPE.EQ.3) TYPE = 7
00940 IF (TYPE.EQ.4) TYPE = 15
00950 IF (TYPE.EQ.2) TYPE = 3
00960*
00970* TRANSFER MICRORDERS INTO MATRIX 'CONMAT' USING THE CORRECT CI
00980*
00990    I = 0
01000 18 I = I + 1
01010 19 DO 20 J = 1,20
01020 20 IF (CONFLIC(I,J).EQ.1) GOTO 21
01030    IF (I.NE.20) GOTO 18
01040    GO TO 24
01050 21 DO 23 K=1,20
01060 23 IF (CONFLIC(I,K).NE.0) CONMAT(K,J)=CONFLIC(I,K)
01070    IF (I.NE.20) GO TO 18
01080 24 DO 25 I=1,20
01090    DO 26 J=1,20
01100       IF (CONMAT(J,I).NE.0) CONMAT(J,J)=1
01110    26 CONTINUE
01120 25 CONTINUE
01130*
01140* FIND CI'S THAT DON'T CONFLIC
01150*
01160    KFLAG = 9
01170    IFLAG = 9
01180    M = 1
01190    N = 1
```

```
01200 27  IF (M+N.EQ.20) GO TO 30
01210     DO 28 I=1,20
01220        IF ((CONMAT(I,M).EQ.1).AND.(CONMAT(I,M+N).EQ.1)) IFLAG = 9
01230        IF (CONMAT(I,M).EQ.1) JFLAG = 0
01240 28  IF (CONMAT(I,M+N).EQ.1) KFLAG = 0
01250     IF ((IFLAG.EQ.0).AND.(JFLAG.EQ.0).AND.(KFLAG.EQ.0))CALL COMBINE(M,M+N)
01260     IFLAG = 0
01270     JFLAG = 9
01280     KFLAG = 9
01290     N = N + 1
01300     GO TO 27
01310 30  IF (M.EQ.19) GO TO 40
01320     DO 31 I = 2,20
01330        IF (NOCON(I,M).NE.0) GO TO 35
01340 31 CONTINUE
01350 32 M = M + 1
01360     N = 1
01370     GO TO 27
01380 35 DO 36 J = 1,20
01390 36 CONMAT (J,NOCON(I,M)) = 0
01400     GO TO 31
01410*
01420* CHECK THAT ALL CI'S ARE IN THE FINAL SOLUTION
01430*
01440 40 DO 41 I = 1,20
01450        IF (CONMAT(I,I).NE.0) GOTO 42
01460 41 CONTINUE
01470     GO TO 45
01480 42 DO 44 J = 1,20
01490        DO 43 K = 1,20
01500           IF (NOCON(J,K).EQ.CONMAT(I,I)) IFLAG = 9
01510 43    CONTINUE
01520 44 CONTINUE
01530     IF (IFLAG.EQ.0) NOCON(I,1) = I
01540     IFLAG = 0
01550     GO TO 41
01560*
01570* NOW ARRANGE THE MATRIX FOR TIDY OUTPUT
01580*
01590 45 DO 47 I = 1,20
01600     DO 46 J = 1,20
01610        CONMAT(I,J) = NOCON(J,I)
01620 46    CONTINUE
01630 47 CONTINUE
01640 DO 55 I = 1,10
01650 55 PRINT 102
01660 PRINT 121
01670 PRINT 122
01680 121 FORMAT (20X,"COMPATIBILITY SETS")
01690 122 FORMAT (21X,"C = CONTROL POINTS")
01700 PRINT 102
01710 DO 60 I = 1,20
01720     IF (CONMAT(I,1).NE.0) GOTO 70
01730 60 CONTINUE
01740 STOP
01750 125 FORMAT (18X,"FIELD",I3,3X,"C=",20I3.0)
```

```
01760 70 ICT=ICT+1
01770    PRINT 125,ICT,(CONMAT(I,J),J=1,20)
01780    GOTO 60
01790 END
01800 SUBROUTINE INITIAL
01810 COMMON CONFLIC(20,20), CONMAT(20,20), NOCON(20,20)
01820 INTEGER CONFLIC(20,20), CONMAT(20,20), NOCON(20,20)
01830 DO 10 I=1,20
01840    DO 9 J=1,20
01850       CONFLIC(I,J) = 0
01860       CONMAT(I,J)=0
01870       NOCON(I,J) = 0
01880 9 CONTINUE
01890 10 CONTINUE
01900 RETURN
01910 END
01920 SUBROUTINE COMBINE(I,J)
01930 COMMON CONFLIC(20,20), CONMAT(20,20), NOCON(20,20)
01940 COMMON/T/ TYPE
01950 INTEGER CONMAT(20,20), NOCON(20,20), TYPE
01960 IFLAG = 0
01970    DO 10 L=2,20
01980       IF (NOCON(L,I).NE.0) GO TO 50
01990 10 CONTINUE
02000    IF (IFLAG.EQ.9) RETURN
02010    DO 20 IK = 2,TYPE
02020 20 IF (NOCON(IK,I).EQ.0) GOTO 25
02030    RETURN
02040 25 NOCON(IK,I) = J
02050    NOCON(1,I) = I
02060    CONMAT(J,J) = 0
02070    RETURN
02080 50 DO 51 IK = 1,20
02090 51 IF ((CONMAT(IK,NOCON(L,I)).EQ.1).AND.(CONMAT(IK,J).EQ.1)) IFLAG = 9
02100    GO TO 10
02110 END
READY.
```

INDEX